Your Church & You

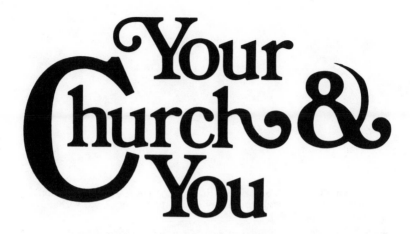

Your Church & You

History and Images of Catholicism

Michael Pennock

Ave Maria Press • Notre Dame, Ind. 46556

Nihil Obstat:
Rev. Paul J. Hritz, S.T.L.
Censor Deputatus

Imprimatur:
Most Rev. Anthony M. Pilla, D.D., M.A.
Bishop of Cleveland
December 14, 1982

Library of Congress Catalog Card Number: 83-070053
International Standard Book Number: 0-87793-268-9

Photography:
Jagdish Agarwal, 204; Associated Press, 112; Camerique, 166; Joseph De Caro, 47, 120, 193; Robert J. Cunningham, 56; G. A. Douglas, 151; J. Murray Elwood, 38, 260 (top); Jack Fitzgerald, 128; Selwyn Image, 157; Carolyn A. McKeone, 64, 88, 278; Joanne Meldrum, cover; Roger W. Neal, cover, 212, 260 (bottom); Notre Dame Sports Information Department, 32; Kenneth C. Poertner, 270; Religious News Service, 10, 19, 72, 84, 95, 98, 170, 173, 182, 199, 220, 242; Paul M. Schrock, 45; Rick Smolan, 228; Bob Taylor, 252; Jim Whitmer, 117; Wide World Photos, 234, 246, 266; Joanna Yates, 26.

DEDICATION

I dedicate this book to Alice Massarella and her late husband John. Their Christian life and marriage taught me and my wife Carol the meaning of Christian community. John also helped me learn how to teach. I am indebted to them both.

Acknowledgments

I extend my love and gratitude to my wife Carol and our children—Scott, Jennifer, Amy Marie and Christopher—for their love and encouragement during the writing of this book.

Next, I want to express my heartfelt thanks to the people who have significantly helped me write this book. Frank Cunningham, both my editor and friend at Ave Maria Press, lent his wisdom, editorial skills and common sense. His observations and suggestions have made this a better book than it would have been. I thank the Lord for Frank's continual encouragement in developing this high school series for Ave Maria Press. He, Charlie Jones, Joan Bellina and Father John Reedy are an important part of the Christian community which is Ave Maria. It is a privilege to know and work with them all.

My friend and colleague, Larry Ober, S.J., is a brilliant teacher, a warm and witty friend, and a church historian with few peers on the high school level. Larry saved me from some embarrassing mistakes and made some wonderful suggestions that brought precision where precision was needed.

Again, I wish to acknowledge my mentor, Father Paul Hritz, and my indebtedness to him for my vocation as religious educator. His work for God's kingdom is an inspiration to me and to many people in the Diocese of Cleveland. His ideas on Christian community and Catholic identity appear throughout this book.

I also wish to express gratitude to one of the finest secondary religious educators known to me: Jim Skerl. I am very proud of Jim, a former student of mine. He now serves as my department chairman. A beloved and creative teacher, Jim contributed many helpful ideas. He is a prime example of the kind of Christian who spreads the Lord's love by the kind of warm, gracious, caring person that he is.

So many others deserve my gratitude. I am most fortunate to teach at an outstanding school, St. Ignatius High School in Cleveland, Ohio. There I have experienced incredible support for my work. I am proud to be associated with this institution and with my colleagues and students. Members of the theology department in particular have greatly encouraged me. Their support has given me much strength. Thanks to Carolyn Capuano, H.M., Marty Dybicz, Tom Healey, Mary Lou Salzano, Tom Frech, S.J., Larry Belt, S.J. and Ron Torina, S.J. Thanks also to the president of St. Ignatius, Bob Welsh, S.J.; my principal Ken Styles, S.J.; and Don Petkash, S.J., who have all supported and encouraged me. Thanks also to all my lay and Jesuit colleagues for sharing a Christian community life with me and the Ignatius students. Special thanks to Mary Jane Treichel for her prayers.

Ted Ross, S.J., of Loyola University (Chicago) deserves my gratitude and respect for giving me a love of history when he taught me in high school 20 years ago. He epitomizes the Jesuit tradition of excellence which I was so fortunate to be exposed to both in high school and in my undergraduate work at Loyola. He and Bernie Streicher, S.J., of St. Ignatius helped me at a critical time to love learning and writing.

Finally, I once again wish to acknowledge all the fine young men I have been privileged to teach at St. Ignatius. Their response to the Lord's word has been a gift of joy to me. Their kind attention, thoughtful reactions and the way they have demonstrated to me the existence of the living Lord have empowered me to dare to write this book for them and the other students who will use it. Two of them, in particular, have made significant contributions to this text: Tad Brown and Steve Crone.

To all these wonderful people and all the others who are part of this book—the story of God's people—thank you and God bless you.

—Michael Francis Pennock

Contents

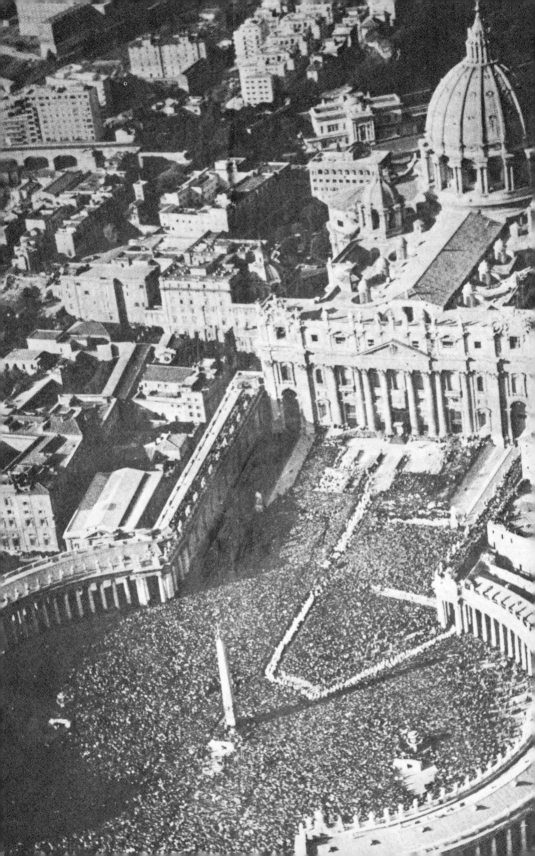

1
Looking at the
Roman Catholic Church

Yahweh called me before I was born,
from my mother's womb he pronounced my name.

See, I have branded you on the palms of my hands.
—Isaiah 49:1,16

"What's your story?"

Have you ever been asked this question? People often ask it
because we all have stories to tell, and our personal story is extremely
important. It tells us and others who we are; it reveals our identity.

What is the raw material of your personal story? For one thing,
your family. Your mom and dad, brothers, sisters and relatives have
all greatly influenced who you are. So have your friends. An old saying underscores this point: You are known by the company you keep.
The schools you have attended, the neighborhoods you have lived in,
jobs you've held, sports you've played, music you've listened to—all
and more are part of your personal story. To this list we should also
add the church you belong to. If you reflect on the elements which
make up your history, you will learn a lot about yourself.

Institutions and organizations also have stories to tell, stories intimately connected to key elements—people, places, events—which
make up their past. This book is about the story of the Roman

11

Catholic Church, an institution/organization that plays an important role in your story. The book attempts to:

- show you something about what the church is.

- point out key elements in the church's story that have contributed to what it is today.

- involve you in the church's story by showing that it exists to support you in your journey to the Father. We together are the church; you as an individual add to its story. In like manner the church has the potential to be an important part of your story.

This chapter will take up the following issues:

- it will offer some definitions of the church.

- it will introduce you to some models of the church.

- it will give you an overview of the rest of the book.

This book contains a number of exercises and projects to help you become more involved with the material under discussion. Let's begin with one of these exercises.

REFLECTING ON YOUR STORY

A. *Who Am I?* All of us are fundamentally mysterious. We can never tell fully who we are because there is so much to us. We change. We grow. What we were yesterday might be a bit different from what we are today. But we can say something about ourselves by using some familiar images. Which image in each of the following pairs is more appropriate for you? Circle your choice.

I see myself more like a _____ than a _____.

Volkswagen...Cadillac   lion .... lamb
swimmer ..... football player   question mark..period
rock song.....symphony   mountain ...... valley
waterfall ..... quiet brook   guest .... host
rose .... dandelion   eagle .... duck
sunset........sunrise   politician ..... movie star

B. *My Story.* Fill in the following blanks to make a short auto-biographical story. Share your story and your responses to exercise A with a classmate.

My name is _____. I was born _____ in
                                             (date)
_____. I graduated from _____
        (city)
elementary school. The most significant experience of my life

was the time when _____

_____.

The person who has most influenced my life is _____

because he/she _____

_____. My best friend is _____

because he/she _____. In my

faith life Jesus Christ is _____

For me the Catholic church means _____

_____.

Right now in my life I am questioning _____.
If you really want to know me, I would have to tell you that I am

_____

_____

WHAT IS THE CHURCH?

Church is one of those richly evocative terms over which many people argue. Why? Simply because people cannot agree on what it means or what it is. Cardinal Newman once said that if we would define our terms, we would have few arguments.

For some, the church is primarily a building, a place where people gather to worship. Others see it as a cold institution, as big as General Motors and equally removed from the lives of ordinary people. Others see the church as a warm, loving community of which they are a meaningful part. Still others only identify the church with priests and nuns and do not really consider themselves part of it.

Let's focus on what precisely church means to the community of Christians called Roman Catholic.

In a speech given to the bishops at the opening of the second session of the Second Vatican Council (1962-1965) Pope Paul VI offered this definition: "The church is a mystery. It is a reality imbued with the hidden presence of God."

The church as mystery is intimately connected to the mystery which is God. We know something about the mystery of God; for example, we believe that he freely created the world, that he wished to share himself with us by inviting us to participate in his own life. He gave us life itself. He extended his invitation in the Old Testament many times through the people of Israel. His invitation became most evident when God the Father sent his son, Jesus Christ, to us. Jesus invited us to be adopted sons and daughters of the Father. He preached and ushered in the kingdom of God and revealed the mystery of his Father. He showed us by his life, death and resurrection that God is love, that he cares for each of his children and wills our healing, our salvation.

Part of God's mysterious plan is to unite his people in a community of love, worship and service. To accomplish this the Father and Son sent the Holy Spirit to dwell in the church and in the hearts of believers.

Jesus Christ is essential to the mystery of the church. He gives it life. He sustains it. He continues his work of salvation through it. Part of the mission of the church is to help people understand better who they are and what they are called to be in Jesus Christ.

Because the church is mystery—intimately related to God—we can never fully define it. However, various images help us get at its divine reality. In the next section of this chapter we will look at six images of the church: community, herald, institution, pilgrim, sacrament and servant. Each helps us understand better the nature and mission of the church.

TO THINK ABOUT AND DO

A. *Closer Study.* You would profit greatly from reading "The Mystery of the Church," Chapter 1 of the *Constitution on the Church.* Make a list of 10 new things you learned from reading this section of the document.

B. *Taking Another Look at Your Story.* Next to each category write the name of the person who has contributed the most to your personal faith story. Then briefly describe how that person is a living sign of God's love to you.

	Who	**A Living Sign**
a parent		
a priest		
a teacher		
a friend		
a godparent		

IMAGES OF THE CHURCH

As we have seen, it is difficult to define the church because it is essentially a mystery. It includes both the human and the divine. It is made up of an observable, visible dimension, but at the same time it includes a spiritual, invisible dimension. Real flesh-and-blood people make up the church, but the glorified, resurrected Jesus Christ lives in the church as well. It is somewhat easy to name and define the human and visible dimensions of the church. It is much more difficult to define the spiritual, invisible dimensions.

Because of an initial difficulty in defining the church many theologians attempt to describe it instead. The *Constitution on the Church* suggests that a proper way to describe the church is with images or figures of speech. Avery Dulles, S.J., has done precisely that in one of the most influential theological works written in the past 10 years or so. His book *Models of the Church* discusses in some detail five major images that are so descriptively rich that he calls them models. A model is a very good image which helps us to reflect deeply and understand critically some reality. A model of the church is an image that helps us understand more clearly the exact nature of the church. Furthermore, a model helps us understand the various functions of the church, that is, what the church does.

Study carefully the diagram on page 17 which contains six symbols of the church. Five of these images, Mystical Communion (which is referred to as Community in the diagram), Herald, Institution, Sacrament and Servant, are used in Father Dulles' book. A sixth image, church as Pilgrim, is added because it too is an important way to help us understand what the church is. We could use other images. In fact, one scholar has named 96 images which he found in the New Testament. The six described here will provide a solid basis for our study of the church.

Let us now turn to a brief description of each of these images.

1. **Church as Community or Mystical Communion.** Most of us know what it means to be a member of a close family or to play together on a team or to participate with friends in a common activity. We sense a spirit of unity. We feel part of something larger than ourselves, but we know that as individuals we have an important part to play as well. The image of the church as community evokes these same kinds of feelings and understandings.

Community is a popular image of the church today. Chapter 2 of the *Constitution on the Church* discusses the church as the People of God with a certain common task and mission. St. Paul also considered this an important metaphor when he referred to the church as the Body of Christ (1 Cor 12:12-30). What Paul had in mind is that we are members of Christ's body, each with our own talents and duties, but all united in the Holy Spirit to the head Jesus Christ who guides our work. Christian art has often depicted this image with a picture of a vine. All the members (the branches) receive their life from the true vine (Jesus). They are to bear fruit by living Jesus' words and doing the Father's will.

The image of the church as community stresses the common fellowship of all believers who are united in faith by the Holy Spirit.

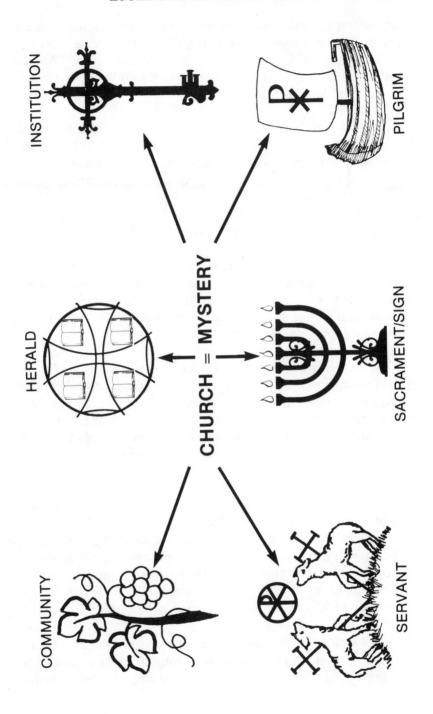

It emphasizes common goals, ideals and intimate sharing. These individuals form one community with a life, a tradition, a story of its own. The People of God who are branches on the vine of Christ and members of his body are responsible for living his life by serving each other and building up the community.

Our first description of the church, then, is that it is the presence of Christ in the world through a community of faith in him as Lord and Savior. The church is a visible community made up of individuals who are united as members of a body. These members are guided by the Lord as they continue his work in the world. The church is like a vine whose branches derive their life from the risen Lord. They share a common life and are one People of God.

2. **Church as Herald**. What would you do if you opened a letter from a prestigious university and read that you had been awarded a generous four-year scholarship? After the initial shock wore off a bit, you would want to share your good news with someone, your close friends, parents, classmates or teachers.

The church performs a similar task of spreading joyful good news. This image of church is herald—one who receives an official message and is given the mission of passing it on to others. Christians believe Jesus gave the church this commission when he instructed the apostles to baptize and to teach in his name. The task of the church is to share the good news that God wills the salvation of all people and has accomplished this through Jesus Christ.

The image of church as herald puts considerable emphasis on the word of God. The diagram for herald on page 17 depicts a cross with one of the four gospels at each corner. It stresses that the church is entrusted with preaching the good news of Jesus Christ to the four ends of the earth, and that Jesus calls people to respond to his word in faith and come together into a community of fellow believers whose main task is to proclaim the good news of God's kingdom.

3. **Church as Institution**. One of the ways to look at the church is as an institution. An institution is a group or organization of people structured in a *formal* way in order to ensure that a job gets done.

The community of faith called the church is organized to carry on the mission of Jesus Christ. This society has its ordained ministers whose task, like the task of the institution itself, is to serve the members through teaching, making holy and ruling. The supreme authority rests with the pope, the vicar of Christ, who is joined with the bishops, the successors to the apostles. Priests and deacons work with their bishops in serving God's people.

One symbol of the institutional church is that of a key. The key is a symbol of authority and calls to mind the church's power to forgive sin and to teach and direct various organizations and activities in the Lord's name.

As institution the church *teaches authoritatively* in matters of faith and morals. *Sharing the Light of Faith* (the National Catechetical Directory for Catholics of the United States) points out the value of this teaching role:

> These teachings give the faithful assurance of truth in their profession of faith and their adherence to moral standards and ideals (No. 69).

The church as institution also *makes holy* through the sacraments and sacramentals, and *rules* by serving all people.

4. **Church as Pilgrim**. Your life is not yet complete. In front of you, God willing, are exciting discoveries and adventures. You have much to learn. You have a career to undertake, friends to meet, perhaps a family to raise. In short, you are a traveler in this life. You are a pilgrim.

The church is also a pilgrim. Although it is the budding forth of God's kingdom on earth, its work is not yet complete. It is like a ship on a stormy sea which has not yet reached its final destination. Along the way individual members might sin and be tempted to give up the journey, but true pilgrims know that they have the strength of the Lord to guide them on their journey. It is the Lord who helps the members combat the temptations within and without the community as he leads the community to its destiny.

This image of the church underscores the truth that the church as pilgrim is going somewhere. It has the continuing work of remaining faithful to the Lord as it moves into an uncertain, even, at times, dangerous future. But it has the confidence that the Lord will help it keep steering in the right direction, correcting itself when it gets off course.

5. **Church as Sacrament/Sign**. In the *Constitution on the Church* the Second Vatican Council offered this definition of the church:

> By her relationship with Christ the Church is a kind of sacrament or sign of intimate union with God, and of the unity of all mankind. She is also an instrument for the achievement of such union and unity (No. 1).

This definition highlights the sacramental nature of the church. A sacrament is a mystery, an outward sign which points to some deeper, invisible reality.

Jesus is God's great sacrament. He is God-in-the-flesh. He was visible, hearable, touchable, human like us, an outward sign. In him God lived, invisible made manifest. His kind face, his forgiving words, his healing touch showed the glory of God's love. Jesus came as the sign of God's great love. If we want to know how God loved, how he desired human love, how he understood and forgave human failure, all we have to do is look to Jesus who said, "To have seen me is to have seen the Father" (Jn 14:9).

But where is this Jesus today? Where can we hear, touch and see the great sign of God's love? When Jesus died, rose from the dead, ascended into heaven to be glorified at the right hand of the Father, he did not abandon his people. He left another sign of his presence. This sign is the church—the sacrament of Jesus Christ. As the Father lived in his Son Jesus, so Jesus lives in the church through the power of the Holy Spirit. We might diagram this reality like this:

This reality is a mystery. Jesus is the mystery of God made flesh, incarnate in history. The church is the sacrament of the Lord and Savior Jesus Christ, his visible presence in history, his Body. The church derives its very life from the continuing presence of the Lord after his resurrection. It is a community for, of and in Jesus Christ. It is a living organism, united in the friendship of the Lord. All members are united in this community as sons and daughters of the Father.

The church, then, is the sacrament of the Lord and Savior Jesus Christ. It is an outward sign which contains the invisible presence of the Lord. It has both a divine and a human aspect. It is visible yet contains the spiritual. It is holy, for example, because of Christ's presence; but it can be sinful because of the human members. As the bride of Christ the church must continuously strive to live up to its true identity, to strive to be like the Lord who dwells in it.

The church is like a candle. It gives off the light of Christ and sheds light on God's kingdom so that people will see what it is like to be united to Christ's love. It is a sign or sacrament which shows people what God's kingdom is like here and now. The church is a true sign when its actions support its message of the coming of God's kingdom. Others can see the risen Lord Jesus in the church only if they can see Christians who are living his message, not merely talking about it. This brings us to the image of church as servant.

6. **Church as Servant.** Who makes a good class officer? Is it the person who only seeks the prestige of the office, or the one who tries to use the office to help others? Do you have much respect for an officer who likes to dominate others? Probably not. You probably have more respect for the officer who wants to serve fellow classmates. We tend to have more respect for elected leaders who use their office to help serve our needs and interests.

A valuable image of the church is that of servant. It reminds us that the church is supposed to follow in Jesus' footsteps. He came as one "not to be served but to serve, and to give his life as a ransom for many" (Mt 20:28). When the apostles wanted to know what it was like to be a leader in Jesus' kingdom, he washed their feet to show them that "anyone who wants to become great among you must first be your servant" (Mk 10:43). The church and its members must be foot-washers.

The church as servant must serve others. It has a mission to heal and to reconcile as Jesus did. It must feed the hungry, give drink to the thirsty, welcome the stranger, clothe the naked, comfort the sick, visit the imprisoned. It must act out of motivations of true concern and love, not out of motivations of personal gain or glory. By serving others, the Body of Christ is a true sign to itself and others that the kingdom of God consists of concern for the least of God's children on its pilgrimage to the Father.

Summary. Each image sheds some light on the mystery of the church. No one alone tells everything there is to say about the church. Each must be thought of as a particular way of looking at the church and what it does. To get a full picture we should study *all* the images because they all have something unique to contribute to our understanding.

Each of the six images puts a particular emphasis on the church's mission. Each has its own strengths and weaknesses. To help see what each of these images contributes to our understanding of the mystery of the church, study the diagram that follows.

IMAGES OF THE CHURCH			
Model/Image	Mission of the church	Major strength of this image	Major weakness of this image
Community	to seek union with God through the power of the Holy Spirit	unites all members by the Spirit of Jesus	lack of emphasis on formal structure can lead to confusion when there are disputes
Herald	to proclaim the good news of salvation to the ends of the earth	emphasizes the Bible and the Word of God	danger of thinking that the *only* task of the church is the proclamation of the gospel
Institution	to teach, to make holy, to rule	gives structure to the church and guidance to its members	danger of identifying the church only with the formal structure
Pilgrim	to be faithful to Christ on a journey through time to eternity	emphasizes that the church needs to be directed to the future	might neglect the responsibility of the church to take risks now in living the gospel
Sacrament/ Sign	to be a meaningful sign to all people, believers and non-believers	reminds the church to be what it is called to be	emphasizes a lot of theology; it is difficult to preach and to teach this model
Servant	to renew the face of the earth in the vision of Jesus Christ	emphasizes the social gospel	danger of doing good works yet neglecting the spiritual side of the church

DEFINING THE CHURCH

This exercise is designed to help you define the church.

Directions:

A.   Divide into six groups. Each group should select a spokesperson and a notetaker to record the group's findings.

B.   In your small groups, arrive at a consensus on these three questions:

  1. How does your group define the church?

  2. What does your group see as the major task of the church?

  3. What are the three most pressing problems your parish should be concerned about right now?

C.   The spokespersons should then share the results with the class.

Discussion:

1. Is it possible or desirable to come up with only one definition of the church? Why or why not?

2. Consider what each of the six groups reported. Does each seem to prefer a particular image of the church? Explain.

3. Make a class list of pressing problems. Which of these are concerned with the church itself? Which are concerned with the church in relationship to the world? Should the church today be more concerned with its own affairs or with what's going on in the world? Explain your response.

4. Consider again the list of pressing issues. Is there anything you can do to help solve these problems? If so, what?

OVERVIEW OF THE BOOK

There are many possible ways to tell the story of the church. In this book we will discuss in greater depth the six images of the church you have read about in this chapter. At the same time we will attempt to touch on some of the high points of the church's story along the way. Thus, *the concepts of image and story will be brought together into the same discussion.*

One thing should be noted from the start. The history of the church is quite detailed and complex. To simplify the story, and at the same time to discuss in greater depth these major images, the book will treat the story of a particular historical era through the perspective of a particular image. For example, the early Christian communities of the first century are the charter communities of the church; they set the stage for later church history. We will look at the story of the church in this first century through the image of community. How did the early church see itself as the Body of Christ? Where did it fail to live up to its lofty vocation?

One additional warning is in order here. Each era of the church could be discussed from the vantage point of *any* image. But to simplify matters, the book will look at a particular era from the vantage point of only *one* image. Only a few comments will be made on how that era demonstrated other images.

With this in mind, here is a brief outline of the other chapters in the book:

- Chapter 2 looks at the first century of the church through the image of community.

- Chapter 3 treats the story of the church from approximately 100-800 through the image of herald. How did the church of this era proclaim the gospel to the world?

- Chapter 4 discusses the Middle Ages (800-1500) through the image of institution. Many church historians believe that the institutional church reached its highest glory during this period.

- Chapter 5 considers the period of the Reformation and post-Reformation up to the Modern Age (1500-1900). The image of a pilgrim struggling with difficult internal and external threats seems an apt image for this age.

- Chapter 6 uses the image of sacrament/sign to discuss the church of the Second Vatican Council, a church which is trying to be an authentic sign to the modern world of the 20th century.

- Chapter 7 looks at some issues and concerns of the church today. Servant seems to be a most appropriate image for the church's self-study and self-understanding today.

Most of the chapters have these common features:

    1. A short reflection on the image under consideration.

    2. A brief overview of the important events in the church's story in the particular era under discussion.

    3. A short biographical sketch of some church "heroes" who are representative of their particular age.

    4. An application of the history of this era in church history to the church of today.

SUMMARY

Here are the major points of this chapter.

1. Reflecting on our personal story helps us to discover our identity. Many factors make up the elements of each person's story.

2. The Roman Catholic Church also has a story to tell. Its story also helps us to understand its identity.

3. The church is primarily a mystery which is intimately connected to the mystery of God's involvement with humanity.

4. Jesus Christ—the great sign and sacrament of God's love for his people—mysteriously lives in the church today.

5. The church is human and divine; it has both spiritual and visible elements. It is made up of both saints and sinners.

6. The *Dogmatic Constitution on the Church*, a key Vatican II document, teaches many profound insights about the nature of the church.

7. Biblical images shed some light on the meaning of the mystery of the church. The following six are especially helpful:

   a. *Community*—stresses the unity of the People of God as the Body of Christ.

   b. *Herald*—emphasizes the church's mission to preach the good news of Jesus Christ.

   c. *Institution*—underscores the need for order in the church.

   d. *Pilgrim*—reminds Christians that they are still on a journey to the Father.

   e. *Sacrament*—calls the church to be a true sign of God's kingdom in human history.

   f. *Servant*—symbolizes the church's mission of serving others, thus pointing to the goodness of Jesus Christ.

8. This book will study the six images of the church listed above as they are reflected in various eras of church history. There are, of course, other ways to study the nature of the church and different ways to look at its history.

EVALUATION

Each chapter of the book will have some questions to test your understanding of what you read. Good luck on this first quiz.

1. *Definition*: Write a good definition of *church* and discuss what it means.

_____

_____

2. *Identify: Dogmatic Constitution on the Church*

_____

_____

3. *Short answer*: The mystery of the church is intimately related

to the mystery of God's_____.

4. *Fill-in*: The church has both a _____ and a human dimension.

Matching: Match the images of the church with the descriptions.

_____5.   Church as footwasher   a. sacrament
_____6.   Church as preacher of the gospel   b. pilgrim
_____7.   Church as united in the Holy Spirit   c. herald
_____8.   Church as authentic sign of Jesus Christ   d. servant
_____9.   Church as a traveler in space and time   e. institution
_____10. Church as authentic teacher of faith and   f. community
          morals

A SCRIPTURE EXERCISE

The New Testament and the Church. Here are some New Testament references to the church. Read each one. In the space provided below each statement briefly summarize what the passage or passages are saying. Then check off four of the descriptions which apply best to your own parish community.

____ 1. A community which forgives the sinner. (Read Lk 19:1-10 and Mt 5:43-48.)

_____

____ 2. A community of love. (Read Mt 25:31-46 and Acts 2:42-47.)

_____

____ 3. A community founded by Jesus Christ on Peter and the apostles. (Read Mt 16:15-19.)

_____

____ 4. A community which derives its life from the Eucharist. (Read 1 Cor 11:23-29.)

_____

____ 5. A community with a universal message. (Read Mt 28:19-20.)

_____

____ 6. A community willing to suffer for Christ. (Read 1 Pt 2:19-25.)

_____

____ 7. A believing community united in one faith. (Read Rom 10:9-13.)

_____

____ 8. A community based on the resurrection of Jesus. (Read 1 Cor 15:12-19.)

_____

____ 9. A community which prays. (Read Mt. 6:5-15 and Mt 18:19-20.)

_____

Sharing. When you share the results of your reading with your classmates, be sure to point out *how* your parish lives up to the particular description. Offer examples.

PRAYER REFLECTION

Father of our Lord Jesus Christ,
    you call us by name, you see in each of us something
      wonderful, you love us as mothers and fathers love
      their newborn infants.

Never let us forget that to you we are special.

Never let us forget your son Jesus who came to draw us near to
    you.
    Help us to see that you are involved in the story of our lives.
    Remind us that we need each other on our journey to you.

We need your Son and our brothers and sisters to grow,
    to live as your children,
    to love as you want us to love.

Father, in the name of our Lord Jesus Christ,
    we thank you for giving us life, for giving us the opportunity
      to hear your good news, for drawing us into the community
      of your church which cares for us.

Praise be to you, O Father. Amen.

2
A Call to Community: The Founding of the Church in the First Century

These remained faithful to the teaching of the apostles, to the brotherhood, to the breaking of the bread and to the prayers.
   The faithful all lived together and owned everything in common; they sold their goods and possessions and shared out the proceeds among themselves according to what each one needed.

—Acts 2:42, 44-45

Sports thrive on team unity. Imagine the disaster which would result on a gridiron if every player "did his own thing." Linemen must work in tandem with the quarterback and the running backs if the team is to advance. The same is true on the baseball diamond. A hotshot shortstop who is not aware of the moves of his second baseman will be quite ineffective at pulling off a double play. The infield must work as a unit or the pitcher is doomed to take an early shower.

Unity on sports teams builds a kind of community. Each member of the team has a particular role to play. Tasks are assigned, usually by the manager or the coach of the team. The team is organized with one goal in mind: win the game by defeating the opponent.

A sports team is an organized and carefully structured kind of community. A second and less-structured kind of community is your family. This kind of community usually lasts a lifetime. Members may have different tasks and roles that can and do change over the years. Family members associate on the most intimate of terms. Unity is also a must for good family life.

Communities like your family and sports teams have the common element of unity. As a matter of fact we might think of community as people "coming into unity." Community is also an excellent way to think about church. The *Constitution on the Church* talks about the church as the People of God who are gathered into the Body of Christ. The Holy Spirit binds believers into one body under the leadership, the headship of Jesus Christ.

From the earliest days of its founding Jesus calls the church into community. The story of the church in the first century tells us how the church struggled to form into the Body of Christ. Sometimes the unity and love in this community were most evident. At other times there were challenges to that unity which seriously threatened the community of the church.

In this chapter we will look at the following:

- the history of the first-century church as it formed into the community of God's people according to Jesus' teaching

- short biographies of Paul, missionary and apostle, and Ignatius, bishop and martyr, two leaders of the early Christian community

- building the Body of Christ in the modern world

IDENTIFYING THE "BODY BUILDERS"

St. Paul described the church as the Body of Christ. This image implies that every member of the church has a certain task in contributing to the work of the church, to building up the Body of the Lord. Break into small groups (four or five). Name a person from your class or parish who seems to fit each of the descriptions below.

_____ *Church Public Relations Director*: a person excited about the good news and glad to share it with others

_____ *Church Bellringer*: a person who calls people together to celebrate

_____ *Church Organizer*: a person who plans things and sees that they get done

_____ *Church Janitor*: a person who works in the background and quietly does things that no one else seems to want to do

_____ *Church Counselor*: a person who can listen to others and bring them the understanding they need

_____ *Church Cook*: a person who adds just the right amount of salt to every event so that everything goes all right

_____ *Church Social Worker*: a person who stands up for others and is concerned with social justice

_____ *Church Social Director*: a person who adds life to every event

_____ *Church Mouse*: a person who can always be counted on to be around

_____ *Other*: (Write your own—either to describe you or someone you know.)

JESUS

Early Preaching About Jesus. Without Jesus of Nazareth there would be no Christian church. He is its foundation. There is no doubt that St. Peter thought as much. When Peter began preaching the good news on Pentecost Sunday, the day traditionally assigned as the birthday of the church, he testified to the magnificent things God the Father had accomplished in Jesus of Nazareth.

The story of Peter's preaching and what took place on Pentecost Sunday is found in Acts 2. Luke, the author of Acts, tells how the Holy Spirit descended on the apostles in the form of tongues of fire. He further records the strange phenomenon of the disciples speaking in foreign tongues to all the devout Jews who were in Jerusalem for the feast of Pentecost. Peter spoke for the apostles when he told these Jews what was taking place in their midst.

Peter proclaimed boldly and enthusiastically that God had raised Jesus up from the dead. This, Peter insisted, was proof that the prophecies of old were fulfilled. Jesus the Nazorean was indeed a prophet. He worked miracles as signs of his credentials. He was delivered over to death by some of the leaders of the Jews, a death accomplished by the Roman authorities. But death did not conquer Jesus; God raised him up. Jesus is indeed both Lord and Messiah. As a result, all men and women are called to turn from their sinful (destructive) ways, be baptized in the name of Jesus Christ and receive the gift of the Spirit.

Luke records that over 3,000 believed Peter and were baptized. This core group constituted the first Christian community. It was the church.

Who Was Jesus? The gospels, written between A.D. 65 (Mark) and A.D. 100 (John), are our primary sources of information about the historical Jesus. Yet the gospels are not primarily history books. They are faith testimonials written to inspire the faithful and to convert nonbelievers. They attest to the marvelous things God has accomplished in Jesus of Nazareth, the Messiah, the Son of the Living God. The gospels tell us very little about Jesus' early life. At best we can conclude that Jesus was probably born around 6 B.C., that is, sometime shortly before the death of Herod the Great in 4 B.C. Most scholars maintain that Jesus died in A.D. 30 on the fourteenth day of the Jewish month of Nisan (which corresponds to the last part of our month of March and the first weeks in our month of April).

Jesus appeared on the public scene around A.D. 28. All the gospels report that he was baptized by John the Baptist, a prophet who called men and women to prepare themselves spiritually for the coming of the Messiah. Shortly after his baptism the carpenter and layman Jesus—from the insignificant Galilean town of Nazareth—began to preach what he called the "good news." Mark's gospel succinctly reports the nature of that preaching:

> After John had been arrested, Jesus went into Galilee. There he proclaimed the Good News from God. "The time has come" he said "and the kingdom of God is close at hand. Repent, and believe the Good News" (Mk 1:14-15).

The essence of Jesus' preaching was that God's kingdom, his reign, had begun. The concept of God's kingdom was very important to the Jews of our Lord's day. It referred to the time when God's will would be done on earth as it is accomplished in heaven. Among other things this meant that sinners would be forgiven. Further, it meant, as Jesus reported to the disciples of John the Baptist, that "the blind see again, the lame walk, lepers are cleansed, and the deaf hear, the dead are raised to life, the Good News is proclaimed to the poor" (Lk 7:22). In other words, God had entered human history and was bringing salvation to everyone, the poor and the rich, women and men, the sick and the well, Gentile and Jew. Salvation—that process whereby God reconciles people to himself—has begun. It is, furthermore, accomplished in Jesus himself.

Jesus: A Wonderworker. All the gospels attest that Jesus performed miracles. They list certain nature miracles, for example, the changing of water into wine, the calming of the storm at sea, the multiplication of loaves and fishes. But above all else they present Jesus as a healer. He cured people possessed of demons. He calmed epileptics. He made the blind to see and the deaf to hear. He helped the crippled to walk. He touched lepers and made them whole.

The gospels tell us that Jesus' miracles dramatically demonstrate that the power of God has broken into human history. His miracles also point to how God is present in Jesus, accomplishing his will of salvation. Jesus called people to respond to him and to God's kingdom with faith. He challenged them to repent of their sins and accept the coming of the kingdom. His miracles authenticated his claim to teach in God's name.

Jesus the Teacher. Jesus was a teacher *par excellence*. Though not a trained rabbi (teacher), he spoke with power and personal charisma. His teaching often took the form of a parable, a story drawn from ordinary life which makes a comparison. The point of comparison most often contrasted Jesus' teaching about God's kingdom with the attitudes of his opponents.

The parables taught the following points:

1. *God's kingdom is in our midst.* Although the kingdom appears small now, it will grow like a mustard bush. God makes it grow by his own design. Salvation is here; one day it will reach a great harvest.

2. *God's kingdom is a free gift, open to all, even sinners.* God is like a generous vineyard owner who will reward us beyond what we earn. God loves sinners beyond measure. He is like a good shepherd who seeks out the lost sheep. He is a merciful father who welcomes back his lost children. His joy over the returned sinner is immense. He asks two things: that we joyfully and gratefully accept God's love; that we forgive those who have harmed us as we ourselves have been forgiven by our Father.

3. *The good news of the kingdom demands an urgent response.* We must be ever watchful for Jesus' return. We must be willing to give everything for the kingdom, like the man who sold all his possessions to buy a pearl or a hidden treasure which he had discovered.

4. *The coming of the kingdom means we must repent.* We must ask for God's forgiveness. We must pray without ceasing, addressing God as *Abba,* Father, always confident that he will answer our prayers. We must share our gifts with the poor, not hoard our goods. Most important, Jesus taught that we must love everyone, even our enemies. The heart of Jesus' message, in fact, is love: *Love God above all things and our neighbors as ourselves.* We show love of God by loving our neighbor, by responding to the least of our brothers and sisters, by feeding the hungry, giving drink to the thirsty, welcoming the stranger, clothing the naked, visiting the sick and the imprisoned.

5. *Living the kingdom is challenging.* Following Jesus and living his message can be difficult. We must be willing to take up a cross to follow Jesus. Following the example of Jesus means that we must be willing to wash feet as he did; we must serve others. But those who respond to Jesus will be rewarded.

Jesus: A Community Builder. Jesus not only preached the good news of God's kingdom, he also created a community of brothers and sisters around him. He ate with his followers, joyfully celebrating the new covenant of love with God and anticipating the heavenly banquet. Although his disciples often misunderstood Jesus and bickered among themselves, he wanted them to be like a family whose devotion to doing God's will would bind them intimately together.

Near the end of his life Jesus celebrated a special Passover meal with his disciples. He took bread and wine, blessed them and shared them with his followers. He transformed the meaning of this tradi-

tional Jewish feast when he told them to repeat what he had just performed for them. His command underscored his desire that his
followers should remember his passion and death and stressed that he
would come again and would continue to be present with them
forever. To this day Christians believe that celebrating the
Eucharist—which is the memorial meal commemorating Jesus'
sacrifice for us—creates and celebrates Christian community. Furthermore, Catholics believe that Jesus is alive and comes to his
followers in the most intimate way when they break bread in his
name. They receive his very body and blood.

Jesus' Death. All the gospels report that the preaching and actions of Jesus met severe opposition. Some Jewish leaders thought
that Jesus committed blasphemy by claiming for himself privileges
which only God had. They also disliked some of his teachings about
the role of temple worship and the role of Jewish law. Others were
worried that his actions and words might lead to a rebellion against
the Romans, a rebellion the Romans would put down with much
Jewish bloodshed.

The gospels tell us that these same leaders conspired with the
Roman procurator of Judaea, Pontius Pilate. Pilate, who seems to
have thought that Jesus was innocent, had him put to death.

The death of Jesus should have put an end to the community
which he had called together. At the crucifixion of Jesus his followers
were confused and disappointed. They questioned whether Jesus was
the Messiah after all. Wouldn't the Messiah defend himself and bring
down legions of angels to fight off the Romans? Most important,
they were extremely afraid for their very lives. They scattered, fully
believing that Jesus of Nazareth had let them down.

Something happened, though, that convinced them that Jesus
was alive. This something was the resurrection, and the resurrection
of Jesus created the church.

DISCOVERING JESUS

A. *The First Preaching About Jesus.* Read Acts 2. Then answer these questions:
   1. What was the first reaction of the Jews when they heard the apostles speaking in tongues?
   2. How did Peter answer this false reaction?
   3. In the space provided, briefly outline the major points of Peter's sermon:

   _____

   _____

   _____

   _____

   _____

B. *Jesus' Parables.* Please read the following parables of Jesus. In a few short words, summarize the major point of each parable. Then decide which of the following themes of Jesus' teaching the particular parable represents. Put the corresponding number in the space provided.

   Themes:
   1. God's kingdom is in our midst.
   2. God's kingdom is a free gift, open to all, even sinners.
   3. The good news of the kingdom demands an urgent response.
   4. The coming of the kingdom means we must repent.
   5. Living the kingdom is a challenge.

PARABLE	Reference	Major Point	Theme
Lost Coin	Lk 15:8-10		
Yeast	Mt 13:33		
Rich Man and Lazarus	Lk 16:19-31		
Wily Business-man	Lk 16:1-13		
The Sower	Mt 13:3-23		
Faithful Servant	Lk 12:42-48		

C. *Test Your Knowledge of Jesus.* Here are some questions about
Jesus. Every Christian should know these basic facts about the
founder of Christianity. Test your knowledge. Then check your
answers by looking at the reference provided.

True or False:

_____ 1. Jesus sometimes broke the Sabbath laws.

_____ 2. Jesus did not have to learn as he was growing up.

_____ 3. Jesus came to throw out the Ten Commandments.

_____ 4. Jesus did not permit divorce.

_____ 5. Jesus told his followers not to pay taxes.

Short Answer:

6. To whom was Jesus speaking when he said, "I am the resurrection and the life"? (Bible versions may vary slightly in
wording.)

_____

7. Which apostle said to Jesus, "You are the Christ"?

_____

8. Whom did Pilate free when he decided to crucify Jesus?

_____

9. Where did Jesus' first miracle take place?

_____

10. When did Jesus say: "All authority in heaven and on earth
has been given to me. Go, therefore, make disciples of all the
nations; baptize them in the name of the Father and of the Son
and of the Holy Spirit, and teach them to observe all the commands I gave you"?

1. Mt 12:1-14	5. Mt 22:15-22	8. Lk 23:13-25
2. Lk 2:52	6. Jn 11:24-25	9. Jn 2:1-12
3. Mt 5:17-19	7. Mk 8:29	10. Mt 28:16-20
4. Mk 10:1-12		

THE CHURCH GETTING UNDER WAY

The resurrection of Jesus Christ was a decisive event in human history for it gave rise to the founding of Christianity. The appearances of Jesus to his close followers in and around Jerusalem and also in Galilee were earthshaking events for the men and women who were frightened and confused at the time of his death. The appearances of Jesus convinced them that he was alive. Decisive, too, for the rise of the church was our Lord's great commission before he ascended into heaven:

> "You will receive power when the Holy Spirit comes on you, and then you will be my witnesses not only in Jerusalem but throughout Judaea and Samaria, and indeed to the ends of the earth" (Acts 1:8).

As you have already seen, the apostles and the early disciples received this power on Pentecost Sunday when over 3,000 were converted to the good news. Many of these early converts formed into a loving community which shared possessions, celebrated the Eucharist together in their homes and preached the good news of Jesus to their Jewish brothers and sisters.

In striving to live the good news of Jesus, they became a Christian community, the model for all later Christians who have struggled to overcome human weaknesses in their attempts to follow Jesus Christ and build up his Body into a strong community of concern and compassion.

The Nature of the Early Religion. The earliest converts to Jesus' message were Jews who either lived in Jerusalem or were there for the feast of Pentecost. These early Christians still considered themselves Jews. They still recited their Jewish prayers and worshipped in the Temple.

Some Jewish groups like the Sadducees, the aristocratic leaders of the Jews who controlled the Temple, were not pleased with the new sect. Almost immediately they tried to suppress the followers of Jesus, but they were cautioned by Gamaliel, a famous first-century rabbi:

"What I suggest, therefore, is that you leave these men
alone and let them go. If this enterprise, this movement
of theirs, is of human origin it will break up of its own
accord; but if it does in fact come from God you will not
only be unable to destroy them, but you might find
yourselves fighting against God" (Acts 5:38-39).

An Initial Church Problem and the First Persecution. After the
Pentecost experience more Jerusalem Jews began to accept Jesus as
Messiah. Numbers of converts increased. But whenever an organization rapidly increases in size, there are bound to be problems. The
first problem that arose was a threat to Christian community. There
were two kinds of Christians in Jerusalem at that time: Palestinian
Jews who spoke Aramaic, the language of Jesus, and Greek-speaking
Jews who came from cities around the Roman Empire but remained
in Jerusalem after the Pentecost experience. It was the custom for the
early Christian community to distribute food and other goods to the
poor widows who lived in the city. Apparently the Greek-speaking
Jews complained that their widows were not getting a fair share.

To solve this matter the apostles decided to appoint seven men
of good reputation to look after the distribution of the goods. The
men chosen were called deacons. Acts tells us that the problem was
solved and the numbers of disciples continued to increase.

You can read the story of one of the most famous deacons,
Stephen, in Acts 6:8-8:3. His preaching of Jesus led to his martyrdom; he was the first Christian to die for Jesus Christ. Following
Stephen's death a general persecution of Greek-speaking Christians
took place in Jerusalem. One of the leaders of this persecution was a
devoted Pharisee, Saul of Tarsus. As a result of the persecution many
of the disciples left Jerusalem and began to preach the good news
around Palestine.

Peter, who was certainly considered the leading apostle, also
engaged in missionary work. He went throughout Judaea to preach
about the Christ. Like his Lord Jesus he cured many people, even
bringing some back to life. At Jaffa he had a strange dream which
later resulted in his baptizing the first non-Jew, a Gentile centurion
by the name of Cornelius.

Other disciples made their way up to Antioch and preached in the synagogues there. Still others went as far as Cyprus and Cyrene. It was at Antioch, though, that two very important things happened: first, the followers of Jesus were for the first time called by the name *Christians;* second, the gospel was regularly preached to *Gentiles,* that is, non-Jews. As we shall see, this second phenomenon had revolutionary consequences for the development of Christianity.

St. Peter

READING ABOUT EARLY CHRISTIANITY

1. Read the story of the deacon Stephen in Acts 6:8-8:3. Discuss the following:

    a. For the most part, Stephen outlined the history of the Jews in his speech. What is the major theme of his historical over-view?

    _____

    _____

    b. How does Stephen's death remind you of Jesus?

    _____

    _____

2. St. Peter played a key role in the development of early Christianity. He was the spokesman for the apostles on numerous occasions. He settled disputes. He performed miracles. He did missionary work. Read the following passages about Peter and answer the questions.

    a. *Acts 3:1-10 and 4:1-22*

        1) What astonishing thing did Peter do?

        _____

        2) Why were he and John arrested by the Sanhedrin, the ruling body of the Jews?

        _____

        _____

        3) What did the Sanhedrin command Peter not to do? Did he obey the command?

        _____

        _____

    b. *Acts 11:1-18*

        1) Summarize Peter's dream.

        _____

        _____

        2) What was the important meaning of this dream?

        _____

        _____

PAUL: AN APOSTLE FOR JESUS CHRIST

Next to Jesus, Paul is the most important figure in the story of Christianity in New Testament times. Sixty percent of the Acts of the Apostles tells about his life's work; half of the New Testament books were written by or attributed to him. He was the key figure in the debate on the church's attitude to Gentile converts held at the Council of Jerusalem (c. A.D. 50). Most important, he founded many Christian communities throughout the Roman Empire.

Paul was not always a glorious Christian hero. His given name was Saul, the name of the first king of the Israelites. Born between A.D. 5 and 15 in the city of Tarsus, the capital of Cilicia, Saul was of the tribe of Benjamin and was trained in the tradition of the Pharisees, a sect of laymen who were strict keepers of the Jewish Torah (Law). Tarsus contained a famous library, second only to the libraries of Athens and Alexandria. Jews of Tarsus enjoyed the protection of Roman citizenship, probably granted by the Romans in 171 B.C. to entice Jews to emigrate there. As a learned Jew of this cosmopolitan city Saul knew Greek, Aramaic and Hebrew, the classical language of the Jewish people.

Saul learned a trade as a young man. He was a tentmaker, a profession that made him economically independent even when he later

Ancient Tarsus

began to preach the gospel. As a young man he also went to Jerusalem and studied the Law under Gamaliel. He fervently persecuted the new sect of Jews who claimed that Jesus of Nazareth was the Messiah. He was present, for example, at the stoning of Stephen. At his request he was commissioned by the Sanhedrin to persecute Christians in the synagogues of the city of Damascus. On his way to Damascus, though, a most important event in the history of Christianity took place.

Paul's Conversion. Saul was literally knocked off his horse on the road to Damascus when Jesus appeared to him and asked, "Saul, Saul, why are you persecuting me?" (Acts 9:4). This powerful experience temporarily blinded Saul and convinced him that Jesus Christ lived and was indeed the Messiah. After his baptism in Damascus by Ananias, Paul began preaching the gospel in Damascus. He made enemies of the Jews there and narrowly escaped to Jerusalem where he presented himself to Peter and the disciples. Barnabas, an important early missionary, took Paul under his wing and helped him win the approval of the Jerusalem community. But Paul's sudden reversal and fervent preaching now on behalf of Jesus made him enemies among the Jews, and he had to flee Jerusalem, returning to his hometown of Tarsus.

Paul eventually made his way to Antioch in Syria where he helped to build up the early Christian community there, the strongest community outside of Jerusalem. After he and Barnabas went to Jerusalem with a donation for the church, they embarked on their first missionary journey to preach the gospel where it had not yet been proclaimed.

First Missionary Journey: A.D. 45-49. Paul's first journey took him and his companions to Cyprus, Perga, Antioch of Pisidia and the cities of Lycaonia. (Refer to the map on page 49.) His practice was to deliver the good news first to the Jews, God's chosen people. If they rejected his message, he would then preach to the Gentiles, thus emphasizing that Jesus Christ came to save all peoples. Many of the Jews violently resisted his teaching and on several occasions Paul had to flee.

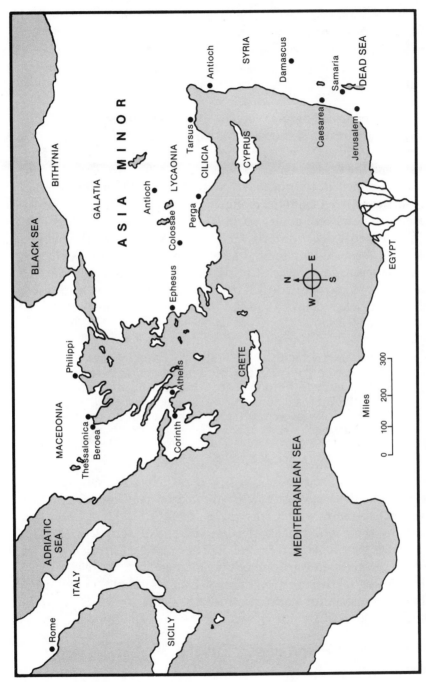

Christian missionaries travel throughout the eastern Mediterranean

When Paul and Barnabas returned to Antioch they were faced with a serious crisis. Some Jewish-Christians from Jerusalem challenged Paul's practices with the Gentiles. Paul argued that belief in Jesus did not impose the obligations of the Jewish Law on the Gentiles.

The Council of Jerusalem: The First Crisis in the Church. This controversy threatened the very unity of early Christianity. To settle the matter Peter and the disciple James, the so-called "brother of the Lord" and the first bishop of Jerusalem, called the first church council, the Council of Jerusalem (c. A.D. 50). Paul's arguments that Gentiles were freed from the requirement of circumcision and Jewish dietary laws and ceremonial washings won the day. Even Peter, the acknowledged leader of early Christianity and the man on whom Jesus had founded his church, had to admit that his former practice of siding with those Jewish-Christians who required submission to Jewish Law (these were called *Judaizers*) was wrong. James, speaking for the Jerusalem church, had the following letter sent to Antioch, Syria and Cilicia:

> "It has been decided by the Holy Spirit and by ourselves not to saddle you with any burden beyond these essentials: you are to abstain from food sacrificed to idols, from blood, from the meat of strangled animals and from fornication. Avoid these, and you will do what is right. Farewell" (Acts 15:28-29).

What was settled at Jerusalem was crucial for the spread of Christianity. Faith in Jesus Christ was sufficient for salvation. As Paul taught time and again: "What makes a man righteous is not obedience to the Law, but faith in Jesus Christ. . . . If the Law can justify us, there is no point in the death of Christ" (Gal 2:16,21). The decision at the council was critical in distinguishing Christianity from Judaism. It clarified Christianity's position as a distinct religion, not a Jewish sect. Christianity was destined from its outset to be a universal religion, meant for all peoples at all times in all places. Soon it was spreading like wildfire throughout the towns of the Roman Empire.

Paul's Further Adventures. Paul's further missionary work provided the kindling wood for this fire. He was engaged in two other major missionary efforts. In his second major journey, A.D. 49-52, Paul and Barnabas set off from Antioch but soon parted ways over an argument caused by Barnabas' cousin, Mark, possibly the author of one of the gospels. On this journey, Paul once again traveled through Asia Minor and eventually reached the European continent. There he established churches in the Macedonian cities of Philippi, Thessalonica and Beroea. Once again the Jews caused him trouble, leading to his arrest at Philippi. When he was released, he went to Athens, the center of Greek culture, but his preaching had little effect on the "sophisticated" Greeks. From there he went to Corinth where he remained for 18 months working as a tentmaker during the week and preaching the gospel on the Sabbath. Corinth was the most important of his churches, but it had a number of problems after he left.

Paul eventually returned to his headquarters at Antioch and rested there a short time. In 53-58 he was hard at work again. He eventually came to Ephesus, the home of a famous temple dedicated to the pagan goddess Artemis (Diana). This temple was one of the seven wonders of the ancient world. When Paul preached *monotheism* (the belief in one God) he raised the ire of the silversmiths of the city against him because they made their livings by creating small shrines for pilgrims to use at the temple. Paul was bad for business! Along with his Jewish enemies, these silversmiths were successful in driving Paul out of the city. From Ephesus he once again went through Macedonia and Greece, eventually making his way to Jerusalem with a collection for the church there. On this third lengthy journey Paul kept up a considerable correspondence, writing important letters to the Galatians, Corinthians, Ephesians and to the Roman Christians.

Paul's Story Concluded. Paul ran into new troubles in Jerusalem when the Jews tried to put him to death. He was rescued by Roman troops when he appealed on the basis of his Roman citizenship for a trial before the emperor. After a precarious journey at sea filled with various adventures, Paul finally arrived in Rome. Clement I of Rome (c. 92-101) wrote that Paul was acquitted and may have even spread the gospel as far as Spain on a fourth journey.

Paul was later imprisoned again at Rome and was probably decapitated by the Emperor Nero in 67 or 68. Thus ended the life of the most colorful and the most dynamic of all the early Christian missionaries. At the time of his death he and other Christian missionaries had firmly established Christian churches in every important city of the Empire. Christianity had arrived!

DISCOVERING PAUL

A. *Paul, the Letter Writer.* Besides being the early church's greatest missionary, St. Paul was also its greatest theologian. Most scholars believe that Paul has had the greatest influence of any theologian in the history of the church. Paul's theology can be found in the letters (epistles) he wrote to the Christian communities he evangelized. Many of his letters were written to correct certain abuses which had crept into his churches after he left them. They often give further instruction in the faith for the new converts.

The eight themes which follow appear often in Paul's epistles. They summarize his theology, his teaching about the good news of Jesus. After studying these themes, see for yourself how they appear in Paul's writings. Read the verses given and decide which theme is illustrated in that particular passage.

1. Salvation takes place through Jesus Christ, the Lord of the universe.

2. The heart of the gospel is the death and resurrection of Jesus.

3. We will participate in the resurrection of Jesus Christ.

4. Salvation is a free gift of God that demands faith. We cannot earn it.

5. We Christians are bound together in one body, the church, of which Jesus is the head. We become sons and daughters to God by union with God's Son.

6. The Holy Spirit is the life of the church who enables us to call God *Abba*, Father.

7. As brothers and sisters of Jesus we should treat each other with dignity. We must love.

8. Following Jesus means that we must suffer for him gladly.

Reading	*Theme Illustrated* (mark number from list above)
a. 1 Cor 15:12-20	_____ _____ (list two themes)
b. Rom 8:14-17	_____

    c. Phil 2:5-11   _____

    d. Rom 3:27-31   _____

    e. Eph 4:31-32   _____

    f. 1 Cor 12:12-30   _____

    g. Col 1:24   _____

B.   *A Threat to Christian Unity.* Celebration of the Eucharist was the main source of unity in the early Christian communities, just as it is today. But like today, early Christians sinned and did not always act the way they should have around the Lord's table. Paul writes of a particularly serious abuse at Corinth. Read 1 Cor 11:17-34 to discover the problem and how Paul solved it.

    1. What abuse was taking place at Corinth?

    _____

    _____

    2. What does Paul say is the true meaning of the Eucharist?

    _____

    3. What solution does he recommend to the Corinthians for the problem?

    _____

C.   *Paul on Unity.* Reread 1 Cor 12:12-30. Paul's major image of the church is the Body of Christ. Jesus is the head of the body. Each of us is a member with different tasks, functions and gifts, but we are united to each other and to Christ because we are united to his body, the church. Here are some of the common gifts which the Holy Spirit gives to the members of Jesus' body. Check off one or two which are strong points with you.

    ____the ability to encourage others   ____the ability to express ideas

    ____the ability to work hard and stick to a task   ____the ability to endure hardships

    ____the ability to lead   ____the ability to adapt to new circumstances

    ____the ability to make peace   ____the ability to help out

    ____the ability to forgive   ____the ability to pray

    ____the ability to handle disappointments

EARLY CHRISTIAN LIFESTYLE

You have already read about some of the things the early Christian community held important during the lifetime of the apostles: shared prayer; celebration of the Eucharist, sometimes preceded by a common meal called an *agape* (love feast); the preaching of the good news; baptism of converts; distribution of goods to the needy, widows and victims of disasters like famine; and the sharing in common of goods and property.

Catholics believe that Jesus established the basic organizational structure of the church when he singled out Peter for the special role of leadership in the church. The apostles, the first *bishops* in the church, and those appointed by them to serve the needs of the community, *deacons,* formed the basis of the early organizational structure in the Christian community. By and large, though, church organization in these early days was rather loose. Everyone was expected to pitch in and be of service to everyone else. Some tasks, however, were designated by the early Christian leaders. People to perform these tasks were chosen by the community in prayer to the Holy Spirit and commissioned by the laying on of hands. In general these selected people were called *ministers.*

The chief ministers of the community were chosen by Jesus himself—the apostles. The Twelve, with Matthias taking the place of Judas, held a special place as the witnesses to the public life of Jesus. Their Christ-appointed leader was Peter; the *popes* are his successors. The chief ministry of the apostles was to witness to the marvelous deeds that had been performed through Jesus. Others, like Paul and Barnabas, were also called apostles. Paul, for example, received a special revelation of the risen Lord and was commissioned by Christ to preach the good news. Although the last apostle died in the late first or early second century, their mission of witnessing to the authentic gospel has been carried out through the ages by their successors, the bishops.

Another office of the early church was *prophet,* a person who interpreted the meaning of Jesus for fellow believers, and consoled, supported and encouraged the community. Prophets were joined by *teachers* who were entrusted with the instruction of converts. Paul also mentions other offices in the apostolic church, offices which seemed to fade from prominence for a number of centuries after this period in church history. Among these were *healers* and *miracle workers,* those who *spoke in tongues* and those who *interpreted* the tongues. These special offices were given as gifts or charisms by the Holy Spirit to help build up the community, the Body of Christ. In all cases the gifts were given for the benefit of the community and not for the personal gain of those holding them.

Further Growth. By the beginning of the second century, the church community needed more organization. The office of *episkopoi (bishops)* became more important. The bishops became overseers who saw to the proper running of the church in their cities. At first the *presbyters (priests)* who advised the local churches and led them in worship were the equals of the bishops, but as time passed priests became subordinate to the bishops and served as their stand-ins. The office of *deacon* remained. Deacons administered the daily concerns of the church, such as taking up collections for the poor, visiting the sick and distributing communion.

By the middle of the second century, the offices of bishop, priest and deacon were fairly widespread, and church authority at the local level was being focused in one man—the bishop. He in turn shared his authority with the priests and deacons. This system ensured that someone was designated to lead the Eucharist and to ordain others to do so. It also guaranteed that someone with authority could carry on correspondence with other Christian churches, represent the local community at a general gathering and be the focus of unity in disputes over doctrine.

By the second century the bishop of Rome, the man we call pope today, had an important position among the bishops. He was the successor to Peter, the first bishop of Rome. It was presumed that his teaching would be in line with that of the apostles. Located at the center of the Roman Empire, he was in an ideal position to lead the church whenever it was attacked by false beliefs. Other bishops often looked to Rome for leadership and made sure that what they taught was in line with what the bishop of Rome taught.

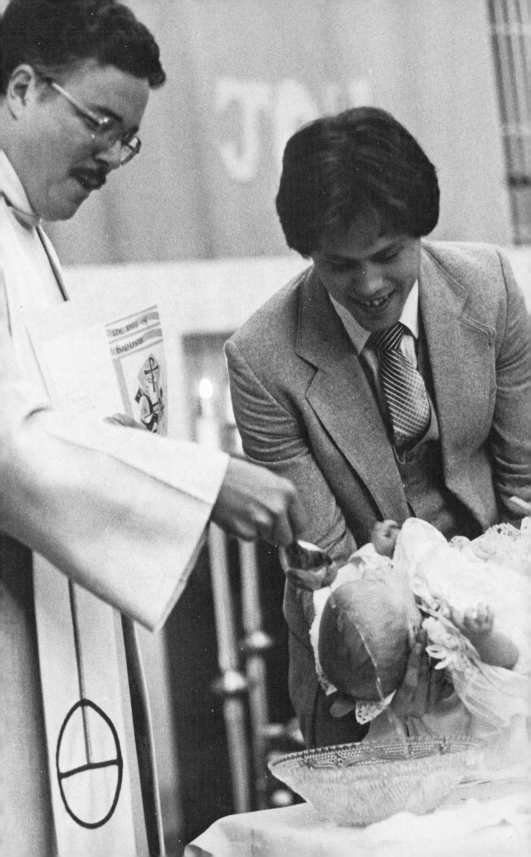

THE *DIDACHE*

In 1873 a small volume of 120 parchment leaves was found in a library of a monastery in Constantinople. Entitled *The Teaching of the Lord to the Gentiles, Through the Twelve Apostles* (or *The Didache, The Teaching*), it dates from the latter part of the first century and contains two major divisions. The first part is entitled "The Two Ways"—The Way of Life of Virtuous Christian Living versus the Way of Death or vices which Christians must avoid. The second part deals with rules of church life such as baptism, fasting, the Eucharist, wandering missionaries, local ministers and so forth.

Here is a selection from *The Didache* about baptism:

> The procedure for baptizing is as follows: After rehearsing all the preliminaries, immerse in running water "In the Name of the Father, and of the Son, and of the Holy Ghost." If no running water is available, immerse in ordinary water. This should be cold if possible; otherwise warm. If neither is practicable, then sprinkle water three times on the head "In the Name of the Father, and of the Son, and of the Holy Ghost." Both baptizer and baptized ought to fast before baptism, as well as any others who can do so; but the candidate himself should be told to keep a fast for a day or two beforehand.
>
> —Maxwell Staniforth, *Early Christian Writings: The Apostolic Fathers* (New York: Penguin Books, 1968), pp. 230-231.

Research:

1. How and when is baptism for children conducted in your local parish?

2. What must an adult in your parish community do before being baptized?

3. With what words is a Catholic baptized today?

PERSECUTIONS AND THE SPREAD OF
EARLY CHRISTIANITY

In the first few centuries, belief in Jesus Christ cost many Christians dearly. You have already seen that the Greek-speaking Christians like Stephen were martyred in Jerusalem for their preaching that Jesus was the Lord. Even the Aramaic-speaking James, the leader of the church in Jerusalem, ran into trouble with the Temple leaders and met his death in A.D. 62.

For about 30 years Rome had a tolerant attitude toward Christianity which it considered just another sect of Judaism. Rome generally protected Judaism, granting it certain privileges, for example, exempting Jews from serving in the Roman armies. This changed, though, under the emperor Nero. He was somehow responsible for a widespread fire in Rome in A.D. 64, and to save himself from the wrath of the populace, he blamed it on the Christians. Nero elicited confessions from some Christians in Rome. He tortured and crucified Christians, igniting their bodies as a spectacle for the bloodthirsty crowds. Both St. Peter and St. Paul died in the 60s under Nero's reign of terror.

Tacitus, the Roman historian who wrote the history of Nero's reign, accused the Christians of hating the human race. He especially disliked their "strange customs" (such as breaking bread in the Lord's name on Sundays) and their refusal to participate fully in Roman civic and religious rites. The Jewish historian Josephus also recorded that the Christians were persecuted because they adored a donkey's head and were guilty of ritual murder and incest. These charges, of course, were false.

Though Christians were martyred for their faith up to the time of the Edict of Milan, a law of toleration passed by the emperor Constantine in 313, they were not always ruthlessly hunted. From time to time the persecutions waned.

The most severe persecution in the first century took place under the emperor Domitian (A.D. 81-96) who required that his subjects worship him as a god. Many Christians refused to do so and were put to death. A letter written by Clement I speaks of persecutions in Rome during the 90s and the Book of Revelations refers to the hunting of Christians in the churches in Asia Minor.

In the second century the Emperor Trajan (98-117) replied to his governor in Bithynia, Pliny the Younger, that Christians were not to be sought out, but if discovered should be required to give up the faith. If they refused to do so, they were to be put to death. Under Hadrian (117-138) Christians enjoyed relative peace, but under other emperors like Marcus Aurelius and Decius persecutions flared up again. Perhaps the most severe took place under Diocletian beginning in 303.

Christianity Spreads. Despite periodic persecutions Christianity spread throughout the Empire. To what can we attribute this phenomenon? Church historian Thomas Bokenkotter lists four important factors responsible for the spread of the new religion in the first couple of centuries:

1. *Favorable Material Conditions in the Mediterranean World.* People spoke a common language—Greek. There was a good system of roads and shipping. There was a common culture. These factors made the job of the Christian missionaries much easier. For example, they could preach everywhere in Greek and be understood, and they could get around the Empire with relative ease.

2. *Roman Peace.* The Roman-enforced peace of the first and second centuries, the *Pax Romana,* enabled Christian missionaries to preach rather easily without worrying about barbarian invasions or the insecure conditions caused by war.

3. *Spiritual Turmoil in the Empire.* Roman religion with its worship of many gods had reached a low point. Many emperors, like Nero, were unbelievably corrupt. People were searching for spiritual meaning to their lives. The new mystery religions and philosophies like Stoicism helped some people. But none of the new religions or philosophical movements had the appeal of Christianity with its message of repentance and its sublime ethical code. Christianity had a wide appeal because of its doctrine of divine grace and forgiveness. Furthermore, unlike other religions, Christianity was based on a real historical person. It also taught people how to live a good life by insisting on sexual purity, marital fidelity, honesty, charity to the poor,

concern for the outcast and the like. This high ethical code attracted many people who wished to live a good life.

4. *Appeal of Christian Ideals.* Perhaps the most important reason for the spread of Christianity was the effective demonstration of the power of love in the lives of the Christians themselves. It caused the pagans to admire the way they lived and to exclaim, "Look how they love one another." Christian love, which took the concrete form of caring for everyone, proved an irresistible magnet to many who were seeking more meaning to their lives than the Roman games, orgies and worship of false idols could ever possibly give.

The periodic persecutions could not and did not stamp out the appeal of Christianity. Despite opposition the new religion grew in numbers and in influence in the Roman Empire.

A MARTYR FOR JESUS CHRIST

For many in the early centuries, the true test of following Christ was the willingness to die for him. Few saints in the history of the church were more willing to die for the Lord than St. Ignatius of Antioch.

Little is known of Ignatius' early life. He was probably the son of a pagan. He spent his early life in self-indulgence. Sometime after his baptism, when he assumed the additional name of Theophorus ("God-Borne" or "God-bearer"), he became the bishop of Antioch, probably around A.D. 69. His life overlapped that of some of the apostles, for example, John, and his leadership as bishop showed how important that office was in the early church.

Ignatius had a successful career as bishop for about 40 years. Then, during the reign of Trajan, he was condemned by the magistrates at Antioch to be thrown to the wild beasts in the circus. They dispatched him in chains to Rome under a guard of 10 soldiers.

They took a northerly route to Rome, stopping for a time in the cities of Smyrna and Troas. Along the way Ignatius wrote several letters to the churches whose delegates greeted him and the churches which entertained him in his stopover cities. These letters are historically famous because they reveal how anxious Ignatius was to die for Christ. He met his death, perhaps on December 19, 108, in the Flavian amphitheater in Rome, torn to bits by lions because of his belief in Christ. His bones were collected by his friends who obtained permission to carry them back to Antioch for burial.

Ignatius' letters show him to be a sensitive pastor, ever concerned that Christians obey their bishops and resist the temptations of false beliefs, that is, heresies. Ignatius attacked the false beliefs of those who did not think Jesus was really human, but only appeared to be. He also attacked the Judaizers, the same kind of men who plagued Paul during his career. To guard against these false teachers Ignatius counseled his flock to cling to the teaching of the bishop who was the focus of unity in the churches at the end of the first century.

Ignatius' greatest influence came with his thoughts on martyrdom, thoughts which greatly influenced Christians for centuries. He believed that the crowning glory for a Christian was to die for Jesus Christ. For him it was a privilege to do so.

Read a selection from Ignatius' *Letter to the Romans* to get a feeling for the kind of man he was.

> . . . Pray leave me to be a meal for the beasts, for it is they who can provide my way to God. I am his wheat, ground fine by the lions' teeth to be made purest bread for Christ. Better still, incite the creatures to become a sepulchre for me; let them not leave the smallest scrap of my flesh, so that I need not be a burden to anyone after I fall asleep. When there is no trace of my body left for the world to see, then I shall truly be Jesus Christ's disciple. . . .

> . . . This is the first stage of my discipleship; and no power, visible or invisible, must grudge me my coming to Jesus Christ. Fire, cross, beast-fighting, hacking and quartering, splintering of bone and mangling of limb, even the pulverizing of my entire body—let every horrid and diabolical torment come upon me, provided only that I can win my way to Jesus Christ!

> . . . All the ends of the earth, all the kingdoms of the world would be of no profit to me; so far as I am concerned, to die in Jesus Christ is better than to be monarch of earth's widest bounds. He who died for us is all I seek; He who rose again for us is my whole desire.

> —Maxwell Staniforth, *Early Christian Writings: The Apostolic Fathers,* pp. 104-105.

Discuss: Do you admire Ignatius? By today's standards would he be considered a fanatic? Why or why not? Is there a parish in your diocese named after this saint?

WHAT ABOUT YOU?

How Do You Measure Up? Today very few of us are called to give up our lives for our belief in the Lord. But we are often put in situations where we have to test the courage of our convictions. Read the following items and respond honestly to them.

_____ 1. If someone were to take the Lord's name in vain in my presence, I would:

   a. ignore the person
   b. show my displeasure
   c. change the subject
   d. I don't know what I would do

_____ 2. If someone were to belittle a handicapped person, I would:

   a. ignore the person
   b. show my displeasure
   c. change the subject
   d. I don't know what I would do

_____ 3. If I were put in a situation where I could skip Sunday Mass, I would:

   a. skip it
   b. go, even if my friends didn't
   c. I don't know what I would do

_____ 4. If someone criticized the Catholic church because of its teachings about abortion, I would:

   a. agree with the criticism
   b. defend the church's teaching
   c. admit that I didn't know what the church taught
   d. remain silent

_____ 5. If others were cheating on a test and expected me to cheat, I would probably:

   a. cheat
   b. not cheat but remain silent about the others' cheating
   c. not cheat and tell the teacher about the cheating
   d. I don't know what I'd do

Discuss: If you'd like, share and discuss your responses.

THE CHURCH AND COMMUNITY

The early church certainly lived the communal dimension. A group of people was called together by the Holy Spirit, engaged in the common task of preaching the good news, prayed together and broke bread in the Lord's name. The members shared their wealth, worked together to overcome internal bickerings, some of which—like the question of what to do with the Gentiles—threatened their continued existence. They also endured attacks from without, most notably the periodic persecutions by the Roman authorities. The church was, and is, a community of people concerned with the welfare of each member and all of God's people.

The early church saw itself as the Body of Christ, his real presence in the world (church as community). All members of the community had an important job to do, the common task of ministry (church as servant). All—precisely as a community—were to be authentic signs of God's love in the world (church as sacrament). All were to struggle together to resist the internal and external threats to community (church as pilgrim). Some were entrusted with the task of preaching the good news (church as herald); others—like bishops and deacons—were chosen to lead and teach and serve the community (church as institution).

Building community is a task of today's church as well. *You* have an important role to play in building up the Body of Christ, in making him present in your world. Our Lord has endowed you with certain gifts and talents to use for the benefit of all. You have the responsibility to discover your gifts and to use them for the good of others. Are you compassionate? Can you think clearly? Can you express yourself well? Do you have a sense of humor? Do you have musical ability? Are you a good listener? Whatever your gifts, they have been given to you so that you can use them for the good of others, your fellow believers and all people. The church needs you!

One of the very best ways you can celebrate and create community with your Catholic brothers and sisters is to participate fully in the Mass. Many people today do not see the value in the eucharistic liturgy. Some are lazy; others are too busy; still others do not like to be with "hypocrites" who do not always do what they profess. Some do not like the boring homilies or the weekly repetition of the same ritual. But consider carefully what really takes place at Mass.

We, rather ordinary sinners who gather together once a week, are very precious in God's eyes both as individuals and as a community. We gather to celebrate our need for the Lord. We receive the Lord Jesus who binds us into a tight community of love. We en-

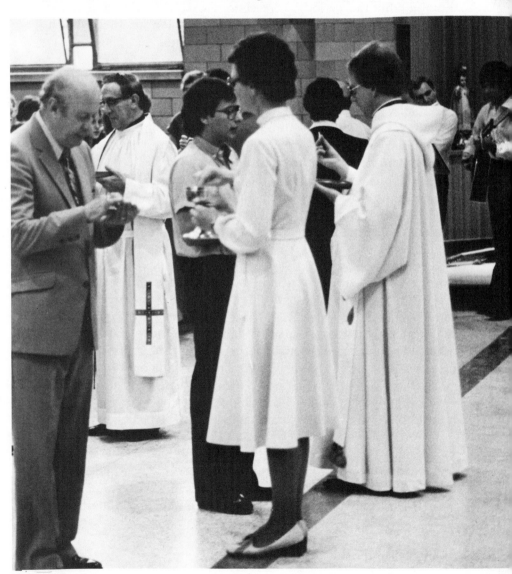

courage each other and acknowledge our need for each other. We love by simply going to Mass and saying we care.

Imagine the power of community-building you as a young person have. By discovering and using your talents for others you help create the church. By going to Mass and worshipping with a community of saints and sinners you are making an important statement. The Eucharist is a body-builder. It tells us that to be united to the church is to be united to Christ, and to be united to Christ is to be joined in some way to his church. This union shows that you care, that you love your Christian community, your church. It shows that you are willing to let the Lord into your life so that you have his love and strength and power to serve your brothers and sisters in the Christian community and your brothers and sisters in the everyday world in which you live. The Eucharist—and your participation in it—is a sign of love and love, above all else, creates Christian community.

REFLECTION

Read 1 Cor 13:1-13, Paul's great passage on the meaning of love. Love builds community. In reference to this passage, think of a recent time when you showed the following expressions of love. Briefly explain how this helped build community.

You were patient:_____

_____

You were not jealous:_____

_____

You were courteous:_____

_____

You were humble:_____

_____

You were kind:_____

_____

_____

SUMMARY

1. From its very beginning, the church was a community bound by the Holy Spirit into the Body of Christ.

2. The early church was founded in Jesus' name when the Holy Spirit descended on the apostles on Pentecost Sunday. Peter preached that Jesus of Nazareth is the Messiah who suffered and died for all and rose from the dead. Peter also preached the need for repentance and baptism in the name of the Lord.

3. The foundation of the church is Jesus Christ who preached the advent of God's kingdom. Jesus performed miracles to authenticate his mission and to display the power of God's kingdom.

Jesus was a teacher *par excellence.* His message included these points:

    a. God's kingdom is in our midst.

    b. God's kingdom is a free gift, open to all, even sinners.

    c. The good news of the kingdom demands an urgent response.

    d. The coming of the kingdom calls for repentance.

    e. God's kingdom demands suffering.

4. Jesus was a community-builder who remains with us in the Eucharist, the great symbol of Christian love and unity.

5. Without Jesus' resurrection there would be no church.

6. Two early threats to Christian community concerned the proper treatment of Greek-speaking Jewish-Christian widows, and how to handle the Gentiles. The first problem was solved by appointing deacons to serve the community; the second was solved at the Council of Jerusalem when the Holy Spirit led the church leaders to decide that one need not be a Jew first to be a Christian.

7. The persecution of the Greek-speaking Jewish-Christians impelled them to spread the gospel in districts outside of Jerusalem. Paul of Tarsus, with the help of other Christian missionaries like Barnabas, engaged in three major journeys to spread the gospel around the Roman Empire. By the end of the first century Christianity was well established in the Roman world.

8. The followers of Jesus Christ were first called *Christians* at Antioch in Syria.

9. Next to Jesus, Paul is the most important figure in New Testament times. A Pharisee, he was converted on the road to Damascus when he experienced the risen Lord. He led three missionary efforts. He converted the Gentiles and was instrumental in winning over James and Peter to the cause of the Gentiles at the Council of Jerusalem in A.D. 50. He wrote many important theological letters which form a significant part of the New Testament. He was finally beheaded under Nero in Rome in A.D. 68.

10. A threat to Christian community arose in Corinth when some Christians failed to recognize the presence of the Lord in their fellow believers during the celebration of the Eucharist.

11. Early Christian organization involved everyone in ministry. The apostles were appointed by Christ with Peter as their head. Some were prophets, teachers, healers and miracle workers. Some could speak in tongues; still others were able to interpret tongues. By the end of the first century the bishops—the successors to the apostles—became the focus of unity in the church. Priests and deacons assisted them. The bishop of Rome (the pope) held a preeminent position among the bishops and was more and more looked to for leadership, especially as the second century got under way.

12. Various persecutions of Christians threatened the existence of Christianity. At times, Rome was tolerant; at other times, especially under emperors like Nero, Domitian, Marcus Aurelius, Decius and Diocletian, persecutions flared up.

13. Christianity spread throughout the Roman Empire because:
   a. There were favorable material conditions.
   b. There was relative peace.
   c. People were looking for spiritual meaning.
   d. The love of Christians for one another and for all people attracted many.

14. Ignatius of Antioch presents an ideal of the Christian martyr, one willing to die for Jesus Christ.

15. The building of Christian community is a vital responsibility for Catholics today just as it was when the church was first established. By recognizing and using our talents for others and by participating in the Eucharist, the great symbol of Christian community, we are contributing to the building of Christ's body.

EVALUATION

1. Briefly discuss the significance of the Council of Jerusalem.

2. Identify the *Didache*:_____

Matching: Match the following names with the descriptions.

____ 3. a companion of Paul's   a. Jesus

____ 4. a Jewish historian   b. Gamaliel

____ 5. man who baptized Paul   c. Paul

____ 6. a leader of the church in   d. Peter
        Jerusalem
                                     e. Ignatius of Antioch
____ 7. the first Christian martyr
                                     f. Barnabas
____ 8. most important of the
        12 apostles   g. James

                                     h. Stephen
____ 9. teacher of Saul
                                     i. Cornelius
____ 10. Peter's Gentile convert
                                     j. Ananias
____ 11. man who replaced Judas
         as an apostle   k. Clement I

____ 12. the apostle to the Gentiles l. Nero

____ 13. an emperor who perse-   m. Matthias
         cuted early Christians
                                     n. Tacitus
____ 14. Jesus-appointed leader of
         the church   o. Josephus

SOME FINAL PROJECTS

Choose one of the following topics for research.

1. Read "The People of God," Chapter 2 of the *Constitution on the Church,* and list 10 important insights you learned about the church from this chapter of the Vatican II document. Report to the class.

2. Research the modern-day charismatic movement in the church. Report to the class on one of these two topics:

    a. the healing ministry

    b. speaking in tongues

3. *Hagiography.* One way Christians learn about the richness of their tradition is to study the lives of the saints. Construct a hagiography (the biography of a holy person) by researching the life of one of the greatest of the Christian saints of the first century, St. Peter the Apostle. Present your report to the class.

Your report should have two parts: first, a short biography of St. Peter; second, a response to your reflections on the following questions:

    a. What did you learn about Peter's personality?

    b. What did you learn about Peter's motivation?

You can approach this topic two ways. The first is to consult a concordance to the Bible, a bible dictionary or resource book on people of the Bible to gather your information. A second way is to consult the New Testament references below:

Luke 5:1-11	Luke 22:54-62	Acts 3:1-4:31
Matthew 14:22-33	Luke 24:1-12	Acts 9:32-10:48
Matthew 16:13-20	John 21:15-19	Acts 11:1-18
Mark 9:2-8	Acts 2:1-42	Acts 15:7-11

Additional Fact:

Tradition holds that Peter was crucified at Rome between A.D. 64-67 under the emperor Nero.

PRAYER REFLECTION

Lord Jesus, thank you for calling us into your community, your
body, the church.

Thank you, Lord, for the gifts you have given us.
>   Help us to recognize them and use them.
>   Help us to know what it means to be members of your body.
>   Remind us that . . .
>>   we are your gentle touch in the world today;
>>   we are your forgiving, understanding eyes;
>>   we are your voice to proclaim the good news;
>>   we are your presence.

Remind us, Lord, of these powerful privileges. And help us to be true
to you. Amen.

3
Proclaiming the Good News:
The Church From 100-800

Christ be with me, Christ before me, Christ behind me,
Christ in me, Christ beneath me, Christ above me,
Christ on my right, Christ on my left,
Christ where I lie, Christ where I sit, Christ where I arise,
Christ in the heart of every one who thinks of me,
Christ in the mouth of every one who speaks of me,
Christ in every eye that sees me,
Christ in every ear that hears me.
                                        —St. Patrick's Breastplate

Today we live in an era of instant communications. Our ancient ancestors had to rely on hand-delivered letters which may have taken months to reach their destination by land route or sea. Today a dial of the telephone can put us in touch with any part of the globe. Radio and television, aided by satellite systems, bring us the voices and faces of people at the very moment they are making news. We have even communicated with astronauts walking on the face of the moon.

All of us both use and are exposed to the various media—television, radio, newspapers, and so forth—yet none of these media can replace face-to-face contact when we want to share our good news with others.

Early Christians were faced with the momentous task of spreading the good news of God's great love for us. Before his ascension into heaven Jesus gave the Christian community the mandate to be heralds of the good news. You read in the last chapter how Christianity had been established in every corner of the Roman Empire by

73

the end of the first century. The task did not end there, though. Christianity was just beginning, and as you have seen, it was being persecuted.

In this chapter we will look at the ways the church spread its message about Jesus during its first few centuries. The task was formidable. There were no mass communications; at the beginning of this era Christianity was a hated religion, hunted and persecuted; and false teachings known as heresies soon developed which threatened the very existence of the church. Later on the barbarians and then the Moslems threatened to destroy the gains Christianity had made.

This chapter will look at three important factors which greatly contributed to the heralding of the good news in the second through eighth centuries:

- the role of some great teachers, the apologists and the church Fathers
- the legalization of Christianity and the cooperation between state and church
- the monastic movement

CHRISTIAN RESPONSIBILITY

Every follower of Jesus is called on to spread the good news, to be a herald for Christ. St. Paul expressed this truth vividly when he wrote to his friends in Ephesus:

> Finally, grow strong in the Lord, with the strength of his power. Put God's armor on so as to be able to resist the devil's tactics (Eph 6:10-11).

> So stand your ground, with *truth buckled round your waist,* and *integrity for a breastplate,* wearing for shoes on your feet *the eagerness to spread the gospel of peace* and always carrying the shield of faith so that you can use it to put out the burning arrows of the evil one. And then you must accept *salvation from God to be your helmet* and receive the word of God from the Spirit to use as a sword (Eph 6:14-17).

Rank your own readiness to be a herald for Jesus Christ by marking the following scale (1 is very low readiness; 5 is very high):

Belt of Truth: I am willing to stand for the truth, unafraid of the consequences of being an honest person as Jesus himself was honest when he admitted to Pilate his true identity.

1   2   3   4   5

Breastplate of Integrity: What I say, I do. I live my commitments. People know where I stand.

1   2   3   4   5

Shoes of the Good News of Peace: I stand ready to share my belief in Jesus Christ with others. I am a person of peace. I am not afraid to explain what I believe and what I value.

1   2   3   4   5

Shield of Faith: I firmly believe that Jesus will help me when I am tempted and raise me up when I fall.

1   2   3   4   5

Helmet of Salvation: I trust in the Lord and accept his good news of love. I take advantage of his forgiveness in the sacrament of reconciliation. I receive his love in the sacrament of the Eucharist.

1   2   3   4   5

Sword of God's Word: I am committed to learning more about my faith. I participate fully in religion classes and read the Bible and other materials that will help me know the Lord better.

1   2   3   4   5

THE FATHERS OF THE CHURCH

As you saw in the last chapter, conditions were ripe in the Roman Empire for the spread of Christianity. The poor, the enslaved and women—who were granted few rights in much of the Roman world—were greatly attracted to Christianity. Paul's teaching helped to draw the exploited like a magnet: "There are no more distinctions between Jew and Greek, slave and free, male and female, but all of you are one in Christ Jesus" (Gal 3:28). The charitable activities and the witness of Christian martyrs greatly helped attract new converts.

Despite the periodic persecutions of the Roman emperors like Decius and Valerian in the middle of the third century, the preaching of the gospel continued. By 310 or so Christianity had rooted itself in many places throughout the Empire. About half of the population of Asia Minor might have been Christian. A sizeable minority of Christians lived in Numidia, Egypt, Rome, lower Italy and Spain. In Gaul and Germany the religion was just getting under way.

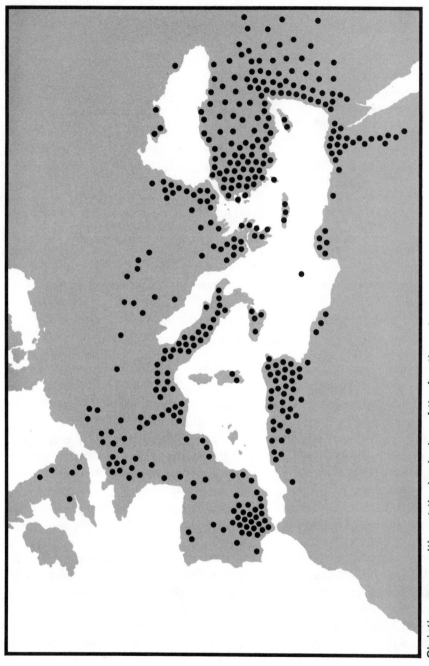

Christian communities at the beginning of the fourth century

The Apologists. Christianity had its critics, though. Many Roman intellectuals attacked it as barbaric, atheistic and disruptive of the life of the empire. These attacks from without were met by a group of Christian writers known as the *apologists* who largely wrote in the second century and attempted to convince the emperors and the intellectuals that Christianity was a respectable religion. One of the most famous of these men was St. Justin the Martyr. He was a converted philosopher who taught that Christianity was the true religion, and that persecution of Christians was unjust.

Gnosticism. More serious than attacks from without, however, were false teachings which cropped up within the church. The period from 100-800 saw a number of heresies arise which threatened the very existence of true belief in Jesus Christ. Perhaps the most dangerous was Gnosticism, which appeared in a number of forms. Gnosticism claimed to give secret knowledge (*gnosis*) to its followers, knowledge which assured them of salvation. Gnostics denied the validity of the scriptures and denied that Christ was really a man. They believed that material things were evil and were created by the Old Testament God while only the spiritual realm was good because it was created by the God of the New Testament.

Among others, St. Irenaeus wrote against Gnosticism. In his famous work *Against Heresies* he stressed that the world was created by one God; that Jesus Christ, son of the Creator, died to save all people; and that there will be a resurrection from the dead. Very significantly, too, Bishop Irenaeus underscored the tremendous importance of the tradition of the church in arriving at religious truth. For Irenaeus, the source of right teaching and right belief resides with the Roman church (with the bishop of Rome, the pope, as the head) because this church was founded by Jesus and entrusted to St. Peter and has best preserved the teaching of the apostles.

Who Is a Church Father? The term "church Father" originally applied to bishops of the church who witnessed to the authentic Christian tradition, that is, men like Irenaeus. By the fourth century it applied to a group of church writers whose teaching on matters of doctrine carried special weight. By the fifth century it applied to great teachers, some of whom were not necessarily bishops—men like St.

Jerome (342-420) and even the   layman St. Prosper of Aquitaine (390-463). All of these men we now call church Fathers were known for the correctness of their doctrine (*orthodoxy*—"right teaching"), their holiness of life (*orthopraxis*—"right living"), their approval by the universal church and their having written sometime during this early era of church history.

The church Fathers were true heralds of the gospel of Jesus Christ. As leading thinkers of their day they attempted to make the Christian message make sense for the people of their time. Their writings are read today because they still help Christians appreciate and understand better the good news. Many church Fathers formulated their teachings in response to internal attacks on Christian beliefs. Mistakes in thinking and in the expression of ideas were made by those who were trying to take the beliefs of the scriptures and make them intelligible to Greek thought patterns. The church Fathers heralded a true understanding of Christian belief by defending the gospel against certain false teachings and beliefs.

Three of the questions with which the church had to deal in these centuries are discussed below. The name of a heresy is mentioned in connection with each question, and the teaching of a prominent churchman and/or church council is given as a response to the problem.

PROBLEM #1: What should be done with Christians who fall into sin after baptism?

This question arose about 220 in regard to those who gave up their faith when threatened by persecution. Baptism included forgiveness of sins already committed, but serious sins committed *after* baptism needed special treatment. Pope Callistus (217-222) held the moderate view that even apostasy, denying Christ, was forgivable if the person was truly repentant. The test of sincerity was often a long penance, one sometimes lasting for years.

This view did not sit well with a much stricter man, Novatian, who was defeated in an election for pope held in 251. He and his followers broke off from the church and set up congregations in

Carthage and in the East. These congregations held that there could be no absolution for anyone who had rejected Jesus Christ, or committed murder or adultery. This heresy was countered by the Council of Nicaea (325) which explicitly directed that the dying be reconciled.

Another overly strict view, this time aimed at priests, was that of Donatus from North Africa. He wrongly taught that the spiritual value of the sacraments depended on the personal holiness of the priest. Donatism was condemned at the regional Council of Arles (314). The bishops at this council taught the important truth that the sacraments convey grace independent of the worthiness of the person who confers them.

Discuss:

What is the value in the teaching that sacraments convey grace independent of the personal holiness of the priest?

Research:

How was the sacrament of reconciliation practiced in the early church?

PROBLEM #2: Who is Jesus Christ?

One of the major doctrinal problems of the early church was how to proclaim the Jesus of the gospels in a way that those familiar with Greek philosophy could understand what was taught about him. By and large this question was hammered out in the Eastern church which was much more given to theological speculation, especially at the two leading theological centers of Alexandria in Africa and Antioch in Syria. In trying to formulate a correct philosophical understanding of Christ, some serious errors were made. These errors were ultimately corrected by some leading church Fathers and some important church councils.

Arianism. The most widespread heresy in the early centuries of Christianity was Arianism. Named after an Alexandrian priest, Arius, this heresy taught that the Word of God was only an adopted son of God and therefore not divine. For Arius, Christ was the greatest of God's creatures made before time, but a creature nonetheless. This dangerous teaching attracted quite a few followers so that the Emperor Constantine called the first *ecumenical* (worldwide) church council to help preserve both the unity of Christianity and the peace of the empire. The Council of Nicaea (325) condemned Arianism by teaching that Jesus Christ has the same nature as God, that Jesus Christ is divine and equal to the Father.

Arianism should have died out at Nicaea, but certain Arians persisted and gained the ear of Constantine's successors, Constantius II and Valens. They were quite successful in imposing Arianism in many parts of the Eastern Empire. Arian missionaries were even responsible for converting many of the invading barbarians from the East.

The Catholics had a champion in the bishop of Alexandria, St. Athanasius, who fought valiantly for the orthodox teaching set down at the Council of Nicaea. Exiled five times by the emperor, Athanasius held firmly that Christ "was made man that we may be made divine." He held correctly that if Christ were not God then he could not be our savior. Only God could restore people to communion with himself. This view of Athanasius, along with the support of two Eastern church Fathers, St. Gregory of Nyssa and St. Basil, prevailed at another church council in Constantinople in 381.

In the Western church the great Father and bishop of Milan, St. Ambrose, helped stamp out Arianism. He clashed with the mother of the emperor Valentinian II when she tried to set up an Arian church in Milan. Later he became a close adviser of the emperor Theodosius and even forced the emperor to make a form of public confession after he had massacred the citizens of Thessalonica. Ambrose was the first church official to successfully use his office to coerce civil rulers.

The creed of the Council of Nicaea, reiterated at Constantinople, is the very creed we recite at Mass today. It reads as follows:

The Nicene Creed

We believe in one God,
   the Father, the Almighty,
   maker of heaven and earth,
   of all that is seen and unseen.

We believe in one Lord, Jesus Christ,
   the only Son of God,
   eternally begotten of the Father,
   God from God, Light from Light,
   true God from true God,
   begotten, not made, one in Being with the Father.
   Through him all things were made.
   For us and for our salvation
     he came down from heaven:
   by the power of the Holy Spirit
     he was born of the Virgin Mary, and became man.
   For our sake he was crucified under Pontius Pilate;
     he suffered, died, and was buried.
     On the third day he rose again
       in fulfillment of the Scriptures;
     he ascended into heaven
       and is seated at the right hand of the Father.
   He will come again in glory
       to judge the living and the dead,
     and his kingdom will have no end.

We believe in the Holy Spirit, the Lord, the giver of life,
   who proceeds from the Father and the Son.
   With the Father and the Son he is worshiped and glorified.
   He has spoken through the Prophets.
   We believe in one holy catholic and apostolic Church.
   We acknowledge one baptism for the forgiveness of sins.
   We look for the resurrection of the dead,
     and the life of the world to come. Amen.

EXERCISES ON THE CREED

A. *The Creed and You.* How much does this creed from the
Councils of Nicaea and Constantinople mean to you? Here are
some beliefs which are central for Roman Catholics. These
beliefs either come directly from this creed or are derived from
it. Rate yourself according to this scale:

    1—I really believe this

    2—I believe this

    3—I think I believe this

    4—I don't know if I believe this

    5—I don't believe this

____I believe in God

____I believe that Jesus Christ is God

____I believe that Jesus died and rose again

____I believe in Jesus as a personal friend

____I believe in the power of the Holy Spirit

____I believe in the Ten Commandments

____I believe that everyone is a child of God and a sister and
brother to me

____I believe that I must respond to the Lord by loving the
poor, the sick, the lonely, the outcast, etc.

____I believe in the power of the sacraments, especially the
Eucharist and the sacrament of reconciliation

____I believe in the authority of the pope as vicar of Christ

____I believe in the Trinity

____I believe that Jesus Christ is my personal Lord and Savior

____I believe that Jesus lives and can be contacted in prayer

____I believe in the power of prayer

____I believe the Lord will judge me at the end of time

____I believe that I must love God above all things and my
neighbor as myself

____I believe in the Catholic church

____I believe that I am destined for an eternal life of glory with
the Lord

B. Write your own creed. Share it with your classmates.

How Many Persons in Christ? The battles over Jesus continued. Nestorius, a patriarch of Constantinople, held that there were two *persons* in Jesus Christ—one divine, the other only human. He refused to call Mary the mother of God, claiming that she only gave birth to the human Jesus. St. Cyril of Alexandria argued strongly for the term *theotokos*; that is, that Mary was the mother of God, the mother of Jesus Christ who was one person, a divine person. Cyril's view was endorsed and Nestorianism condemned at the Council of Ephesus held in 431.

How Many Natures in Christ? Christological questions did not end in Ephesus! A certain Eutyches, the chief abbot of the monks at Constantinople, preached that Christ's human nature was absorbed into his divine nature "like a drop of honey into the water of the sea." This heresy was known as Monophysitism (Christ had only one nature—a divine one) and ultimately denied that Christ was really a human being. Pope Leo I in his work entitled *The Tome of Leo* taught that Jesus Christ was one divine person subsisting in two distinct natures—one human, the other divine. Leo writes:

> In this preservation, then, of the real quality of both natures, both being united in one person, lowliness was taken on by majesty, weakness by strength, mortality by the immortal.

Leo's views prevailed at the Council of Chalcedon (451). Despite repeated attempts by the emperors to dilute this teaching and strike a compromise with the Monophysites—and thus to keep religious peace in the empire—the Second Council of Constantinople (681) adopted the teaching of the previous councils, St. Leo and the popes who followed him: *Jesus Christ is one divine person with two distinct natures—one human, the other divine.*

PROBLEM #3: Can people save themselves?

The Western church was more interested in practical issues than the kind of theological speculation on Christ's nature which occupied Eastern Christians. A typical problem was that posed by Pelagius, a popular priest-teacher from Britain. In defending the concept of free will and one's obligation to strive for personal holiness, Pelagius denied original sin and the need for divine grace. In effect, Pelagius held that people could save themselves without God's supernatural help. (Pelagianism is still a common problem of American Christians in fact if not in faith.)

St. Augustine

Pelagius met his match in the person of the greatest of the church Fathers, St. Augustine of Hippo (354-430). Augustine eloquently demonstrated that people have fallen natures and are subject to the effects of original sin. He taught that God's grace is absolutely necessary for personal salvation.

St. Augustine. Following St. Paul, Augustine had the greatest influence on the development of Christian theology. Born in Africa in 354, Augustine received a Christian upbringing—his mother, Monica, was a Christian—and a good Latin literary education. He studied at the university at Carthage and became a noted lecturer in rhetoric there. During this period he abandoned Christianity and also took a mistress with whom he lived for the next 15 years. Their son, Adeodatus, was born in 372. Several years later his interest in philosophy took him to Rome and eventually he made his way to Milan where he came under the powerful influence of St. Ambrose. Ambrose helped him see that Christianity contained many answers to the questions which had plagued him: the nature of the spiritual world, the relationship between good and evil, the nature of the Old Testament writings, and so forth. He experienced a profound desire to change his life, a life he now saw as sinful and devoid of Christian ideals, and was baptized in 387. He returned to Africa where he was ordained and, in 396, was elected bishop of Hippo. He became a pre-eminent preacher and pastor, judge and intercessor, organizer of charity, minister of the sacraments, tireless defender of the Catholic faith and author of some of the world's greatest theological works.

His autobiographical book, *Confessions,* tells about his spiritual journey. His tract *On the Trinity* influences Christian theologians to this day. Another book, *The City of God,* was written in the wake of the Visigoth Alaric's sack of Rome in 410. This book divides history into the struggle between the sinful inhabitants of the City of Man, typified by the dying Roman Empire, and the pilgrims or believers in God who live in the City of God. Citizenship in these cities depends on commitment to the important values in life. The church is not necessarily the same as God's City. Made up of sinners, the true task of the church is to act as a sign of God's love for the world.

Augustine spent the rest of his life after his conversion defending

Catholicism against the Pelagians, the Donatists and the Manicheans, a gnostic group which also argued that material reality was evil and that there were two gods—one of evil and one of good. He also prepared for the attack of the Vandals, opening up his city to refugees who were escaping the onslaught of the barbarians across Africa. Augustine died in 430; a year later, the Vandals sacked Hippo.

AUGUSTINE'S CONVERSION

"I probed the hidden depths of my soul and wrung its pitiful secrets from it, and when I gathered them all before the eyes of my heart, a great storm broke within me, bringing within it a great deluge of tears. . . . For I felt that I was still enslaved by my sins, and in my misery I kept crying, 'How long shall I go on saying "Tomorrow, tomorrow"? Why not now? Why not make an end of my ugly sins at this moment?'

"I was asking myself these questions, weeping all the while with the most bitter sorrow in my heart, when all at once I heard the singsong voice of a child in a nearby house. Whether it was the voice of a boy or a girl I cannot say, but again and again it repeated the chorus, 'Take it and read, take it and read.' At this I looked up, thinking hard whether there was any kind of game in which children used to chant words like these, but I could not remember ever hearing them before. I stemmed my flood of tears and stood up, telling myself that this could only be God's command to open my book of Scripture and read the first passage on which my eyes should fall. . . .

"So I hurried back to the place where Alypius was sitting, for when I stood up to move away I had put down the book containing Paul's Letters. I seized it and opened it, and in silence I read the first passage on which my eyes fell: 'No orgies or drunkenness, no immorality or indecency, no fighting or jealousy. Take up the weapons of the Lord Jesus Christ; and stop giving attention to your sinful nature, to satisfy its desire.' I had no wish to read more and no need to do so. For in an instant, as I came to the end of the sentence, it was as though the light of faith flooded into my heart and all the darkness of doubt was dispelled."

—Augustine's *Confessions,* VIII.12

To Do:

Write a few paragraphs describing any profound religious experience you've had, perhaps on a retreat or renewal. How did it differ from Augustine's?

Or:

Interview a convert to Catholicism. Ask the person what experience helped him or her to convert. Report to the class.

TWO HERALDS OF THE WORD:
JEROME AND JOHN CHRYSOSTOM

St. Jerome. One of the great church Fathers was St. Jerome (345-420). Born in northeast Italy, he studied the Latin scholars of ancient Rome. He was baptized in Rome and spent some time in a strict monastic community near his home at Aquileia. Later in Antioch (374), Jerome had a vision which criticized him for his devotion to secular learning, for being "a follower of Cicero and not of Christ."

Jerome was ordained in Antioch, traveled to Constantinople and studied under the church Father Gregory of Nazianzus in 380 and eventually came to Rome as the secretary to Pope Damasus. Jerome had a fiery temper and used his sharp pen to write fierce letters to his opponents. But the pope recognized his talents and commissioned him to translate the bible into Latin. After the death of Damasus, Jerome traveled to Antioch, Egypt and the Holy Land, eventually making his home as a monk in a cave. He founded a monastery, convent and church. For the next 23 years Jerome spent his time translating the entire bible into Latin and making scholarly comments on it.

With the third-century church Father, Origen, and St. Augustine, Jerome ranks as one of the greatest of all biblical scholars. His translation, known as the *Latin Vulgate* (382-405), became the authorized bible used in the Catholic church up to modern times. His efforts made it much easier for churchmen to preach God's word throughout the ensuing centuries.

St. John Chrysostom. A contemporary of Jerome, John was born in Antioch in 350. Baptized at the age of 18, he became a reader in the church and then lived for two years in a cave in the mountains, damaging his health in the process. Ordained a priest in 386, he began preaching in the principal church in Antioch, gaining the reputation as the "Golden Mouth" (Chrysostom) orator.

Against his will he was chosen as bishop of Constantinople in 397. John met with opposition when he attempted to raise the moral climate of the city. The Empress Eudoxia did not like his attacks on sin in high places; the local clergy found him too strict; and the patriarch of Alexandria was jealous of him. They had him deposed by the emperor who reinstated John when the people rioted. He again took up his preaching against sinners and was driven out of the city a second time, an exile which ended in his death in 407.

John Chrysostom is honored for his piety, for his defense of the faith, for his moral teaching, and especially for his way of heralding the good news. His methods of preaching from the pulpit are still studied today as excellent models of how a preacher should present the word of God.

CLASS PROJECT:

Construct and discuss a list of traits which you think all good preachers should have.

INDIVIDUAL PROJECT:

Using a reference tool like *The New Catholic Encyclopedia,* research and report on the life of one of these church Fathers.

St. Polycarp (died around 156)
Tertullian (second/third century)
St. Hippolytus (died around 235)
Origen (died around 254)
St. Hilary of Poitiers (315-367)
St. Basil the Great (330-379)
St. Gregory Nazianzen (330-389)
St. Ambrose (333-397)
St. Prosper (died around 463)
St. Isidore of Seville (died around 636)
St. Bede the Venerable (died around 735)

CHRISTIANITY COMES OF AGE:
CHURCH-STATE RELATIONS

Great changes took place in both the church and the political scene in the Western Roman Empire during the fourth, fifth and sixth centuries: Christianity, a persecuted minority religion at the time of Constantine's conversion, became the official religion of the empire by 380; the Germanic barbarian invasions extinguished the Western Roman Empire; and the prestige, importance and power of the pope in Rome greatly increased.

Constantine's Conversion. Few events in the history of the church can match the conversion of the Emperor Constantine in 312. He later told church historian Eusebius of a vision he had before the battle of the Milvian bridge outside Rome. He claimed that Christ appeared to him in a dream and instructed him to use the Chi-Rho (☧—the first two letters of Christ's name) on the shields of his men and victory would be his. Constantine followed the promptings of his dream, won the battle and became convinced that the Christian God was the most powerful of all gods.

In 313 Constantine and his co-emperor issued an edict tolerating Christianity. The wheels of official recognition had begun turning. Constantine began to shower favors on Christian clerics; for example, by the end of the fourth century they were exempt from civil taxation. Confiscated church property was returned. Churches were built. In 321 Constantine outlawed manual labor on Sunday. By 324, when Constantine was sole emperor, the Catholic church could be truly considered the state religion. Except for a brief period of persecution under the Emperor Julian, who tried to reestablish the old pagan religions, Christianity was on the upswing. In 380 the Emperor Theodosius issued a decree making Christianity the *official* religion of the empire.

Drawbacks and Benefits. What have been the long-term effects of the wedding of church and state which took place in the fourth century? On the negative side the church became too dependent on the whims of the state officials. Now that people almost had to be Christian to be Roman citizens, the quality of religious commitment declined. Many pagan superstitions hung on. Religious conversions often seemed lukewarm at best; for example, the cult of relics began to develop. People sometimes thought the remains of Christian saints had magical powers. Before the time of Constantine, Christians rarely supported war efforts. By the fifth century, a soldier had to be a Christian. Through its history the church often has had to water down its spiritual interests for political considerations.

On the positive side the conversion of Constantine greatly aided the church's heralding of the gospel. With all the resources of the empire at its service, the church was able to preach to pagans in the empire and later on to the barbarians. The marriage with the state also helped church unity. More often than not it was the emperors who called the early church councils to settle the divisive doctrinal disputes. For example, Constantine convoked the Council of Nicaea and helped enforce its decrees against the Arians.

Roman methods of organization were adopted for church government. The diocese system was used with five great patriarchates in Rome, Constantinople, Alexandria, Antioch and Jerusalem governing the churches in their respective areas. Rome was considered preeminent, though, for two reasons: First, it claimed descent from Peter who died there. Other churches looked to the practices and beliefs of Rome to endorse their own beliefs and practices. Second, when Constantine moved his capital to Constantinople (the old city of Byzantium), the Bishop of Rome (the pope) stepped into a power vacuum and with time became a kind of temporal ruler (as well as the spiritual guide) in the West.

In addition, the church adopted the code of law issued by the Emperor Justinian who tried successfully for a time to wrest the western empire back from the barbarians. The Justinian Code was imitated by the church in its own government for many centuries. Finally, with Christianity no longer a persecuted religion, it took the time and effort to incorporate some positive features of the pagan religions into its own practice; for example, the use of candles and incense, the cult of saints and martyrs (who took the place of the many gods of the pagans), the building of elaborate cathedrals and churches.

CHURCH-STATE RELATIONS

Class Project:

1. Make a list of items which show that the American government today does not want to get overly involved in the affairs of the church. Here are three examples:

   a. The church can run its own religious schools.

   b. Priests and those in religious life are exempt from military service.

   c. Christians are free to worship as they please.

2. *Discuss these questions:*

   a. Is each of the items you listed a real benefit for the church?

   b. Is the American separation of church and state generally a good thing? Why or why not?

   c. List some dangers for the church if the government became more involved in church life.

The Barbarian Invasions and the Rise of the Papacy. The fifth century was noteworthy for the migrations of the barbarians from the East. The Visigoths settled in Gaul and Spain, the Vandals in North Africa, the Ostrogoths and Lombards in Italy. They destroyed an already internally weak empire, an empire which lost the will to be great, an empire characterized by decaying morals and softness of life. Since the capital was now in Constantinople, the West was left vulnerable. The fall of Rome is linked to the sack of Rome in 410 and the deposition of the last western emperor in 476.

Barbarian kingdoms in the fifth/sixth centuries

The barbarian invasions posed a serious threat to Christianity. Some barbarians had converted to Arianism. These Arian Christians persecuted the Roman Catholics and one of their leaders, Theodoric, even imprisoned the pope. The Catholics, though, found a powerful ally in Clovis, the king of the Franks. He was baptized in 496 at the urging of his Catholic wife, Clotilda. Clovis broke the power of the Visigoths and forced them to accept baptism. The Franks thrived and their alliance with Rome helped Catholicism grow among the barbarians. This arrangement had its drawbacks, however, as future Frankish kings began to appoint their own bishops, an arrangement which would cause many problems in later centuries.

During these treacherous times the church was the preserver of Roman culture. It provided stability. It was the custodian of the law. Its bishops were men of rank and authority. Fortunately, the barbarians admired the Roman civilization and wanted to adopt many of its customs. In Southern Europe both bishops and missionaries won many Visigoths and Burgundians to Roman Catholicism. In the Northern countries of Scotland and Ireland, missionaries like St. Patrick converted the Celts.

Pope Leo the Great. Pope Leo the Great, who died in 461, managed all the affairs of Rome, even seeing that the poor were fed. He was so highly regarded that a popular but untrue story circulated claiming that he met Attila the Hun outside the city walls of Rome and persuaded him not to attack Rome. His greatest contribution was establishing the primacy of the pope, convincing the bishops of the church that as bishop of Rome and successor to Peter he was the *supreme teacher, supreme ruler* and *supreme judge.* He was most influential in settling the matter about Christ's two natures at the Council of Chalcedon (451).

Pope Gregory the Great. In the next century, Pope Gregory the Great (590-604) further enhanced the reputation of the papacy. A great spiritual writer and church Father, Gregory was the first to use the title "servant of the servants of God" to describe the office of the papacy, a title still used today. Gregory has entered the history books for three momentous achievements: 1) He established the popes as the rulers of central Italy. He did so by mustering up opposition to the Lombards and winning a general peace. 2) He strengthened the papal primacy over the churches of the West. Gregory accomplished this by directing the churches throughout the empire, corresponding with them and persuading them by virtue of his moral guidance. 3) He was responsible for the conversion of many barbarians. Gregory sent the monk Augustine to England where he converted the Angles and the Saxons. A thriving church developed there and in turn sent missionaries like St. Boniface (d. 754) to convert inner Germany. These churches in England and Germany looked to Rome for guidance and helped bring most of Europe under the influence of the pope.

Pope Stephen II. The work of the popes in helping to unify European Christianity had just begun. The emperor, now located in Constantinople, was too weak to stem the continuing invasions of the Lombards into Italy. To compensate for this harsh reality Pope Stephen II turned to Pepin, the son of Charles Martel. (Martel had stopped the Moslem advance into Europe in the year 732 at the famous Battle of Tours.)

Pepin had recently usurped the Frankish throne from the descendents of Clovis and was seeking approval for what he did. Stephen II endorsed Pepin's rule in 754; in return, the grateful Pepin recognized the pope as ruler of a large part of Italy and backed up his recognition with troops. The Donation of Pepin, the grant of land and the right to rule it, was a key event for the papacy, making it a secular ruler in Italy. The bargain struck up between the pope and Pepin's heirs (known as the Carolingians, after Charlemagne—Pepin's son) was instrumental in making them the protectors of Italy and the driving force in the Christianization of Europe.

Charlemagne in particular became the epitome of the Christian ruler. A huge man, he was a good father, the model of medieval knights, a man of firm Christian conviction and popular with his subjects. He used military force and political strategy to unify Europe. His greatest conquest was against the Saxons in the East whom he finally pacified and won over to the Christian faith. By 800 Charlemagne's kingdom extended from the Atlantic to southern Italy, from the Pyrenees to the Elbe.

Charlemagne Crowned Holy Roman Emperor. Charlemagne's official title was King of the Franks and Lombards and Patrician of the Romans. A highly symbolic act took place on Christmas Day in the year 800. Charlemagne had come to Rome to investigate the case of Pope Leo III whose enemies had accused him of perjury and adultery. Leo III proved to Charlemagne that he was innocent of the charges against him. In gratitude for Charlemagne's approval, Leo III crowned him emperor at the Christmas Mass. Charlemagne's biographer suggested that Charlemagne was not too delighted with the pope because the pope's action signified that Charlemagne was ruler of Europe through the good graces of the church's highest authority. At any rate, he accepted the crown. The new empire was established, this time as a holy one. Christianity had arrived.

A new era—the Middle Ages—was about to begin. Church and state were linked in a tight union, a union that would cause many problems in the coming centuries. The influence of the popes had enabled Christianity to survive the turmoil of the barbarian invasions. The West was now Catholic both in name and in reality!

The coronation of Charlemagne

MORE ON CHURCH/STATE RELATIONS

In the United States today Catholics and some other Christians have two major issues in which they would like the government to take an active role. These issues are:

1. *A human life amendment* which, in effect, would reverse the 1973 Supreme Court decision which allows abortion on demand. The purpose of this human life amendment would be to protect the innocent life which is now being mercilessly taken in our country today.

2. *Tuition tax credits or a voucher system* which would help parents who choose to send their children to private schools, for example, to Catholic schools where young people can be taught religious values.

Project:

In small groups, research one of these proposals. Discover and then discuss the answers to these questions:

1. What exact proposals are now before our lawmakers? Does your group think these are good proposals?

2. What has the United States Catholic Conference of Bishops said about these two issues?

3. What are the arguments of the opponents of these issues? In your judgment are they good arguments?

4. What would be the good effects of these proposals? Can you anticipate any bad effects?

THE MOSLEM INVASION

While Europe was coping with the barbarian invasions, the East and later Africa and Spain had to deal with the Moslems. Founded by Mohammed after his religious call in 610, this new religion proclaimed the message of Islam (Arabic for "submission to the will of God"). The religion imposed the following five main obligations on its believers: confession of faith ("There is no god but Allah, and Mohammed is his prophet"); prayer five times a day; charitable giving; fasting during the holy month of Ramadan; and pilgrimage to Mecca.

Part of the Moslem call was to conquer the world. Deeply devoted, armed men swept through Asia and into Europe. Syria, Palestine, Egypt and Africa were lost to them. Christianity went into an eclipse in these areas and the great patriarchates of Alexandria, Antioch and Jerusalem lost all influence in the church. The Moslems entered Spain in 711 but were stopped in France at Tours by Charles Martel.

What saved Christendom more than anything else was that the Moslem world was deeply divided with three distinct political centers—Baghdad, Cairo and Cordova (in Spain).

The Moslem invasion effectively isolated Europe from the rest of the world. By controlling the Mediterranean Sea the Moslems shut down the commerce of Europe. This helped to give rise to feudalism. It took five centuries before Europe began to reach out beyond itself.

Optional Assignment: Read about and report on the life of Mohammed.

MONASTICISM

During this period of church history the monastic movement made an important contribution to heralding the good news. It was from the monasteries, for example, that many missionaries spread the gospel to the barbarians who had overrun the European countryside. Monasticism is one form of asceticism. Ascetic Christians attempt to practice the faith more rigorously than the average believer. It involves practices like abstaining from good things (for example, food) and adding further requirements and routines (for example, setting aside certain hours for prayer).

Perhaps two factors were instrumental for the beginning of the monastic movement: 1) With the influx of new converts there was a lowering of standards in the living out of the Christian message. Monks tried to raise the standard of Christian practice. 2) When Christianity became the official religion the age of the martyrs and the confessors (those who admitted to their faith when faced with persecution) was over. Monasticism was a substitute for the kind of pure Christianity these men and women had represented.

St. Anthony. St. Anthony the Hermit (c. 256-356) is considered to be the first Christian monk. He lived in a cave in Egypt as a hermit. It was believed that in the desert the devil could be directly confronted, since deserts were supposed to be where devils dwelled. (Recall that Satan tempted Jesus in the desert.) Anthony lived an intense Christian life of prayer, meditation, bible reading, fasting and penance. For example, he would stand in one position for hours.

Monasteries. An important contribution to Christianity came from monks who gathered in monasteries. During Anthony's lifetime

St. Pachomius founded a monastery in Egypt (320) to answer the desire of monks to gather together on Sundays for the Eucharist and a common meal. Monks were to undergo a period of trial before they were allowed to join the group. Pachomius also discouraged extreme practices. Since he wanted the monastery to be self-sustaining, his monks grew fruits and vegetables to sell. Before his death Pachomius founded numerous monasteries, including one for women.

Pachomius' monks provided the model for many subsequent monasteries. St. Basil in the eastern part of the empire imitated the Egyptian practice. In the West St. Athanasius spread the ideal of Egyptian monasticism while he was in exile in Trier. Also in the West St. Honoratus founded a monastery on the island of Lérins in France. It became famous as a training ground for many monk-bishops. Also in France St. Martin of Tours set up important monasteries from which he and his fellow monks preached to the barbarians.

A typical medieval monastery

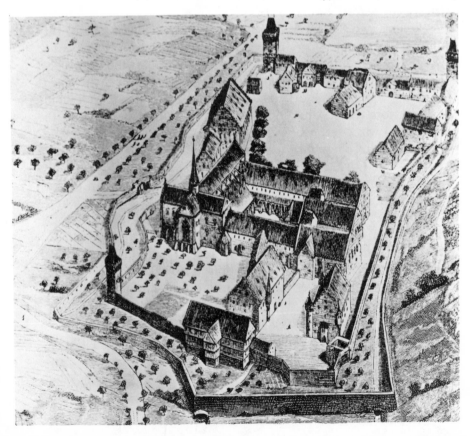

The Influence of Ireland. St. Patrick is credited with founding many monasteries in Ireland (though some historians doubt that Patrick actually did so). The Celtic monasteries were basically set up on the Egyptian pattern. The influence of these monasteries spread wide and far. Because the counties had tribal villages, with no big cities, the monasteries became the center of church life. Monks engaged in learning and copying and illustrating sacred texts. The monasteries were also the center of missionary activity. From them, monks like St. Columba went to Scotland and northern England and founded even more monasteries. Irish monks also established communities in central Europe and went as far as Switzerland and Italy.

St. Benedict. The patron saint of Europe, Benedict of Nursia, a rich young Italian, was responsible for the most influential form of monasticism of all. His monks, the Benedictines, established communities all over Europe.

St. Benedict's community was set up at Monte Cassino in the 520s. The Rule he wrote for his followers represents a gentle monasticism, widely imitated by monks in later centuries. Pope Gregory the Great wrote Benedict's biography and was largely responsible for spreading his ideas. Pope Gregory also sent Benedictine missionaries to England. In turn, the Anglo-Saxon monks returned to Europe and made many converts. Two of the most important of these monks were St. Willibrord, the apostle to the Frisians, and St. Boniface, the apostle to the Germans. Part of their strategy in converting the barbarians was to absorb some of their customs and take over their shrines. According to legend, St. Boniface chopped down the sacred oak tree of Germans. When nothing happened to him, he claimed that the Christian God had proved more powerful than the pagan gods who were supposed to reside in the tree.

Contributions of Monasticism. Monasticism made some very important contributions to the life of the church and the life of Europe: 1) The monks widely heralded the good news to the barbarians and were responsible for many converts. 2) Monasteries were an island of stability in a tumultuous time. Monks worked from their monasteries to help clear the land and re-establish agriculture after the barbarian invasions. 3) Monasteries were centers of learning and helped the West weather the storms of the Dark Ages. 4) The monks provided a spiritual ideal, setting the pace for holiness, piety and reform in the church. Many monks became bishops and many had powerful influence at church councils. 5) During the Middle Ages monasteries provided refuge for travelers.

On the negative side we might note two bad effects of monasticism: 1) Some monks went overboard in their penances; for example, the church Father Origen castrated himself so that he would not be tempted by sexual sins. Other monks tortured themselves in their desire to follow Christ. St. Jerome, in praising the ideal of celibacy, seemed to think of marriage as a necessary evil. 2) Monasticism taught a double standard of spirituality—one spirituality for the "higher" Christian and the "normal" spirituality for those in the world. It helped to contribute to a lay-clerical split in the church. There are very few canonized lay saints in the church and spirituality for laity living in the world has been neglected over the centuries.

ST. BENEDICT'S RULE

Here are some of the provisions laid down by St. Benedict in his famous Rule for community life:

> A monastery should, if possible, be so arranged that everything necessary—that is, water, a mill, a garden, a bakery—may be available.

> For bedding, a mattress, a woolen blanket, a woolen underblanket, and a pillow shall suffice.

> We read that wine is not suitable for monks. But because, in our day, it is not possible to persuade the monks of this, let us agree at least that we should not drink to excess. We believe that one pint of wine a day is enough.

> For the daily meal let there be two cooked dishes, so that he who happens not to be able to eat of one may make his meal of the other. Avoid excess—above all things, that no monk be overtaken by indigestion.

> At the brothers' meal times there should always be a reading. . . . There shall be complete silence at table, and no whispering or any voice except the reader's should be heard.

When the brothers rise for the service of God, let them gently encourage one another, because the sleepy ones are apt to make excuses.

To abolish private property everything necessary shall be given by the abbot: a hood, tunic, shoes, long socks, belt, knife, pen, needle, handkerchief, tablets, so that they can have no excuses about needing things.

Discuss:

1. What do you think of these rules? Are they good rules for communal living?
2. What would you add to this list?
3. Benedict's motto was *Ora et Labora* ("Pray and Work"). Is this also a good motto for lay people? Explain.

To Do:

If there is a monastery in your area, try to arrange to visit it. Report on what you learned.

Invite a monk to class and ask him to speak about his religious community. You might also invite a nun to explain how she and her sisters live in Christian community.

HERALDING THE GOOD NEWS TODAY

We have been studying the church during the period 100-800 using the image of herald. We saw that the church Fathers, the alliance of the church with the state, the influence of the popes, and the movement known as monasticism all contributed to the preaching of the good news during this era. The church, of course, also reflected the other five images. For example, Christians continued to band together in *community;* in fact, communities led by bishops worked hard both to resist the onslaught of the barbarians and to convert them.

During this period, too, the church became more *institutionalized.* Roman patterns of organization were adopted; the role of the clergy became more clearly defined. St. Augustine also wrote extensively on the church as a *sacrament.* He insisted that the church on earth must be a believable sign which points to the activity of God in the world.

Without a doubt, the church also played the role of *servant* during this period. In many cases the bishops and the popes acted as civil servants during the barbarian invasions. They provided the populace with food and other basic needs. Finally, the church was very much a *pilgrim* in this tumultuous time. It ventured into an exciting new era, adapting to new circumstances. At times it faltered, but in the end, under the guidance of the Holy Spirit, the church came through these centuries with its numbers, its influence and its prestige greatly increased.

Heralding Today. The mandate to preach the good news which Jesus gave to the apostles before his ascension remains in effect today. The church and each Christian have the serious responsibility to preach to all the good news of Jesus. The institutional church takes this obligation most seriously by engaging in worldwide missionary activity. With great risk to their own lives, dedicated priests, nuns, brothers and lay people serve overseas in mission countries. They can be found in Latin America where they proclaim social justice. (You might recall recent martyrs in El Salvador and other countries torn by civil strife.) They can be found in the jungles of Africa and the Far East. They can be found underground in communist countries, preaching God's love in lands which are officially atheistic. The Society for the Propagation of the Faith coordinates these activities. All of us are called to sacrifice in order to support our Christian brothers and sisters in the field.

At home the church is also busily engaged in the proclamation of the good news. There are home missions, like those of the Glenmarys who minister to sections of our country with small Catholic populations. There are numerous priests and others involved in trying to involve ordinary Catholics more deeply in Catholic life. Also, at considerable sacrifice and cost, the Catholic church supports a massive educational system which has basically one purpose: the proclamation of the good news of God's love to our young people. This school system is without parallel in the world. Its quality is high and the level of dedication exhibited by the religious and lay people who staff it is admirable. Most parishes, in addition, have religion classes for both adults and young people. They also provide inquiry classes for converts.

The mass communications media are becoming even more important today for heralding the good news. Most dioceses have their own newspapers; in addition, there are countless excellent magazines and journals which treat religious and theological topics of interest to both Catholics and non-Catholics. Many dioceses also have radio and television programs which help to get the message of Jesus across to the public.

All of these efforts are part of the mission of the church to herald the gospel. Each of us must support them. But, above all else, we each have the responsibility to proclaim the good news to those around us. We do this best by living a joyful life in the Lord. We proclaim the gospel to others when we show them that the Lord makes a difference in our lives. When we are honest and loving, faithful to the commandments and the beatitudes, joyful about our faith—then we are doing missionary work, we are sharing the gospel with others. Good news is not something we keep to ourselves. It is something that our Lord commands us to share with others, to proclaim, to herald. Our Lord's voice in the world today is your voice!

HERALDING THE GOOD NEWS

A. *What would you do if*

   1. You were at a party and someone your age began to make snide remarks about Catholics?

   2. A non-Catholic asked you why you go to Mass on Sundays?

   Discuss your responses. Would you be heralding the gospel in both cases? Explain.

B. From the following list check off the five most important ways which you think—as a Catholic—you would be *proclaiming* your faith. Be prepared to discuss the reasons for your responses.

   _____ giving to the Sunday collection
   _____ reciting the rosary
   _____ writing a pro-life letter to a newspaper or legislator
   _____ wearing a scapular or a cross
   _____ participating in a parish youth renewal
   _____ reading the bible

_____ abstaining from meat on Ash Wednesday and the Fridays of
Lent
_____ giving a quarter to a bum who asked for it
_____ belonging to the parish youth group
_____ helping a friend with homework
_____ receiving the Eucharist on Sunday
_____ volunteering at an old folks' home
_____ not swearing at work
_____ going to a Catholic school
_____ offering your seat on a bus to an elderly person

C. *Heralding Through Service.* As a class devise some money-
raising project to aid the overseas missions. Do it in such a way
that you make donors aware of the recipients of your fund-rais-
ing activity. Check with your diocesan office of the Propagation
of the Faith to get the names of some missionaries from your
diocese. Arrange to have money sent in the name of your class.

Some ideas:

1. a school-wide bake sale
2. snow shoveling or yard work
3. parish youth dance or concert
4. homeroom mission collection
5. door-to-door solicitation (begging)

D. *Guest Speaker.* Invite a guest speaker from one of the missionary
orders in your area to class.

SUMMARY

1. One of the chief tasks of the church is to be herald of the good news, to proclaim and spread it to every corner of the globe.

2. Apologists for the faith, like St. Justin Martyr, helped defend Christianity against pagan critics.

3. Church Fathers aided the spread of Christianity during the period 100-800. They did so by attacking heresies, false teachings which had crept into Christianity. Prominent church Fathers included St. Irenaeus, St. Athanasius, St. Gregory of Nyssa, St. Basil, St. Cyril of Alexandria, Pope St. Leo I, St. Augustine of Hippo, St. Ambrose, St. Jerome, St. John Chrysostom and Pope St. Gregory the Great.

4. Some of the heresies during this period, and the Catholic church teachings given as a response to them, are listed here:

   a. *Novatianism* taught that serious sins could not be forgiven. The church held that they could be if the sinner was truly repentant. Novatianism was condemned at the Council of Nicaea (325).

   b. *Donatism* held that a priest must be holy if the sacraments are to be valid. The Council of Arles (314) held that the sacraments convey grace independent of the personal holiness of the priest.

   c. *Arianism* denied that Jesus was really God. The first ecumenical (worldwide) council of the church, the Council of Nicaea (325), taught that Jesus has the same nature as God. St. Athanasius argued against the Arians. The Council of Constantinople (381) reaffirmed the teaching of Nicaea and published a famous creed which we use at Mass today.

   d. *Nestorianism* claimed that Jesus was two persons and that Mary was not the mother of God. St. Cyril of Alexandria and the Council of Ephesus (431) held that Jesus is one divine person and that Mary is truly the mother of God.

   e. *Monophysitism* taught that Jesus Christ only had a divine nature, thus denying the humanity of Jesus. This view was attacked by Pope Leo the Great in his *Tome* and at the Council of Chalcedon (451) which taught that Jesus Christ is one divine person with two natures—one human, the other divine.

f. *Pelagianism* denied the doctrine of original sin and the need for divine grace to attain salvation. Pelagius' heresy was attacked by the greatest church Father, St. Augustine of Hippo, who held that people need God's supernatural help to be saved.

5. The spread of Christianity in this era was greatly aided by the conversion of the Emperor Constantine who issued an Edict of Toleration in 313. By 380, under the Emperor Theodosius, Christianity had become the official religion of the empire. These events tended to involve the state too much in the affairs of the church. Also, since everyone had to be a Christian, the quality of religious commitment declined. On the positive side, the official recognition of Christianity enabled it to preach God's word freely and fostered church unity. Roman methods of organization and Roman law were also adopted for the benefit of the church.

6. The popes were instrumental in heralding the good news during this period of church history. To stem the tide of the barbarian invasions the papacy became allied with Clovis, whose Frankish tribe converted to Christianity. Pope Leo the Great helped protect Rome from the barbarians, and Pope Gregory the Great spearheaded missionary efforts into barbarian lands. Both of these popes assured the strong influence of the papacy in the worldwide church. Pope Stephen II further allied the church with the Franks by striking a bargain with Pepin who donated land to the papacy. The popes remained rulers in central Italy until 1870.

7. When Charlemagne was crowned emperor in 800 by Pope Leo III, the church and state became united in an alliance which would prove decisive in the Middle Ages.

8. The Moslem invasion was responsible for the loss to Christianity of Syria, Palestine, Egypt, Africa and Spain. It effectively isolated Europe and contained the spread of Christianity for over five centuries.

9. Monasticism greatly aided the heralding of the good news. St. Anthony is considered to be the first Christian monk. St. Pachomius is credited with founding the first monasteries. St. Benedict of Nursia is the most important monk during this era. Honored as the patron saint of Europe, his Rule was followed by many monastic communities during the Middle Ages.

10. Monasteries served as centers of operation for the preaching to barbarians. They were centers of learning and stability during the Dark Ages. They provided a spiritual ideal for Christians to follow and gave many bishops to the church.

11. Christians today must heed the Lord's call to herald the good news. The church does this through its missionary activity both at home and abroad, through its educational activities and through its use of the media. Individual Christians do it best by living the good news as a sign to others that the Lord lives.

EVALUATION

To help you review some of the material of this chapter, please work through this short quiz. In the objective part many important names, events and terms are given as possible answers to the questions. You should know something about each of the choices.

Multiple Choice: Choose the best answer.

____ 1. This saint is known as the "Golden Mouth" orator:
       (a) St. Gregory of Nyssa   (b) St. Irenaeus   (c) St. John Chrysostom   (d) St. Gregory Nazianzen   (e) St. Basil

____ 2. Who translated the bible into Latin?
       (a) St. Augustine   (b) St. Jerome   (c) St. Ambrose
       (d) St. Benedict   (e) Origen

____ 3. This church council taught that Jesus Christ has both a divine and a human nature: (a) Second Council of Constantinople   (b) Council of Chalcedon   (c) Council of Nicaea   (d) Council of Arles   (e) Council of Ephesus

____ 4. This man crowned Charlemagne emperor: (a) Pope Stephen II   (b) Pope Leo I   (c) Pope Gregory I (d) Pope Leo III   (e) Pope Callistus

____ 5. Who wrote the *City of God*?   (a) St. Ambrose (b) St. Jerome   (c) St. Athanasius   (d) St. Cyril (e) St. Augustine of Hippo

____ 6. Which ruler did *not* make a significant contribution to the development of church-state relations in the period 100-800?   (a) Clovis   (b) Valentinian II (c) Theodosius   (d) Constantine   (e) Charlemagne

____ 7. Who is known as the Apostle to the Germans? (a) St. Columba   (b) St. Patrick   (c) St. Willibrord (d) St. Boniface   (e) St. Honoratus

____ 8. Who founded the first Christian monastery? (a) St. Anthony the Hermit   (b) St. Benedict of Nursia (c) St. Martin of Tours   (d) St. Patrick (e) St. Pachomius

Matching: Match the heresies with the descriptions.

____ 9. Gnosticism

____ 10. Donatism

____ 11. Nestorianism

____ 12. Monophysitism

____ 13. Pelagianism

____ 14. Arianism

a. people can save themselves without God's help

b. Christ has one nature

c. Christ has two persons

d. Christ is God's greatest creature, but he is not God

e. material reality is evil

f. sacraments have no value unless the priest is holy

Briefly identify:

15. the primacy of the pope:_____

_____

16. asceticism:_____

_____

17. orthodoxy: _____

_____

18. apologist: _____

_____

19. church Father:_____

_____

20. heresy: _____

Briefly discuss the significance of:

21. the Donation of Pepin:_____

_____

22. the Edict of Toleration:_____

_____

23. the Moslem invasion:_____

_____

Short Essays:

24. What were some of the contributions of monasticism?

25. Discuss three ways the message of Christianity was heralded in the period from 100-800.

FURTHER EXERCISES

Choose one of the following:

1. Research and report on one of the heresies or church councils mentioned in the chapter.

2. Read and report on one of the saints mentioned in the chapter.

3. Make a list of the Roman emperors from the time of Christ to the fall of Rome in 476.

4. If you lived in this era of church history, which of the following vocations would have attracted you?
   a. church scholar who fought heresies
   b. a monk or nun
   c. a Christian soldier who fought the barbarians/Moslems
   d. other (please specify) _____
   Write a short essay explaining your choice and your qualifications for that vocation.

5. Write an imaginary dialogue which might have taken place between one of the following pairs of people:
   a. Augustine of Hippo and Alaric
   b. Pope Leo III and Charlemagne
   c. Arius and St. Athanasius
   d. St. Benedict and a novice

6. Write a short imaginary history based on one of the following suppositions:
   a. St. Jerome never translated the bible into Latin
   b. Clovis converted to Arianism
   c. Constantine did not move his capital to Constantinople

7. Research and report on one of these topics:
   a. relics
   b. Christianity's use of pagan customs
   c. the influence of Roman law on the Christian church
   d. the development of the influence of the clergy

  e. places of Christian worship in the early church
  f. places of pilgrimage in this era of church history

8. Make a slide presentation or a picture collage which depicts how Christians and the church herald the good news today.

PRAYER REFLECTION

Lord Jesus, you have commissioned me to proclaim your good news,
  to be your herald.
  to spread your message in the world today.
Send me your Holy Spirit to help me
  challenge statements made against you,
  know my faith so I can share it with others,
  be courageous in living a life of love and service,
  be a person of truth.
You ask great things of me.
  But you also know I am weak and a sinner.
  Give me your help to be the kind of person you want me to be.
In return, I'll try my best. Amen.

4
Building an Institution:
The Church in the Middle Ages

Lord, make me an instrument of your peace:
where there is hatred, let me sow love;
where there is injury, pardon;
where there is doubt, faith;
where there is despair, hope;
where there is darkness, light;
and where there is sadness, joy.

Grant that I may not so much seek
to be consoled as to console;
to be understood as to understand,
to be loved as to love.

For it is in giving that we receive,
it is in pardoning that we are pardoned,
and it is in dying that we are born to eternal life.
—St. Francis of Assisi

Walt Whitman once wrote:

I hear it was charged against me that I
sought to destroy institutions,
But really I am neither for nor against
institutions.

Probably few people today can remain as neutral to institutions as the poet Whitman claimed to be. For many *institution* means bigness—big government, big business, big church. Those who see institutions this way often fight to reduce their size and influence. They point to the danger of *institutionalism*, a trait where the institutional element of the organization rather than another element (for example, people) is given primary treatment. Organizations which suffer from institutionalism manifest three unhealthy symptoms:

113

1. Power is wielded by the upper echelon which has little desire to share decision-making with other members.

2. Institutional survival is of "first" importance. Change is often risky and adaptation to new ideas may seem too dangerous for organizations which have lasted a long time. Thus organizations infected with institutionalism rest content doing the same old things the same old ways.

3. Communication is cut to a minimum. The average members of the organization don't know what's going on and hence don't feel as though the organization is truly their own. In a crisis situation blame and responsibility are shifted to the top—"*They* made the decisions." "It's *their* problem."

But all is not bleak with institutions. Webster offers a positive definition of the word *institution*:

> a significant and persistent element (as a practice, a relationship, an organization) in the life of a culture that centers on a fundamental human need, activity, or value, occupies an enduring and cardinal position within a society, and is usually maintained and stabilized through social regulatory agencies.

This definition underscores the truth that any good value worth preserving needs some ordering and structuring to help it last. Life, for example, is a value; so is freedom of movement. Thank goodness we have the governmental institutions of traffic laws and traffic police so drivers don't indiscriminately choose where they want to stop or how fast they want to go. Eating food is also a value. Luckily for most of us there are organizations of farmers, food transporters and food retailers which make it quite easy for us to shop and buy the food we need.

We can't escape institutions or organizations, nor is it desirable to do so. At their best, institutions (for example, governments) help us pool our individual talents so that all may benefit from our collective gifts. Structured organizations (for example, research institutes) can give support to individuals, to their ideas and efforts, helping them to survive. Finally, organized groups like institutions (for example, banks) build in leadership roles. *Someone* does make decisions. Someone is the *focus of authority* and can help people get things done. By organizing into institutions, the operation of the given enterprise can often function even with poor leadership (for example, schools).

The church is an institution. As an organization it can't help but have structure and order to it. Imagine the organization needed to put on a school dance. Students need to divide up the responsibility of decorating the hall, providing refreshments, securing a band, selling tickets and taking care of the countless other details necessary for a successful evening. Imagine how much more complex is the organization needed to carry on the worldwide mission of proclaiming Jesus' good news, of carrying on his work in the world!

Founded by Jesus Christ and sustained by him, the church is a unique kind of organization. The values it keeps alive are the values of Jesus; the activity it is engaged in is the work of salvation; the human need it speaks to is everlasting life. It has a spiritual as well as a human aspect to it. In a sense the church has a body and a soul. We Christians are the body, and Jesus is the soul. While studying the body of the church it is possible to look at its *skeletal makeup*, how it is organized, how it operates, how it works. Just as our body needs a skeletal structure to move about, so the church needs a structure to carry on the Lord's work. This view of the church can be studied under the image of the church as institution.

More than any other period of church history, the Middle Ages (800-1500) forged the *institutional* church as we know it today. This chapter will take a look at the story of the church in the Middle Ages, a period in Western civilization when Christianity reached its greatest influence.

The following outline will help organize our discussion:

- the prelude: the Dark Ages of the 9th and 10th centuries
- the heart of the matter: the rise of the medieval papacy

- the unfortunate schism with the East
- the influence of the church on medieval life: the Age of Faith
- the autumn of the Middle Ages: the church in decline

SOME THOUGHT PROVOKERS

A. Analyze an organization with which you are quite familiar—your school. List some specific good things which are accomplished because individuals have gathered together into an organization (that is, the *institution* of the school) rather than remain isolated. At the same time, list some negative traits of your school, perhaps some examples of institutionalism. A couple of examples are given to help you get started:

Positive Traits:

1. A collection of books and other media are gathered into a library—these pooled resources help people learn.

Negative Traits:

1. Kids have little say in decisions that affect them.

2. _____   2. _____

   _____   _____

3. _____   3. _____

   _____   _____

4. _____   4. _____

   _____   _____

Share your responses. Then discuss what, if anything, you as an individual or a class can do to help cure your school of any symptoms of institutionalism.

B. *Priorities.* One of the major problems of any institution is how it will use its resources to meet human needs. The church has the ongoing mandate of Jesus to respond to all people, especially the outcast. Unfortunately the institutional church has only limited resources to meet the many human demands made on it.

How should the institutional church distribute its resources? Role play the following: You are a member of your parish budget committee. Your parish council has limited funds and can undertake only *three* of these projects in the next fiscal year. Which would you vote for and why?

_____ The church basement leaks. Without repairs there is a good chance that there will be structural damage to the building.

_____ There is a crisis hunger center located in the parish. It needs volunteer support and money to feed the poor in the neighborhood.

_____ The church organ is broken and beyond repair. Without music parish liturgies will be much less meaningful.

_____ Teachers in the parish elementary school have not received a salary increase in three years. Many of them are having a difficult time making ends meet.

_____ The bishop has asked for a large contribution to open a drop-in center for runaway and abused young people.

_____ The parish does not yet have a youth group. To start one the parish must hire a youth minister and rent a hall.

As a Class

1. Share your choices and your reasons for them.

2. List at least four criteria the church as institution should employ in the distribution of its resources (for example, people are more important than things). Discuss these and apply them to the six choices above.

THE PRELUDE: THE DARK AGES OF THE
9th AND 10th CENTURIES

Historians usually acknowledge that Christianity's strong influence on the medieval world resulted from two factors: 1) a strong papacy that provided vision and leadership, and 2) a sense of unity in the area that had been the Holy Roman Empire.

The Political Scene. Charlemagne's coronation promised a bright future for church-state relations. Unfortunately the ideal of this harmony soon hit a discordant note. Three of Charlemagne's grandsons fought for control of the empire. At the Treaty of Verdun (843) they effectively fragmented the kingdom into three portions: France, central Europe as far south as Italy, and eastern Europe. With this breakup the papacy also went into decline.

This subdivision continued as the 9th and 10th centuries saw Europe devastated by civil war and bitter rivalries. Added to this sad state of affairs were new barbarian invasions which came close to destroying Europe. The Norsemen ravaged England and demolished churches and abbeys on the continent until they were halted by King Alfred (878). The Magyars tore up eastern Europe and were only halted by Otto I in 955. The Moslems renewed their attacks, even making a successful raid on Rome and sacking its sacred shrines. The disruption caused by these new invasions sent the empire reeling, contributed to the decline of learning and discipline among the clergy, and weakened the papacy.

Feudalism. The economic and social upheavals of this period fostered the growth of feudalism. Feudalism rested on strict division among social classes: nobility, clergy, serfs, and later on, freemen. The laws in feudal society were based on local custom. Landholding was based on the fief or fee; feudal economy was local, isolated and agricultural. This system grew out of the turbulent times; the lords of the manors needed armed warriors and their vassals needed protection for the lands they held.

The church became enmeshed in feudalism because of the lack of political structures. The bishops controlled large diocesan lands and were forced to concern themselves with the regulation of manors and vassal relationships, the collection of tolls and the conduct of wars. Some bishops even became warriors and manifested a bloodthirstiness like that of many barons.

Emperor Otto I (936-973) of Germany temporarily revived the empire. Crowned by Pope John XII, he typified the kind of control the political arm of medieval society gained over the church in the Dark Ages. Otto was most concerned with controlling the election of bishops because he found in them potential allies against his enemies, the dukes. Feudalism contributed to the wresting of the election of bishops from candidates put forth by the clergy and laity. More and more local lords and feudal monarchs (like Otto) began to approve candidates for important church positions. This lay control of the bishops became known as *lay investiture*, a serious encroachment by the state on church authority. In practice it meant that lay leaders chose and invested bishops with their spiritual signs of office (a ring and the staff) as well as their temporal signs (the scepter).

Coupled with lay investiture were two other serious problems: *simony* and the *lack of clerical celibacy*. They also led to the breakdown of church authority and independence during this age. Simony was the buying and selling of church properties and offices to the highest bidder, often a layman. In a feudal society there was much potential for personal financial gain by controlling church lands. Also, although various popes and church councils had insisted on clerical celibacy, it was not vigorously enforced. Some priests married; others took mistresses. These abuses, the general lack of church discipline and the lack of education led some of the clergy to try to pass church properties to their heirs.

The Dark Ages and Papal Reform. The history of the papacy in the Dark Ages tells the story of a weak and ineffective institution. The spiritual and temporal authority of the popes during the period of the Holy Roman Empire had been dramatically eroded to the point where they had little influence on the fractious kings and bishops.

One notable exception was Pope Nicholas I (858-867) who

vigorously sought to establish papal authority. He forced Lothair II of Lotharingia to take back the wife whom he had put aside without a papal annulment. He influenced the most powerful bishop of France, Hincmar of Rheims, to reverse a decision made without papal approval. He also became actively involved in the affairs of the church in Constantinople, in the so-called Photian Affair (see page 135). Finally, he gained the support of the French bishops in the publication of a collection of conciliar documents, papal decrees and other church documents. Some of these documents contained forgeries like the Donation of Constantine which records Constantine's alleged transference of control of the western empire to the pope. These documents were used by Nicholas I and by later popes to bolster the papal claim to supremacy, papal rights to censorship and approval over faith and doctrine, and the authority of popes to decide on the validity of the decrees of church councils.

Pope Nicholas I was *the* exceptional pope of the Dark Ages. For quite a time after his reign the papal office was subject to many political pressures. Many of the popes died violently, and many were mere pawns at the hands of a powerful Roman family. The emperor Otto, who effectively exercised authority over the church, was so appalled at the corruption of Pope John XII that he deposed him. Then he and his successors worked for the reform of the papacy. Ironically, when the papacy did emerge strong in the 11th century, the popes forcefully fought against the German rulers who tried to control the church.

The Benedictine Abbey of Cluny

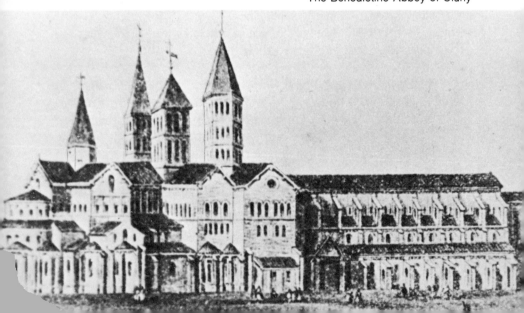

Another breath of the fresh air of reform came from the Benedictine Abbey of Cluny in Burgundy, France. Founded in 910 Cluny was unique in several regards:

1. It was directly under the control of the pope and not subject to the local control of corrupt bishops and secular leaders.

2. It was a model for several hundred daughter monasteries which were ruled from Cluny by some excellent, disciplined and holy abbots.

3. Several of these able abbots at Cluny, like Odo and Odilo, called for a general reform of the church. The seeds they planted took root in the 11th century when Hildebrand, a rather remarkable cardinal greatly influenced by the Clunaic ideas, became Pope Gregory VII.

RESEARCH EXERCISES

Choose one of the following:

A. *Job Description.* Because of the social disruption of the Dark Ages, one of the key problems facing the church was the poor quality of many of her clergy. Luckily for Catholics today, the clergy is of the highest caliber. Reflect on how our priests should serve us and then write up a job description for one of the following: parish priest, pastor, bishop. Include the following elements:
   1. job title
   2. statement of purpose
   3. key responsibilities
   4. qualifications (including educational)
   5. salary

Share and discuss your description with your classmates.

B. Read Chapters 3-6 of the Vatican II *Decree on Priestly Formation.* Make a list of 10 guidelines which go into the making of a good priest today. Report on your list to your classmates.

C. *Feudalism.* Research and report on the topic of feudalism.

D. *Command Into Action.* Jesus left the church with a general blueprint on how to love others and how to preach the good news. He left it up to succeeding generations of Christians to put his mandates into action, to organize so that his good works are done.

Following are three scripture references which express our Lord's will for us. Read each reference and summarize the thrust of Jesus' message in the space provided. Then name one organization in your parish or diocese which was formed precisely to put this mandate of Jesus' into action. Share your list with the class.

Quote	Summary	Organization
Mt 28:18-20	1. _____	1. _____
	_____	_____
Mt 5:9	2. _____	2. _____
	_____	_____
Mt 25:31-40 (Find three examples)	3a. _____	3a. _____
	_____	_____
	3b. _____	3b. _____
	_____	_____
	3c. _____	3c. _____
	_____	_____

E. Interview the director of one of the organizations listed in exercise D. Report on the kind and the scope of the work done by the organization.

F. List some institutions which touch your life and give a brief picture of their structure and organization.

1. your family _____

_____

2. your school _____

_____

3. _____

_____

4. _____

_____

5. _____

_____

THE HEART OF THE MATTER:
THE RISE OF THE MEDIEVAL PAPACY

During the Dark Ages (9th and 10th centuries) the efforts of some of the German emperors like Otto, and the Clunaic movement, were attempts to reform an institutional church in decline. These same factors in turn greatly influenced the renewal that took place in the medieval church in the 11th through 14th centuries.

By the middle of the 11th century Pope Leo IX made strong, though largely unsuccessful, efforts to upgrade the clergy and prohibit lay investiture.

More successful was Pope Nicholas II's wresting of papal elections from external influence. During this era the popes were chosen by the seven deacons of Rome, the German emperors and certain aristocratic families. In 1059 Nicholas II created the college of cardinals to elect the pope, thus saving the office of the papacy from undue external influence.

Pope Gregory VII: Hildebrand. The influence of Cluny came to full fruition during the reign of Pope Gregory VII, a former Clunaic monk. Because of his fiery temperament, fierce devotion to the cause of the church and overall brilliance, his name was turned by some into the equivalent of "Hellbrand." His program for reform, called the Gregorian Revolution, was widespread, thorough and influential for the next two centuries.

Gregory VII is remembered best for his confrontation with Emperor Henry IV over the question of lay investiture. In 1075 Gregory issued his famous *Dictatus Papae* (*Dictates of the Pope*) which forcefully stated his ideas on papal power and the proper relation between church and state. Among his dictates Gregory VII claimed: 1) only popes may depose bishops; 2) only the pope may use imperial insignia; 3) no one can judge the pope; and 4) the pope may depose emperors and release vassals from fealty (loyalty) to a sinful emperor.

Henry IV was appalled at Gregory's dictates, made serious

charges against him and demanded his abdication. In return Gregory excommunicated Henry. He was supported in his decision by the German dukes and populace. In addition the German princes invited Gregory to participate in a council to choose the next German emperor. On his way to the council Gregory was confronted by a wily Henry who begged for the pope's forgiveness by standing barefoot in the snow outside a castle at Canossa. Gregory finally gave in and forgave Henry. Henry displayed his true colors, however, when he went back to Germany, re-established himself as emperor and moved on Rome to punish Gregory. The pope was rescued by some Normans but eventually died in exile proclaiming: "I have loved justice and hated iniquity; therefore I die in exile."

The gain of Gregory at Canossa bolstered the reform image of the popes and served as an object lesson which later popes used to assert church claims. The issue of lay investiture was finally solved in 1122 with the *Concordat of Worms*. This compromise distinguished between the spiritual and temporal aspects of the investment. The emperor could invest the bishop with the temporal signs of his office; but only churchmen could invest him with the spiritual signs.

The Gregorian Revolution Continued. Gregory had won a victory of sorts in the issue of lay investiture. He also condemned simony and clerical marriage, two reforms enthusiastically pursued by his successors. The prestige of the papacy was on the upswing. Bishops and lay leaders looked to the pope for leadership. When Pope Urban II called for the First Crusade at the Council of Claremont of 1095, the lords of Europe rallied around the papal banner.

The new spirit of the age brought with it the energetic building of new churches, abbeys and the great Gothic cathedrals. A spiritual revival was also in the making. New religious orders were founded for the purpose of making up for past sins. St. Bruno established the Carthusians in 1086, and the Cistercians, an important new order of reformist Benedictines, were given their Rule in 1119 by an Englishman, St. Stephen Harding. The most influential Cistercian was St. Bernard of Clairvaux who advised popes, preached throughout Europe and fostered popular devotions, especially to the Blessed Mother. His *"Memorare,"* as well as the "Hail, Holy

Queen" and the "Hail Mary" became popular prayers during the 12th century. St. Bernard and St. Stephen Harding made the new spirit of the Benedictines so popular that in a century the Cistercian monasteries numbered over 500. The Cistercian monks chose forest and swamplands for their abbeys and through their sheer hard labor transformed these areas into rich farms in many areas of northern Europe.

During this period the church helped organize Christian charity by building hospitals, orphanages and homes for the aged. Through movements such as the *Peace of God* and the *Truce of God* the church worked to help control the violence of the private wars and unending feuds which characterized this age. Through the *Peace of God* the church attempted to protect the clergy, the poor and their property from war; that is, it attempted to limit the effect of the outbreaks of violence. The *Truce of God* forbade war itself, under the threat of excommunication, during Advent and Lent and on certain important church feasts.

The papacy developed into a monarchy and used its influence throughout the Christian world to help Europe weather its growing pains. Popes worked hard at centralizing church authority around their papal office in Rome. They intervened in secular affairs through the use of papal legates, letters, councils and church courts. Among their chief political tools were:

1. *The Powers of Excommunication and Interdict.* Kings and lords feared excommunication because it put them outside the church. Interdict declared that the sacraments could not be celebrated in a certain territory. Kings and lords dreaded this because their subjects clamored for a full life in the church. As a result, they would often recant and stop any abuses which offended Rome.

2. *The Levying of Taxes on Clergy and Nations.* The popes needed funds to support the many charitable activities of the church, the Crusades and the ever-growing church structure with its lands, courts, churches and the like.

3. *A Strong System of Church (Canon) Law.* Canon law pro-

vided many clear-cut rules on many aspects of Christian life—rules regarding baptism, confirmation, confession, communion, penance, alms, moneylending, wills, burials, graveyards and clerical dress. The popes reserved the right to grant indulgences and to canonize saints. The papal court became a supreme court in which cases could be appealed by diocesan courts.

4. *The Formation of Political Alliances.* Popes strengthened their political influence by allying themselves with friendly monarchs. When the emperor Frederick Barbarossa wished to take over Italy and suppress the Lombard League, for example, Pope Alexander III, who had been driven from Rome by Frederick, allied himself with the Lombards and the major European powers and dealt a crushing blow to Frederick's cause at the Battle of Legnano (1176). Barbarossa surrendered to the pope and paid homage to him by kneeling before Alexander in St. Mark's Square in Venice. The English King Henry II also had to yield to papal authority after he had killed the great St. Thomas Becket who refused, on behalf of Pope Alexander III, to relinquish strong papal claims over the English church.

5. *The Inquisition.* One of the sadder chapters in church history is the story of the Inquisition created by Pope Gregory IX in 1233 to investigate the Albigensian heresy, a gnostic sect which had crept up in southern France. This sect taught that marriage was evil and that starvation, suicide and abortion were good. This anti-Christian movement was a threat to society in general and when a Holy War called by Pope Innocent III failed to stamp it out, priest-judges were sent to ferret out the heretics. Torture was used to force confessions and the guilty were handed over to the state authorities for execution.

Today we consider the methods used by the Inquisitors to be barbaric and, in fact, there have been many church statements which have condemned the use of force in converting people to the faith. But in the Middle Ages church and state were so bound together that a crime against one was considered a crime against the other. At the time almost everyone thought that these measures were both necessary and right. The Inquisition was a child of its time. Churchmen have learned that coercion, torture and secret trials do violence to the message of peace and love taught by Jesus.

Innocent III (1198-1216). Papal prestige reached its greatest height when a trained and able canon lawyer, Lothario Conti, assumed the papal throne as Innocent III. He believed that the pope should be the moving moral force in society. He held that if sin were involved in the secular affairs of rulers, the pope had the right to get involved in their affairs.

In enhancing the growth of the papal monarchy, Innocent III used many of the means discussed above: papal legates, church appointments, a refined system of taxation. In an extraordinary way he brought about a political alliance with Frederick II of Germany and Philip-Augustus of France to enable Frederick to claim the throne in Germany against another claimant. He placed England under an interdict and forced King John to accept the papal candidate, Stephen Langton, as Bishop of Canterbury. King John submitted himself as a vassal to the pope and agreed to pay 1000 marks per year as feudal aid to the pope. In addition Innocent successfully used the interdict against his sometimes ally, Philip-Augustus of France, when Philip discarded his Danish wife Ingeborg in violation of church law.

Innocent III's greatest achievement was the calling of the Fourth Lateran Council which was held in Rome in 1215. The Fourth Lateran Council was the most important council of the Middle Ages and took up many important issues and made many significant pronouncements. Here is a partial list of its teachings:

- instituted church reforms and eliminated clerical concubinage and simony

- condemned heresies

- forbade the clergy to participate in ordeals

- required papal permission for new saints, relics or religious orders to be recognized

- ordered Jews and Moslems to wear clothing that distinguished them from Christians

- set the number of sacraments at seven

- warned priests not to reveal any sins confessed to them in the sacrament of penance; the penalty for doing so was loss of priestly office with a life of penance in a monastery

- required all Catholics to confess serious sins at least once a year and to receive the Eucharist at least once during the Easter season or suffer excommunication
- declared officially the belief in transubstantiation. The text reads as follows:

There is one Universal Church of the faithful, outside of which there is no salvation, in which there is the same priest and sacrifice, Jesus Christ, whose body and blood are truly contained in the sacrament of the altar under the forms of bread and wine; the bread being changed (transubstantiation) by divine power into the body, and the wine into the blood, so that to realize the mystery of unity we may receive of Him what He has received of us. And this sacrament no one can effect except the priest who has been duly ordained in accordance with the keys of the Church, which Jesus Christ Himself gave to the Apostles and their successors.

A CHANGING CHURCH

In the teachings listed for the Fourth Lateran Council you may have noticed a couple of things: 1) In the teaching on the Eucharist there is a clause which says, "outside the church there is no salvation"; and 2) The council taught that Jews and Moslems must wear different clothes so they could be easily identified.

What does the first statement mean for today? Can only Catholics be saved? No! The church, from the time of St. Cyprian who first used the expression "outside the church there is no salvation," has wanted to communicate to others that salvation comes through Jesus Christ. And it is the belief of the Catholic church that Jesus continues his work through the church which he founded, a church which finds concrete, historical expression in the Roman Catholic Church. But, Vatican II taught, if through no fault of their own people do not belong to the church, God's saving grace and love can extend to them. God wills the salvation of all people. The church teaches that in some way the light of Christ reaches all people and that if non-Christians respond to the light as they have received it, they can be saved. However, people who know the truth of God's revelation in Christ must not turn away from that truth. Those of us who have been given the gift of faith have the obligation to let the good news of Christ shine through us.

Let us now look to a second controversial teaching of Lateran IV, this time concerning the Jews and the Moslems. The historical reasons for this harsh treatment of non-Christians seem to stem from the wedding of church and state in the Middle Ages. Somehow medieval Europeans—who inhabited a society that was thoroughly under the influence of Christianity—viewed the non-Christians as a threat to civil peace and unity. The medieval mind saw *uniformity* as the ideal and anyone who did not conform was seen as a danger to the unity which Christendom had achieved.

The church is made up of men and women who are in constant need of God's love and forgiveness. In the quest to share the good news of Jesus through the ages, some Christians have tried to force on others Christ's message of peace, freedom and love. Christians have even harshly persecuted non-believers for their lack of Christian faith. The story of the church's attitude to the Jews, for example, is a shameful one. Over the centuries the Jews as a people have been blamed for Jesus' death. All kinds of crimes have been tolerated against them because of this false belief.

The church is made up of sinners, limited men and women. Sometimes the church is too much a product of its times and reflects the prejudice and narrowness of vision of a particular age. But Christ continually calls his church to renewal: to rid itself of false understandings and to practice better his message of love. Jesus calls his people to rid themselves of prejudice and hate and lack of sensitivity to others who are different. Thus the church's teaching can and must change, develop and evolve over the centuries. For example, today the church has deplored its own past part in persecuting the Jews:

The Church repudiates all persecutions against any man. Moreover, mindful of her common patrimony with the Jews, and motivated by the gospel's spiritual love and by no political considerations, she deplores the hatred, persecutions, and displays of anti-Semitism directed against the Jews of any time and from any source. (*Declaration on the Relationship of the Church to Non-Christian Religions,* No. 4.)

STRUCTURE IN THE CHURCH

Popes of the Middle Ages saw the church as a pyramid with the pope as the chief administrator. In a real sense the entire church was identified with the local church of Rome; the liturgical and disciplinary customs of Rome became the law for the rest of Western Christianity. Authority was centered on the pope and trickled down to the laity through the bishops and the priests.

The organization of the church today still resembles the basic pattern which was worked out in the Middle Ages. The pope is still the head of all Catholics. The bishops set policies and issue directives for the faithful in their country. In the United States, the church divides into various provinces (regions) composed of the dioceses of one or more states. Each diocese is broken down into deaneries which include the various parishes.

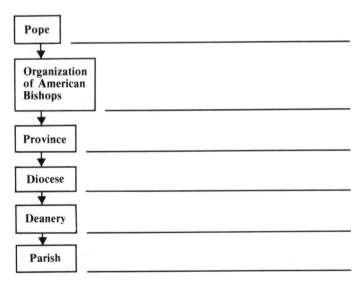

The United States bishops belong to an organization called the National Conference of Catholic Bishops (NCCB) which meets periodically to share problems and make decisions. The bishops have a formal organization called the United States Catholic Conference (USCC) which carries on the many works of the American church.

The pope is assisted in his work by a complex organization called the *curia*. The curia is made up of various congregations, secretariats, tribunals, offices and commissions. Each diocese in the United States is organized in a similar way to the Roman curia, but on a smaller pattern. The bishop has a staff of workers to help in the various tasks conducted by the church—education, missions, hospitals, charities, clergy administration, social issues, and so forth.

Finally, parishes have their various activities and commissions which conduct the church's work on the immediate scene. Many parishes have an active parish council which helps the pastor make decisions affecting the people of God.

Although the pope is still the final authority, the Second Vatican Council (1962-1965) has revived the concept of collegiality. Vatican II teaches that the bishops are a kind of fraternity and that every bishop has power insofar as he is a member of the community of bishops with the pope as the head. This community is called the college of bishops and continues the witness of the college of the apostles. *Collegiality* refers to the bishops advising the pope and teaching with him. They do this in a vivid way in a worldwide council, called an ecumenical council. There have been 21 of these councils in the history of the church, Vatican II being the most recent. Pope Paul VI instituted a new kind of collegial cooperation in the church in 1965: the Synod of Bishops. The Synod is made up of a representative group of bishops from around the world which meets periodically with the Holy Father to discuss certain pastoral questions facing the church. It is the job of the Synod of Bishops to keep the pope informed of the concerns of the bishops and all the faithful throughout the world.

An Image of Church Structure Today. Structure in the church makes continuity possible. Jesus gave the church its initial structure when he appointed the apostles and gave Peter a special role as leader among them; this pattern provided the basis for later developments. The structure of the church is essential to its identity and helps express its fullness, its universality. The purpose of church structure is to call us out of ourselves into the family, out of the family into the parish, out of the parish into the diocese or local church, out of the local church into the universal or worldwide church, and out of the worldwide church into the entire human family. The ministerial leadership of pastor in the parish, bishop in the diocese, and pope in the universal church serves the unique role of keeping that movement going but also acting as a source of unity. Thus we can also picture church structure today by using circles.

In the illustration here, the *P* represents the pope with the Synod of Bishops as advisers, the *B* represents the bishop of the diocese, and the little circles represent the parishes with the pastors as symbols of unity. The task of the parishes is to move out to the larger community; the job of the bishop is to provide a sense of unity for the local church, but also to remind the church that it must move out to the universal church and to the entire human community. The pope, of course, provides the central unity and authority.

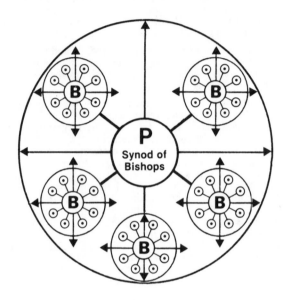

Some Exercises:

1. *Identify* the names which correspond to the flow chart on church structure on page 130. Use the names of your diocese, deanery and parish.

2. *Discuss*: What are some advantages of the organizational pattern of the Catholic church? Can you see any disadvantages?

3. *Consider*: Chapter 3 of the *Constitution on the Church* discusses the hierarchical nature of the church. The hierarchy—the pope, bishops and pastors—are to teach to make holy and to guide the people. The council also insisted that this leadership is organized precisely to *serve* the people of God, to act as a shepherd.

   In the space provided, draw another diagram of church leadership emphasizing the hierarchy's main function as that of service. Don't use either diagram presented above. Be prepared to explain your diagram.

THE EASTERN SCHISM

One of the truly tragic events in the story of Christianity was the *schism* or split which took place between Eastern and Western Christianity in 1054. Some fundamental differences over a long period of time contributed to the break between East and West. Easterners spoke Greek; Westerners, Latin. On the question of authority Easterners relied on the decisions of the church councils; Westerners looked to the pope as the chief source of authority and as one who could reject particular decisions of the councils. In the East the patriarch of Constantinople was appointed by and subject to the emperor; in the West popes more and more asserted their rights over the state. Theologically Easterners were more speculative and laymen took a more active and learned role in religious questions; Western theology was more practical and there was a wider gap between the educated clergy and the usually uneducated believers.

An Eastern Rite ceremony

Four conflicts eventually led to the break between the Eastern church and the Roman one. In one way or another these conflicts were related to differing views of church authority.

The first came from Pope Leo I's condemnation of a teaching of the Council of Chalcedon (451) which seemed to elevate the church of Constantinople to a position of pre-eminence as the New Rome. As the center of church authority traceable to St. Peter, the church in Rome could not recognize this claim.

The second dispute concerned the Byzantine Emperor Leo III's attempt to condemn the veneration of images (called *iconoclasm*). He tried to impose a policy on the worldwide church against Roman wishes. Some Christians in the East and many in the West had the custom of venerating holy pictures and statues called ikons. Ikons were an important means used to educate a largely illiterate laity in the sacred mysteries of the faith. The Second Council of Nicaea (787) supported the Western view of this emotion-laden issue by permitting the use of ikons.

The third shock wave was the Photian controversy in the ninth century. Pope Nicholas I became involved in a dispute over the selection of the patriarch of Constantinople. He rejected a candidate by the name of Photius who got his revenge by condemning Western theology and practice. Photius criticized the Western practice of fasting on Saturday, the use of dairy products in Lent and the papal demands for clerical celibacy. He condemned the Western church's addition of the phrase *filioque* ("and from the Son") to the Nicene Creed, a phrase added without the benefit of an ecumenical council. *Filioque* became a fighting word because the Eastern church was more sensitive to theological language which emphasized the omnipresent and pervasive power of the Holy Spirit. The Eastern church wanted to say that the Holy Spirit descended *through* the Son, not *from* the Son. The pope condemned Photius' views. A permanent break would have happened then had not both Nicholas I and Photius' rival claimant died. The new pope smoothed matters out by confirming Photius as patriarch of Constantinople. Photius, in turn, softened his harsh views.

The final rift took place in the 11th century when Michael Cerularius, the patriarch of Constantinople, closed all Latin churches in the city and excommunicated all priests who continued to say Mass in Latin. He violently opposed the Western practice of clerical celibacy, the use of unleavened bread for the Eucharist and the *filioque* clause added to the Nicene Creed.

Pope Leo IX sent legates to Constantinople to investigate and also to demand Cerularius' submission to papal authority. The patriarch refused. Meanwhile the pope died and the legates, led by a rather uncompromising Cardinal Humbert, excommunicated Cerularius. He, in turn, called a council and excommunicated the pope. Most Eastern churches sided with the patriarch and refused to recognize the authority of the pope. They took the name Orthodox because they would accept only the teachings of the first eight councils of the church. All these were held in the East and were considered true (orthodox). The rift which took place in 1054 remains in effect to this day.

Above all else we can look at the Eastern schism as a split in the institutional church. The argument was not over a matter of belief in Jesus Christ. The split was primarily a question of authority, a question of how much the Eastern churches were to be subject to the ruling authority of the bishop of Rome. Stubborn, uncompromising churchmen were responsible for this tragedy. Matters became worse in 1204 when crusaders who were allegedly engaged in a crusade to *help* Eastern Christians barbarously sacked and pillaged Constantinople. They proclaimed the Western emperor king of Constantinople and put a Latin bishop in charge of the ancient Eastern church. Some attempts were made later in the Middle Ages to heal the breach, but political turmoil prevented reunion.

In our own day there are many hopeful signs that the Greek Orthodox Church and Roman Catholicism are moving to restore total union. Because of the efforts of recent popes and patriarchs of the Eastern Orthodox Church, high-level ecumenical commissions are meeting today in the prayerful hope that true union will result. The most significant development took place when the late Pope Paul VI and the late Patriarch Athenagoras I lifted the excommunications imposed by the two churches on each other in 1054.

ECUMENISM

One of the major documents of Vatican II is the *Decree on Ecumenism*. It wholeheartedly endorses the spirit of *ecumenism,* the movement which seeks to achieve unity of Christians within the church and ultimately of all of humanity. The document recognizes that both sides were to blame for the schism between East and West and also at the time of the Protestant Reformation in the 16th century. In addition the document affirms the ecclesial elements of other Christian churches: the same Bible; the same life of grace; the same faith, hope and charity; the same gifts of the Spirit; the same baptism and faith in the Lord; and the many other common elements which make up the church. In the case of the Orthodox churches, there is a very close relationship to the Catholic church. They possess true sacraments and a true priesthood traceable to the apostles.

The Ecumenical Movement and You. Many church documents in recent years teach that *all* Catholics must work towards unity. Here is a check list of some of the things we can do to help foster Christian unity. Check off those which you, as a young Catholic, can do.

_____ Know your faith so that you can explain it to others

_____ Pray for union

_____ Refrain from judging those who have a different religion

_____ Learn about the beliefs of others

_____ Engage in common projects of service with members of different religions

_____ Approach others and tell them what you believe

_____ Join in common prayer services for Christian unity with members of other Christian groups

_____ Live your faith to show you truly believe it

_____ Study the Bible in ecumenical sharing groups

_____ Engage in ecumenical study groups

Discuss:

1. Add to the preceding list.

2. Which of these are you working on now?

3. In striving for Christian unity, should the Catholic church compromise on its beliefs concerning the role of the papacy? Why or why not?

Action Project:

Visit an Orthodox church. Report on its liturgy and the artwork in the church. Note similarities and differences.

AGE OF CHRISTENDOM

The Middle Ages in Europe was the age of Christendom. The Catholic church and European society were one. In the mind of the average person of the Middle Ages there was no Europe as we know it today. Rather there was a Christian world in which the church played an essential role. The age of Christendom brings to mind images of Ivanhoe, Robin Hood and Richard the Lionhearted. It was an age of the crusades, new religious orders like the Franciscans and Dominicans, the beginning of universities and the revival of learning called scholasticism. Christianity's influence can be seen in popular piety as well as in the artistic expression of the day.

The Crusades. In 1095 Pope Urban II appealed at Claremont for aid against the Turks who had recently captured Jerusalem. With the help of popular preachers like Peter the Hermit who led an army of the poor, and with the promise of many privileges to the crusaders (like the granting of a plenary indulgence—the cancellation of all punishment due for past sins), Urban II rallied the European knights under his banner with the call "God wills it."

The First Crusade (1097-1099) was, in the short run, successful. The knights captured Jerusalem in 1099 and established a Latin kingdom in the East. Pilgrims flocked to the Holy Land to visit the sacred shrines. Crusading orders were founded. They were associations of knights who took semimonastic vows. The Knights of the Hospital of St. John of Jerusalem was founded during the First Crusade to assist the sick and the injured. The Knights of the Temple (Templars), founded in 1118, vowed to protect pilgrims and to wage war perpetually against the Moslems.

In all there were eight crusades, none as successful as the first. The Latin kingdom in the East was always in a precarious situation because of dissension among the crusaders, lack of regular reinforcements and the difficulty of defending a long strip of land in a foreign territory far away from home. The Christian hold on the Holy Land depended on Moslem disunity. When the Moslems recaptured the Kingdom of Edessa in 1144, the Second Crusade (1147-1149), led by the French and German kings, was unable to recapture it. When the Moslems united into a powerful force under Saladin, they were almost unstoppable. The Third Crusade (1189-1192), led by King Richard the Lionhearted of England and the French and German kings, was somewhat successful but could not recover the recently conquered Jerusalem.

Pope Innocent III called the Fourth Crusade (1202-1204) which ended in the shameful capturing of Constantinople discussed above. One of the saddest of the Crusades was the Children's Crusade (1212) which was a spontaneous movement among several thousand children based on the idea that only the pure of heart could lead a successful attack against the Moslems. The French children perished in storms or were sold into slavery. The German group of children disbanded in Italy with only a few making it home.

The only successful crusade of the 13th century was led by the emperor Frederick II (1228-1229) who received Jerusalem by negotiation. Jerusalem fell again in 1244 and even the great crusade of King Louis IX of France in 1248-1254 could not regain it. The Mameluke Sultans of Egypt gradually recaptured the states taken by the cursaders until Christian rule in Syria finally ended completely in 1291.

The crusaders failed in their original aims. Popes more and more began to turn the crusades against heretics like the Albigensians and even against rulers like Frederick II. The crusades were not entire failures, though. Economically they nurtured the revival of commerce in western Europe and opened up the West to new ideas. Furthermore, by attracting people from all over Europe, they were a striking example of both the unity and the religious fervor of medieval Europe.

The Begging Orders. One of the reasons the Albigensian heresy gained favor in southern France in the late 12th century was the relatively weak moral life of the clergy of the day. Another heretical group of the day was the *Waldensians,* founded by Peter Waldo (c. 1170) who preached absolute poverty, favored the translation of the bible into the vernacular language and encouraged his disciples to preach without the church's approval. He attacked the hierarchical system of the church and preached an anti-sacramental and anti-priestly religion. The Waldensians were excommunicated and fled to mountain regions in the Alps.

Fortunately for the church, the rise of the begging orders helped renew the church which was being attacked by the heretics. The begging or *mendicant* orders were devoted to apostolic poverty and the uprooting of heresy. Several orders including the Carmelites and the Augustinian friars were founded at this time, but the two most important were the Dominicans and the Franciscans.

The Dominicans. Born in Castile, Spain, in 1170, St. Dominic founded his order to curb the growth of heresy through the pious example of his friars and through fervent preaching. The Dominicans were known as the Order of Preachers and followed the rule suggested by St. Augustine. They took a vow of absolute poverty and sustained themselves begging. Dominic wanted his friars to be able to go from place to place as the need arose. The Dominicans became extremely influential in medieval universities and became leaders in the court system of the Inquisition. They received their approval to preach from Pope Honorius III who wrote of them:

> Let those invincible athletes of Christ, armed with the shield of Faith and the helmet of Salvation, continue ever, in season and out of season, despite all hindrances and every tribulation, to preach the divine Word.

The Franciscans. One of the most popular of all Christian saints is Francis of Assisi (1182-1226). He was the son of a wealthy Italian cloth merchant who became quite angry when, after a carefree life as a youth, the 20-year-old Francis renounced all worldly goods. Greatly influenced by the words of Jesus in Matthew 10:7-10, Francis interpreted the gospel to mean that goods should be given freely to the poor. He left his home and wandered through the countryside with a few followers, preaching the gospels and begging from the rich to give to the poor.

In 1210 Francis obtained approval from Pope Innocent III for his simple rule of devotion to "Lady Poverty." He began to call his followers the Friars Minor, a humble term meaning "the Lesser Brethren." A society of women, the Poor Clares was founded in imitation of Francis when St. Clare, a rich woman of Assisi, converted to his ideals. The nuns of St. Clare were called the Second Order while a Third Order of laymen and laywomen devoted to the ideals of Francis was also established.

Thwarted by misfortune St. Francis unsuccessfully attempted to do missionary work in Syria and Morocco. He did go to the Middle East in 1219 where he unsuccessfully tried to convert the Moslem Sultan of Egypt.

During Francis' lifetime a split took place in his order. Some friars wanted a more elaborate organization and decided that it was impractical not to own some goods for the sustenance of the many men who had joined Francis' movement. Francis, and a few others, kept his original spirit and retired to a pilgrimage on Mount Alvernia where he received the *stigmata*, the five wounds of Christ. During his last years Francis composed the lovely "Canticle to the Sun," his *Admonitions* and his *Testament* before submitting joyously to "Sister Death" in 1226.

Francis was an original. He loved nature and saw in created things the splendor of the Creator. He did not flee from the world like some monks. His major concern and contribution was ministering to the poor in the growing cities of the medieval world. He spent most of his time in cities preaching the good news while living in utter poverty among ordinary people. To this day he is revered as one who walked in the footsteps of the Master: Jesus Christ.

St. Francis of Assisi

The Franciscans and Dominicans were a moving force in the Catholic church in the Middle Ages. They brought a renewed sense of the gospel spirit to a church which had grown too worldly. They preached and witnessed the gospel in the growing cities. Later they became the intellectual leaders at the new universities. They reminded popes and peasants alike what it means to follow Jesus Christ.

EXERCISES

A. *Some Research Possibilities*:
  1. Read about and report on one of the crusades.
  2. Make a report on the Franciscans and Dominicans today.
  3. Read a life of St. Francis, St. Dominic or St. Clare.

B. *Read and Discuss.* This is the passage from Matthew which turned Francis' world upside down:

> And as you go, proclaim that the kingdom of God is close at hand. Cure the sick, raise the dead, cleanse the lepers, cast out devils. You received without charge, give without charge. Provide yourselves with no gold or silver, not even with a few coppers for your purses, with no haversack for the journey or spare tunic or footware or a staff, for the workman deserves his keep (Mt 10:7-10).

  1. Do you admire Francis' devotion to absolute poverty? Why or why not?

  2. Is it practical today? Explain.

  3. Will the Lord provide for those engaged in his work?

C. *Test yourself on your commitment to the gospel.* Rank yourself on the gospel attitudes/values/practices which influenced Francis so much. *Scale:* 1—a high level of commitment; 5—a low level of commitment.

1. I'm involved in some kind of good work which helps those less fortunate than me.

    1   2   3   4   5

2. I give some of my money to the poor or to the church.

    1   2   3   4   5

3. I recognize the goodness of God in the beauty of nature.

    1   2   3   4   5

4. I am ecology-minded; I know that all of nature is related to me.

    1   2   3   4   5

5. I trust that God will provide good things for me.

    1   2   3   4   5

6. I study hard to prepare myself for a life of serving others.

    1   2   3   4   5

7. I refrain from spending my money on frivolous things.

    1   2   3   4   5

8. I look on others as my brothers and sisters in the Lord.

    1   2   3   4   5

9. I proclaim the good news by giving good example to others.

    1   2   3   4   5

The Universities. One of the major contributions of the Middle Ages was the university, a favorite institution used by medieval popes to further the cause of the church. Universities came about when students and teachers or masters organized themselves into guilds. As craftsman had done before them, students and teachers grouped together for mutual interest and protection and called themselves a *universitas,* the medieval term for a kind of corporation. The forerunners of the university were cathedral schools used by bishops to supply an elementary education for future priests.

There were two major types of universities. The southern type was modeled on the University of Bologna in Italy, founded in the late 12th century. While students in the north tended to major in theology, canon law or liberal arts, students at Bologna usually majored in law or medicine. At Bologna students hired and paid teachers, determined the curriculum, fined and even fired teachers. Professors in the Middle Ages lectured to their students from required texts. Repetition and memorization were the hallmarks of learning. Teachers had to post a sum of money in the city bank from which students could deduct penalties for poor lecturing. Students did not have to attend classes and would present themselves for an oral exam when they felt ready for it. No written exams were given. The equivalent of a bachelor of arts degree took four to six years of study; the master's degree, equivalent to the modern doctorate, could take as long as 14 years and required many oral tests.

In the north, at the University of Paris (late 12th century) and Oxford (c. 1200) and Cambridge (1209) in England, the professors had more power. They forbade student swearing and gambling and fined them for breaking curfews and for bad table manners. Students, though, could sample several lectures of different teachers before joining a class and paying the professor.

Student life in the Middle Ages was most interesting. At first lectures were given in the sheds at Oxford and Cambridge, in the town square in Italy, and in the cathedral choirs in Paris. Eventually teachers rented rooms where students sat on straw-covered floors. University study began at about 13 to 16 years of age. All lectures were in Latin, so a student could easily enroll at a university in a foreign country. Since both the church and the state needed trained and educated personnel, the students were given special status. They were free from most forms of taxation and were exempt from military service. They took minor orders in the church and as such were exempt from civil law; they could only be tried in the more lenient church courts. Poor students could beg their way through college. And, since there was little extracurricular activity, students would often "live it up" in the towns. Police records of the day record many examples of "town and gown" strife caused by frisky college students.

SOME DISCUSSION IDEAS

1. What do you think of the student power in the southern style of medieval university? Is it a good idea today for students to have the major authority in the running of a college? List some benefits. What might be some bad effects?

2. As a class activity, write 10 good rules for students at a Catholic college. Also discuss:

   a. Should students be exempt from the draft while in college? (This was the practice in the United States during most of the Vietnam War.) Why or why not?

   b. In a drug bust in a college dormitory, should the school officials hand the students involved over to the civil authorities, or should they use their own disciplinary procedures? Explain.

3. Examine the catalogue and student handbook of a Catholic college.

   a. What is the philosophy of the school? Is it what you would consider to be "Catholic" enough?

   b. Do students have any say in what affects their lives? Should they? If so, what would you suggest?

   c. Examine the theology requirements at this school. Any reactions or comments?

Scholasticism. The universities were largely responsible for the development of a systematic philosophy known as scholasticism. A major teaching technique in the medieval schools was the disputation in which two or more masters, and sometimes the students, debated text readings. This technique along with questioning, postulating, examining and logically arranging details into a meaningful whole helped forge a new philosophy much used by the church: scholasticism.

By the 13th century Christianity needed a new system of thought. Ancient Greek thought, especially as typified by Aristotle, was coming into Europe and helped spawn a lot of heresies. The philosophies of the Moslem Averroes from Spain and the Jewish philosopher Maimonides were causing people to question the faith.

The church was much concerned about the new ideas and sent Thomas Aquinas to the University of Paris to tackle the new thought. Born of nobility, Thomas Aquinas was a Dominican monk who was known for his courtesy, his incredible work habits and his possession of one of the most brilliant minds known to humanity. Although his classmates nicknamed him "The Dumb Ox" because of his weight, seriousness and slow movement, Thomas was anything but dumb. At Paris he forged what many consider to be the most truly magnificent synthesis of philosophy and religion ever devised.

Aquinas was convinced that human reason and faith were compatible. He examined point by point the major ideas of Aristotle and other philosophers, accepting some and rejecting others. The result was an incredible 21-volume work entitled *Summa Theologica* (a summary of theological knowledge). Thomas believed that religion was reasonable, and that we could apply our rational abilities to try to understand it. Human reason, he believed, can lead us to the truth. But when human reason is exhausted, Thomas taught, a Christian should appeal to divine revelation to search out the truth. Revelation picks up where human reasoning leaves off.

Not everyone accepted Thomas' ideas in his own day. Other philosophers, like the Franciscan Bonaventure, distrusted Thomas' well-developed and ordered theological system. Bonaventure emphasized prayer, contemplation and a mystical approach to God. Furthermore, the brilliant Aquinas, though highly regarded by some churchmen, was not always considered orthodox. Some distrusted his attempt to reconcile Aristotelian philosophy with Christian beliefs. With time, though, Thomism (the philosophy of Aquinas) became the official philosophy of the Roman Catholic Church. Even up to our own times his theological approach has influenced church teachers and church dogma in the most powerful way. His clarity of thought, his insistence on truth, his respect for human reason, and his defense of Christian revelation have all helped form the Roman Catholic Church as we know it.

THOMAS AQUINAS

A. *Does God Exist?* Here is a very small selection from that portion of the *Summa* which deals with a most important topic—the question of God's existence. Thomas offers five proofs. This is the first. Read it carefully.

First Part, Question 2, Article 3

The first and more manifest way to prove the existence of God is the argument from motion. It is certain, and evident to our senses, that in this world some things are in motion. Now whatever is in motion is put in motion by another, for nothing can be in motion unless it is in potency to that towards which it is in motion. But a thing moves in so far as it is in act. For motion is nothing else than the reduction of something from potency to act. But nothing can be reduced from potency to act except by something in a state of act. Thus that which is actually hot, as fire, makes wood, which is potentially hot, to be actually hot, and thereby moves and changes it. Now it is not possible that the same thing should be at once in act and in potency in the same respect, but only in different respects. For what is actually hot cannot simultaneously be potentially hot, though it is simultaneously potentially cold. It is therefore impossible that in the same respect and in the same way a thing should be both mover and moved, that is, that it should move itself. Therefore, whatever is moved must be moved by another. If that by which it is moved be itself moved, then this also must be moved by another, and that by another again. But this cannot go on to infinity, because then there would be no first mover, and, consequently, no other mover, seeing that subsequent movers move only because as they are moved by the first mover, just as the staff moves only because it is moved by the hand. Therefore it is necessary to arrive at a first mover which is moved by no other. And this everyone understands to be God.

Discuss:

1. In your own words, what is Thomas saying?

2. Is his argument convincing to you?

3. *Optional*: Obtain a copy of the *Summa* and read the other four proofs. Try to explain each proof to your classmates.

B. *Disputation*. Role play a medieval disputation. Several individuals should argue for God's existence; several others should argue against it. Prepare your arguments by doing some research into this question in addition to "dreaming up" your own approaches.

Discuss:

What is the most important proof to you that God exists?

Cathedrals. The artistic expression of a people tells a lot about what they value. Medieval cathedrals are a superb symbol of the ideals of the Middle Ages. Originally a cathedral was a church, usually quite simple, which contained a bishop's *cathedra* (chair), the symbol of his teaching authority and power. The cathedral provided a place for the bishops and his assistant priests to say Mass and sing daily services. In time cathedrals developed in size and magnificence, reflecting the religious spirit of the age and oftentimes civic pride.

The large cathedrals had many rooms: a choir (chancel) which contained a high altar, the bishop's chair and stalls for the priests who chanted daily prayers; a main room (the nave) which took care

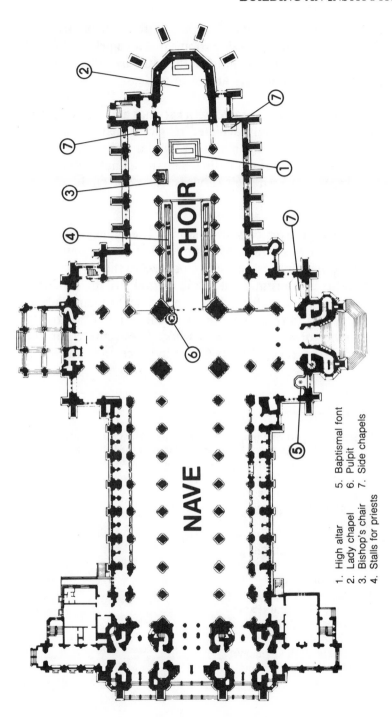

1. High altar
2. Lady chapel
3. Bishop's chair
4. Stalls for priests
5. Baptismal font
6. Pulpit
7. Side chapels

Floor plan of a typical medieval Gothic cathedral

of the needs of the laity—an altar for Mass, a font for baptisms, a pulpit for sermons; and many smaller rooms in which private Masses were said. As the largest building in town the cathedral also served as a meeting place for social activity and even trade.

Cathedrals were richly decorated with carvings and stained glass. These artistic works commonly depicted religious themes and were used to instruct the faithful, many of whom could not read. Everyone took part in cathedral building. The rich donated vast sums of money; tradesmen offered their services; the poor made gifts of foodstuffs.

Cathedrals were prayer carved in stone. The money and time needed to build them was a faith-offering to God. They conveyed a sense of peace, power, timelessness and closeness to the divine. They rose to the heavens as a testimonial to the eternal striving of Christians to be one with the Creator. They stand today as memorials of the effort, energy and faith of a people whose lives revolved around the bustling activity of a cathedral and whose lives centered on the church, the *visible* presence of Jesus Christ in space and time.

CATHEDRALS

1. Research and report on the story of one of these great cathedrals. In your research, report on the difference between the Gothic and Romanesque style of architecture used in cathedral building.

   Cluny Abbey Church, France
   Abbey of St. Denis, France
   Trier Cathedral, Germany
   St. Martin, Cologne, Germany
   Santiago de Compostela Cathedral, Spain
   Canterbury Cathedral, England
   Winchester Cathedral, England
   Milan Cathedral, Italy
   Toledo Cathedral, Spain
   Notre Dame Cathedral, Paris
   Chartres Cathedral, France
   Rheims Cathedral, France
   Cologne Cathedral, Germany
   Glasgow Cathedral, Scotland

2. Report on the building of a cathedral. A good resource, if you can find it, is David Macaulay's, *Cathedral: The Story of Its Construction* (Boston: Houghton Mifflin Company, Inc., 1973).

3. Visit the cathedral located in your diocese. Report on:

   a. its style of architecture

   b. its history

   c. the scenes depicted in its stained glass and other artwork

St. Patrick's Cathedral, New York

THE AUTUMN OF THE MIDDLE AGES:
THE CHURCH IN DECLINE

The unity of Christian Europe (Christendom) depended on the papacy and the concept of the empire. But during the 14th and 15th centuries the power and prestige of the church began to lessen. The process began with the weakening of papal influence over the European kings. Several other forces at work in these centuries, including the Great Plague, contributed to the decline.

The Black Death. One of the real setbacks to the church in this period was the Black Death or Great Plague which ravaged Europe in the middle of the 14th century. It was a highly contagious disease which caused glandular swelling and brought death in a matter of hours. Some cities lost half of their population. The clergy suffered great losses, especially the parish priests and the Franciscans who ministered wherever they were needed. Whole monasteries were wiped out. To replace these losses priests were sometimes ordained without adequate preparation. The spiritual life of Christendom suffered greatly as poorly trained priests greedily sought after wages for their services and even moved from place to place to get higher pay. Many Christians took to extremes, roaming the streets and doing bizarre penances in the hope of warding off the ever-beckoning hand of death.

Pope Boniface VIII (1294-1303). The prestige of the papacy began to decline when Pope Boniface VIII assumed the throne of St. Peter. Pope Boniface VIII was like Pope Innocent III in that he tried to make the pope the central power in Europe. Unfortunately the leaders of the day did not pay too much attention to him. King Edward I of England and King Philip IV of France both attempted to tax the clergy without Boniface's approval. Boniface met this threat by issuing a bull entitled *Clericos Laicos* which, among other things, forbade taxation of the clergy without his permission and threatened excommunication. The English king retaliated by removing the clergy from police protection. Many clergy chose to pay the tax to show loyalty to the crown. Philip IV answered Boniface's challenge by forbidding the exportation of silver and gold from France.

Philip later took the bold step of refusing to recognize a papal candidate for a post as bishop. In return Boniface issued the bull *Unam Sanctam* (1302) which asserted that the pope is superior to the French state. In this bull Boniface made the boldest claim to papal authority of any medieval pope: "We therefore declare, say, affirm, and announce that for every human creature to be submissive to the Roman pontiff is absolutely necessary for salvation." Philip IV retorted by arresting the pope at Anagni. Boniface was roughly treated and died soon thereafter at the age of 86. Philip's action signaled that strong kings would no longer take directions from the pope.

Exile at Avignon. After the brief reign of Boniface's successor Philip engineered the election of a Frenchman: Pope Clement V. More startling, he influenced the pope to withdraw the decrees of Boniface VIII and take up residence at Avignon in southern France. This began an exile of the papacy which lasted 70 years. All seven of the Avignon popes and almost all the cardinals they supported were French. The papacy, which had fought so hard to rule the universal church, now became a mere puppet of the French kings. The exile was likened to the Jewish exile and dubbed the Babylonian Captivity of the Church. The pope's absence from Rome disturbed pious Christians around Europe. The move to Avignon drained the church treasury. As a result, some of the French popes resorted to simony to help support the luxurious court life at Avignon. Politically, the English especially resented a papacy controlled by the French, and passed a law prohibiting papal appointees from assuming office.

The Great Schism (1378-1417) and Conciliarism. The Avignon papacy ended when Pope Gregory XI returned to Rome in 1376. After his death in 1378 mob pressure in Rome helped elect Pope Urban VI. Some cardinals claimed that Urban's election was due to pressure and elected another pope, the Frenchman Clement VII. Neither pope was willing to give up his claim to the throne of St. Peter, so the church found itself in a schism which was to rock Christianity to its very foundations.

Europe split into two camps. The French and their Scottish allies backed Clement VII, who took up his residence in Avignon; the

English and the Germans backed the Roman pope, Urban VI. Even great saints split over the issue, backing one or the other pope. Matters worsened when some cardinals elected Alexander V as a compromise candidate in 1409. There were now three popes. The institution of the papacy had become a source of great anxiety for Christians who didn't know which pope to listen to. It was a matter of grave concern for them because they felt their eternal salvation rested on following the right pope. In the meantime, each pope excommunicated the others.

The matter was finally resolved at the Council of Constance (1414-1418). One pope was persuaded to resign; a second was declared to be false; and the third, the pope from the Roman line, voluntarily abdicated. (His name was Gregory XII; many historians today recognize that he was the legitimate pope.) In 1417 the cardinals at the Council of Constance elected Martin V. He was the first universally recognized pope in over 10 years. This whole episode shows the value of a strong institution and its ability to survive stress.

The Great Schism of the Western church did much to foster the theory of *conciliarism,* a theory that the decisions made by a council hold more weight than the teachings of the pope. At this time many of the main proponents of this theory were truly pro-papal and only resorted to it in the grave crisis of the schism. Previous writers on the topic were more radical; for example, William of Ockham held that the ultimate authority in the church is the Bible and Marsiglio of Padua argued that church authority resides in a representative council of all Christians and that the pope should merely function to carry out the wishes of a council.

Pope Martin V reluctantly followed the decrees of the Council of Constance because he recognized the important function this council played in resolving the scandal of the schism. He and his successors, though, worked against conciliarism. In 1460 Pope Pius II condemned the "deadly poison" of conciliarism and threatened to excommunicate anyone who would appeal to a general council over the pope.

Toward the Reformation. The Great Western Schism was a severe blow to the church. Papal prestige and power were also severely weakened by rising national feelings which put the interests of the state ahead of those of the church. Along with a growing interest in religion and spirituality, the schism and rising nationalism contributed to the Protestant Reformation which was to take place in the 16th century.

Other factors were working to change the influence of the church. New heresies abounded. John Wyclif in England, for example, severely criticized the Avignon popes' practice of taxation. His valid points of criticism led him to such extremes that he ended up denying transubstantiation, the validity of the sacraments celebrated by unworthy priests, and papal authority in teaching on matters of faith and morals. His ideas were taken up by John Hus who circulated Wyclif's ideas in Bohemia. Condemned at the Council of Constance, Hus was turned over to the state authorities who burned him to death. News of his death caused a 20-year civil war in Bohemia and greatly hurt the cause of the church there.

The world was changing. Commerce was on the upswing. It brought with it a new middle class which thought more independently and was more involved in the secular affairs of the day. Monasticism declined in popularity as Christians found new ways to live in the world.

The movement known as the Renaissance, the "rebirth" of Greek learning, stressed the human more than the divine. Whereas "medieval man" looked heavenward, "renaissance man" focused on human creative efforts. Many great advances in learning and art resulted from the Renaissance, but its spirit tended to make people look away from God. The church was no longer looked on as the *only* source of beauty, wisdom and guidance. Many of the post-schism popes were infected by the spirit of the Renaissance and manifested a worldliness that was unbecoming in men of God. Popes like the notorious Alexander VI had reigns marked by nepotism, simony, military expeditions, political and financial intrigue and even murder. It was in this spirit that the period of the Middle Ages ended. It was this spirit which helped to contribute to the next chapter in the church's story.

CHRISTIAN HEROINES

A. *St. Catherine of Siena.* The church has produced some remarkable women during its long history. The Middle Ages was notable for giving birth to outstanding and forceful leaders in a time which needed them.

Catherine was born in 1347 in Siena, a city ravaged by the Black Death. She was the 24th child of pious parents. As a child, she was known for her spirituality, which was marked by visions and deep devotion to Jesus and Mary.

At 16 Catherine took the black and white habit of the Third Order of St. Dominic. She lived at home until the age of 19 caring for the sick and poor and ministering to the victims of the petty vendettas which plagued the Italian families of the time. Her personal holiness attracted a number of disciples, both men and women, who worked for the renewal of the spiritual life in Siena. Catherine herself was known for the severe penances which she inflicted on herself to atone for the many sins committed against the Lord.

Catherine had no formal education and didn't learn to write until she was 30. But she carried on a tremendous correspondence with leaders and others throughout Europe, often dictating to three or four secretaries at once. Her *Dialogue* is a rich treasury of mystical prayer. For Catherine, love of God is most dramatically demonstrated in love of neighbor. In her later years she was known for the unselfish care she gave to the victims of plagues and to prisoners.

In time this single-hearted woman of peace exerted a profound influence on church politics. Many of the problems in the Italy of her day resulted from the pope's exile in France and his despised system of taxation to support his courtly lifestyle in Avignon. Catherine wrote continuously to the pope's legates, and to Pope Gregory XI himself, condemning the immorality, greed and pride of the clergy. She had a deep respect and reverence for the papal office and insisted that the pope live up to his vocation. She took the extraordinary measure of visiting the pope and demanding his return to Rome. Remarkably, the pope heeded her pleas and returned to Rome, thus ending the Babylonian Captivity of the Church.

Catherine's life demonstrates the power of one deeply devoted, peaceful yet forceful Christian on the course of history. Convinced of Jesus' love for her, she moved mountains in serving others and calling the church to reform.

B. Research and report on one of these other great women who lived in or close to the Middle Ages:

St. Clare (1194-1253)	St. Colette (1381-1447)
St. Elizabeth of Hungary (1207-1231)	St. Joan of Arc (1412-1431)
	St. Teresa of Avila (1515-1582)
St. Bridget (1303-1373)	

You may want to consult one of the following references:

Butler's Lives of the Saints (London: Burns & Oates, 1956; reprinted in 1980 by Christian Classics, Inc.)

Dictionary of Saints by John J. Delaney (Garden City, New York: Doubleday & Co. Inc., 1980)

The Oxford Dictionary of Saints by David Hugh Farmer (Oxford: Clarendon Press, 1978)

C. *Some Optional Research Ideas*

1. Look into the past and current history of the Black Death (bubonic plague). Report to the class.

2. Obtain a book on the works of *one* of these Renaissance artists. Prepare a short illustrated talk using an opaque projector.

Michelangelo	Botticelli	Titian
Raphael	Cellini	Dürer
Leonardo da Vinci	Corregio	Holbein

3. Write a one-page essay with this thesis: In today's world, one convinced Christian can make a difference.

St. Joan, wounded while leading the French troops at Orleans, France

THE INSTITUTIONAL CHURCH TODAY

This chapter has studied the church's story under the image of *institution*. The Middle Ages cathedral, towering above the world and seeking to draw everyone through its doors so that all peoples might believe that Jesus Christ is Savior of the world is an appropriate symbol for this period in the church's history. But the church exhibited the other images as well. Great saints like Francis of Assisi formed Christian *communities* which put themselves at the service of God and the church. Others like Thomas Aquinas developed a sophisticated theology to enable the church to *herald* its message with philosophical precision. The institutional church also involved itself in many *service* activities, becoming *the* charitable organization of the Middle Ages. Also, when certain churchmen became tainted with a spirit of worldliness, saints like Catherine of Siena boldly reminded them that the church was meant to be a true *sacrament* of God's presence in the world. Finally, the church still saw itself as a *pilgrim*, a traveler with the final goal of eternity.

You and the Church Today. As a Catholic you belong to one of the most influential organizations to grace the face of the earth. It is fashionable today to criticize big institutions. The church, in fact, has come under attack for its bigness and its alleged wealth.

Consider for a moment, though, the value of the institutional church. As a worldwide community organized into a well-functioning institution, the church has been able to carry out many important charitable ministries for people. It takes organization and financial wherewithal to run schools, orphanages, retirement and nursing homes, hospitals, clinics, counseling centers, hospices, mission centers and the like. The Roman Catholic Church is the largest charitable organization in the world. Through the support of many Catholics around the world, the church's efforts to bring Christ's love to people is visibly present in every corner of the world.

A second value of the institutional church, organized into a hierarchical structure, is that there is a central authority to safeguard Jesus' authentic teaching. The pope—and the bishops teaching with him—serve the important function of settling disputes and teaching clearly on matters of faith and morals. They help preserve unity and are also an important symbol of unity. Without this authority the church would fragment into many smaller communities, often at odds with one another. This, in fact, is what happened in the Reformation when many Christians turned away from the authority of the pope. Today, more than ever, Christianity needs to stand as one in its presentation of Jesus and his gospel. The world needs the Lord and a united community can present him more authentically than bodies of Christians quarreling among themselves.

You belong to this institution. As a Catholic you have your part to play. You can learn about the organization of the church so that you can explain to others how it functions. Through financial support and volunteer work you can become part of the church's worldwide mission. By participating in your parish organizations you can experience the institutional church in miniature. Above all, you can take a kind of humble pride in being part of something bigger than you, a community which the Lord has organized to carry on his work.

REFLECTION

The institutional church is always in need of good leaders. Do you qualify? Here is a leadership grid which lists three leaders and a list of leadership qualities. Add to the list of qualities suggested here. Check off those which you think each of the leaders exhibits. Then check off those you think a potential leader—you—exhibit. Share your grid with your classmates.

QUALITIES / LEADERS	patient	self-confident	courageous	willing to stand alone	warm personality	person of conviction				
Jesus										
The Pope										
A respected Christian _____ (add name)										
You										

SUMMARY

1. The church functions as a good institution when it keeps alive the values of Jesus, engages in the activity of salvation and addresses the human need for everlasting life.

2. The 9th and 10th centuries are called the Dark Ages. They were characterized by the breakup of Charlemagne's Empire, the advent of feudalism, new barbarian invasions and an ever-increasing control of the church by the state. Pope Nicholas I and the abbots of Cluny encouraged efforts at church reform during this era, especially concerning these three abuses: simony, lay investiture and the lack of clerical celibacy.

3. In the Middle Ages the church emerged victorious over the state largely due to the efforts of some outstanding popes. Here is a list of key popes and their major achievements:

Popes	Achievements
Nicholas II	created the college of cardinals to elect the pope
Gregory VII	*Dictatus Papae* and victory over Emperor Henry IV in the investiture controversy
Urban II	called the First Crusade
Alexander III	important political victories over Frederick Barbarossa and Henry II of England
Innocent III	political victories in Germany, France and England; Fourth Lateran Council

4. Medieval popes gained ascendency in Europe through the use of excommunication and interdict, by levying taxes and developing a strong system of canon law, through the formation of political alliances, by use of the Inquisition and the Crusades, and by calling church councils.

5. The Eastern Schism took place in 1054 and was the result of many centuries of differences between the Western and Eastern churches. The Photian Controversy and the affair with Michael Cerularius, Patriarch of Constantinople, were key events which helped bring about the split.

6. The Middle Ages has been called the Age of Christendom because the church affected many aspects of peoples' lives. The Crusades, the founding of the begging (mendicant) orders, the rise of universities, the development of scholasticism and the building of cathedrals all characterized this age.

7. The autumn of the Middle Ages during the 14th and 15th centuries was characterized by the decline of the papacy and the rise of the spirit of nationalism. The Babylonian Captivity of the church (when popes resided in France) and the Great Western Schism did much to foster disrespect for the papacy. The Black Death was responsible for the loss of the lives of many clergy. New heresies arose. The spirit of the Renaissance which focused on this world, rather than the next, also contributed to the decline of the church's influence.

8. The Middle Ages contributed to the rise of the institutional church as we know it today. At its best the church as institution is organized in such a way that Christ's good works can continue in the world today. Also, a strong organization, with the pope as the supreme teacher, can demonstrate a unity in belief and practice which is most important in attracting others to the Lord.

EVALUATION

The church's story in the Middle Ages contains many important names, events, terms, and so forth. To help you measure your learning of this material, here is a quiz which contains many of the most important concepts covered in this chapter. Good Luck!

Short Essays:

1. Discuss three important factors which helped the rise of the papacy in the Middle Ages.

2. Why is the Middle Ages properly called the Age of Christendom? Be sure to back your reasoning with facts and examples.

Terms: Fill in the blanks with terms chosen from the list at the top of page 163.

_____ 3. the movement which works for unity among Christians

_____ 4. sacred leadership

_____ 5. the bishops teaching with and cooperating with the pope

_____ 6. a division in the church, usually over the question of authority

_____ 7. a negative attitude to the veneration of holy images and statues

_____ 8. a refusal of permission to celebrate the sacraments in a certain area

_____ 9. the condemnation of fighting during certain church holy days

_____ 10. the selling of church offices

_____ 11. an organization which centers on a fundamental human need, is enduring, and is maintained by a society

_____ 12. the theory that a representative group of Christians and its decisions are more important than the pope's authority

Peace of God	conciliarism	ecumenism
inconoclasm	institution	schism
lay investiture	simony	heresy
collegiality	institutionalism	excommunication
Truce of God	interdict	hierarchy

Multiple Choice:

____ 13. Hildebrand is associated with all of these except:
(a) Pope Gregory VII   (b) *Dictatus Papae*   (c) the
Crusades (d) Investiture Controversy   (e) Henry IV

____ 14. Fostered devotion to the Blessed Mother:
(a) St. Colette   (b) St. Bernard of Clairvaux   (c) Odo
of Cluny   (d) St. Catherine of Siena   (e) St. Norbert

____ 15. Founded the Order of Preachers: (a) St. Stephen
Harding   (b) St. Thomas Aquinas   (c) Peter the
Hermit   (d) St. Dominic   (e) St. Francis of Assisi

____ 16. Ended the Great Western Schism: (a) Council of Constance   (b) Council of Pisa   (c) Fourth Lateran Council   (d) Council of Claremont   (e) Second Nicaean
Council

____ 17. Greatest of the medieval popes: (a) Boniface VIII
(b) Innocent III   (c) Urban II   (d) Gregory VII
(e) Gregory XI

____ 18. All of these are associated with the Dark Ages except:
(a) Cluny   (b) feudalism   (c) Treaty of Verdun (d) Pope
Nicholas I   (e) Concordat of Worms

____ 19. Which Crusade recaptured Jerusalem? (a) First   (b) Second   (c) Fourth   (d) Children's   (e) Seventh

____ 20. Which medieval heresy originated in southern France and
was responsible for the establishment of the Inquisition?
(a) Hussitism   (b) Waldensianism   (c) Islam
(d) Albigensianism

____ 21. Known as the Dumb Ox: (a)   St. Dominic   (b) St. Francis of Assisi   (c) St. Thomas Aquinas   (d) St. Bruno
(e) St. Thomas Becket

____ 22. Which of the following is *not* associated with the Eastern
Schism? (a) Pope Nicholas I   (b) *filioque*   (c) Michael
Cerularius   (d) Gregorian Revolution   (e) Photius

Short Answers:

Briefly explain the *significance* of each of the following for the development of the church in the Middle Ages:

23. Canossa: _____

_____

_____

_____

24. cathedrals: _____

_____

_____

_____

25. Babylonian Captivity:_____

_____

_____

_____

PRAYER REFLECTION

St. Bernard Clairvaux wrote a beautiful prayer to Mary called the *Memorare*. In the Middle Ages Christians more and more turned to our Lady for help and guidance and looked to her as a mediator between them and our Lord. Mary serves the same function today. Recite this beautiful prayer as a class while keeping in mind your special intentions.

Remember, O most gracious Virgin Mary,
that never was it known that anyone who
    fled to your protection,
    implored your help,
    or sought your intercession
    was left unaided.

Inspired by this confidence, we fly unto you,
O Virgin of virgins, our Mother!
To you we come, before you we stand,
    sinful and sorrowful.

O Mother of the Word incarnate,
despise not our petitions,
but in your mercy hear and answer us.

                    Amen.

5

The Pilgrim Church:
Protest, Reform and Crisis
in the 16th Through 19th Centuries

I pray not only for these,
but for those also
who through their words will believe in me.
May they all be one.
Father, may they be one in us,
as you are in me and I am in you,
so that the world may believe it was you who sent me.
—John 17:20-21

Imagine the incredible perspective you would have if you could stand on the very edge of our solar system and focus a powerful telescope on the earth. You'd see a tiny orb silently floating through the darkness of space. From such a distance you might think the earth was a spaceship bound on some journey, mysteriously drawn to a final destination. You might even imagine the passengers on this spaceship cooperating to make sure that the earth keeps on a steady course.

The close-up view of the earth is quite different. Nations war among themselves. People fail to care for one another. Race and religion and language and economics cloud the vision of our common lot and destiny.

In truth, we are pilgrims traveling together on the spaceship earth. We *ought* to be concerned about one another.

The concept of pilgrim has many religious overtones. Students of history know that the Pilgrims were among the founders of the United States of America. These pioneers boarded ships which braved stormy seas in order to escape persecution and settle in a land which would allow them to worship God in their own way. They stuck together—they had to—in order to survive the trip to the "Promised Land."

167

Pilgrim is also a vital image used to describe the Catholic church today. It brings to mind a community with a definite goal, a community on its way, even if it often finds itself in the midst of distress, imperfection, uncertainty and perplexity. Despite these dangers, the community of the church keeps in mind a definite though distant aim: perfect salvation and redemption in the Lord Jesus Christ. It trusts that Jesus and those who died in him (the saints) will strengthen and aid the pilgrims who have yet to attain their final goal. This strength and aid provided by the Lord and his saints give us present-day pilgrims the courage to go on and strengthen our hope that the victory they have won will one day be ours.

The concept of church as pilgrim is often pictured in Christian art as a ship on a rough sea. This is an especially apt image for the church in the period we will study in this chapter: the 16th through 19th centuries. Many perils beset the church in this era. The unity of the church was severely shaken by the Protestant Reformation. The security of the Middle Ages and the privileged status achieved by the church began to crumble. New ideas and historical movements—nationalism, the Enlightenment, the French Revolution, liberalism—assailed all that had been achieved. Like a pilgrim, the church weathered these rough storms.

As a result of these internal and external perils, the church was forced to reform itself and to stress those things which were essential for its survival. Like a pilgrim it rid itself of excess baggage. At times it was quite defensive and conservative, but in the light of history we can understand that this approach grew out of the need to survive some very rough times. Jesus' promise to be with the church always, in good times and in bad, was evidenced during this era of upheaval and change.

We will study the story of the pilgrim church during this era by looking at the following themes:

- the Protestant Reformation
- the Catholic Reformation

- the marks of the church: what they are, tensions which tended to obscure them in this era, and evidence of the church's faithfulness to them

---

ON PILGRIMAGE

A. *Your Values.* The pilgrimage has been a very important part of Christian spirituality from about the fourth century up to our own day. Values—repentance, prayer, respect for the holy, sharing and an eternal destiny animated the pilgrims who left home for far-distant lands.

As a member of the church you too are a pilgrim on a journey through life. What values do you take along on the journey? Check any of the following which help define what you are—or what you are not.

I place much
value on (✔)

_____ having friends
_____ my freedom
_____ my family
_____ my church
_____ having lots of money
_____ having enough money
_____ my achievements
_____ saving my soul
_____ loving and being loved
_____ helping others
(Add others)

I don't place much
value on (X)

_____ recreation
_____ prayer
_____ traveling
_____ working for peace
_____ helping others be happy
_____ exploring and/or risking
_____ keeping busy
_____ silence
_____ my heritage
_____ my future

___ _____   ___ _____

___ _____   ___ _____

In small groups discuss any insights into yourself that this exercise triggered.

B. *Destiny.* When your life's pilgrimage is over, what would you like to be remembered for? Check two of the following traits. Then list some things you are *now* doing that demonstrate that the traits you selected are truly descriptive of you.

Traits

_____ famous
_____ idealistic
_____ hard worker
_____ loving
_____ good family person
_____ individualist

_____ religious
_____ open-minded
_____ dependable
_____ helpful
_____ cooperative
_____ rich
_____ patriotic and/or loyal

List

1. _____

   _____

2. _____

   _____

3. _____

   _____

Discuss: Do you see any connection between what you now value
(exercise A) and what you'd like to be remembered for (exercise
B)? Explain.

Zwingli and Luther at the Marburg Conference, 1529

THE PROTESTANT REFORMATION

Like the Eastern Schism in the 11th century, the Protestant Reformation in the 16th century dealt a shattering blow to Christian unity. The Reformation did not happen overnight. Reformers like William Ockham, Marsilius of Padua and John Wyclif in the 14th century and John Hus in the 15th century had been calling for church renewal, especially in regard to the popes and the papal curia. Through their writings Catholic humanists like the famed Erasmus of Rotterdam and St. Thomas More gently prodded the church to reform even while the Reformation was taking place. But the church did not act fast enough and was finally forced to take steps at self-reform when the Protestants revolted.

Causes of the Protestant Reformation. Rev. Richard McBrien, in his important book, *Catholicism,* lists the following specific causes of the Protestant Reformation:

1. *The Renaissance.* Despite the literary and artistic achievements of the rebirth of Latin and Greek learning, the Renaissance turned away from God to celebrate the human. A series of popes was infected with the spirit of the Renaissance. Their reigns were characterized by nepotism (appointing relatives to church offices), simony, financial manipulation, political intrigue, military expeditions and even murder.

2. *Debasement of Catholic piety and an anti-intellectual Catholic theology.* Religious art and spirituality of this period appealed almost exclusively to the emotions. Crude depictions of the sufferings of Christ, for example, became commonplace, with statues of Christ dripping blood appearing everywhere. Scenes of the Last Judgment filled believers with dread and terror. The precision demanded by scholasticism fell into disfavor, and a new form of philosophy known as nominalism came into vogue. Nominalism taught that nothing can come between God and humankind. The sacraments, church authority and good deeds are worthless; only God's mercy revealed in Jesus Christ can bridge the gap between us and God. This utterly simple message—which did away with many of the church's institutions—greatly influenced leaders of the Reformation.

3. *Great Western Schism.* The era of the three popes had caused people to lose respect for the pope and lessened his power as a symbol of unity in the Western church. The Eastern Schism of the 11th century had also played its part in weakening the credibility of the papal office.

4. *Rise of nationalism.* As kings united their lands they became the centers of authority in their own territories. They resented the papal claim to authority over their subjects, openly fought with the popes and increasingly were able to diminish the church's ruling power in their countries.

5. *The church too closely identified with Western civilization.* By modeling its government along the lines of Western monarchies, the church denied itself a necessary measure of flexibility. It became less a people of God than a hierarchical, perhaps an absolutely monarchial society. Western cultural customs were imposed as a matter of faith.

6. *The role of personalities.* Some remarkable men came on the scene at this crucial time, men who were able to command a large following from a confused and often unhappy laity. Prominent among these men were four who can be considered the leaders of the Protestant Revolt: Luther, Zwingli, Calvin and Henry VIII of England.

Martin Luther (1483-1546). Except for Jesus, more books have been written about Luther than any other figure in history. Luther became an Augustinian monk as the result of a vow he took during a frightful thunderstorm. He was sent by his order to the University of Wittenberg in Germany to teach moral theology and the Bible. During the course of his study and preaching Luther was engaged in a serious personal religious crisis. He knew his own unworthiness and sinfulness and was tormented by the realities of death, judgment, heaven and hell. Nothing he did—including prayer and penance—would settle his conscience. Then, while studying Paul's Epistle to the Romans, Luther came to the conclusion that only God's mercy justifies a sinner. Faith in God's mercy and love alone saves.

As a result of this conclusion Luther rejected all other means of reaching God's mercy: church authority, the sacraments, good works and especially indulgences. Indulgences, the remission of temporal punishment in purgatory due to sins already forgiven, were a sore point with Luther. The church taught that it could dispense indulgences from the richness of graces left from Christ's saving act on the cross. The problem was that abuses had crept into the practice of issuing indulgences. In Luther's day they were being sold to raise money to build St. Peter's Basilica in Vatican City.

Luther reacted to this abuse and some of the gross materialism and low-level commitment of many churchmen by tacking up his famous *95 Theses* on the church door in Wittenberg in 1517. Luther wanted desperately to reform the church; he did not want to break away from it. The means used, though, led to a revolution. When confronted by the pope's representative in Augsburg, Luther refused to recant and eventually denied the supremacy of the pope. He burned the pope's edict of excommunication which finally came in 1521.

Martin Luther at Wittenberg, 1517

In an earlier day Luther may well have been burned at a stake for his heresy. As it was, he found a protector in Frederick of Saxony who offered him refuge. He translated the Bible into German and spread his ideas through many pamphlets which were enthusiastically read by the laity in Germany. His ideas spread and many people, especially in Germany and the Scandinavian countries, followed the lead of their rulers in adopting Luther's reforms. They rejected many of the customs and beliefs of the Roman Catholic Church and established churches patterned on Luther's. The basic creed of Lutheranism—the *Augsburg Confession*—was drawn up by Luther's disciple, Philipp Melanchthon.

Ulrich Zwingli (1484-1531). Zwingli was a Swiss humanist who established a branch of Reform Protestantism which became popular in Zurich. He believed in a form of democratic rule for the church, a rule which he put into practice in Zurich. More anti-clerical and anti-institutional than Luther, Zwingli removed images from churches, banned all church music and abolished fast days. He and Luther could not agree on the Real Presence of Christ in the Eucharist; Zwingli held only to a spiritual kind of presence. He died in a battle against Swiss Catholic cantons (provincial rulers).

John Calvin (1509-1564). John Calvin, a former priest from France, fathered what became the most international form of Protestantism. He formulated the theological base for the Presbyterian and Reformed churches and systematized his beliefs in one of the most important books of the Reformation, *The Institutes of Christian Religion* (1536). He founded the Geneva Academy which attracted students from all over Europe, especially France.

Calvin taught that the Bible is the only source of the truth needed for salvation, and the absolute sovereignty of God who reveals himself to man in scripture through Jesus Christ.

He also espoused the doctrine of predestination by which God determines people for salvation or damnation before they are born. Nothing they do by their own efforts can win salvation or make them members of the elect. He also taught that grace was a total free gift from God and not dependent on the person's behavior.

Although he held no political or civic office in the city of Geneva, he established a church-state there to control all civil affairs. He and his followers were able to enforce a strict discipline in all modes of behavior. Calvin's ideas won over a great part of his native France, the area we now call Holland. His disciple, John Knox, brought Calvinism to Scotland in the form of Presbyterianism which held that every believer is a priest (presbyter) and that there is no need for a special clergy.

Henry VIII. Henry VIII was responsible for a schism that led to the establishment of the Church of England which is variously known as the Anglo-Catholic and Protestant-Episcopal Church.

Before Henry broke from the church in Rome, he had eloquently defended Catholicism against Luther and was given the title "Defender of the Faith" by the pope. His problem in the church was not one of faith. Rather, Henry wanted his marriage to Catherine of Aragon declared invalid so he could marry Anne Boleyn. Like the schism between the Orthodox and Roman churches, the controversy became one of authority.

After lengthy negotiations with the pope, Henry's marriage to Catherine was declared valid and he was forbidden to divorce her. The king then took matters into his own hands and declared himself head of the church in England. He forced the populace to take an oath acknowledging his headship. The penalty for refusal was death. Some brave Catholics, most notably St. John Fisher, bishop and cardinal, and St. Thomas More, a close friend of Henry's and Lord High Chancellor of England, refused to accept royal supremacy over the church in England. They both were beheaded in 1535.

Henry VIII's political differences with Rome were precipitated by a moral issue, not a fundamental doctrinal one. He even issued *Six Articles* (1539) which insisted on Catholic doctrine and imposed severe penalties on anyone who denied transubstantiation, private Mass and confession, or the need for clerical celibacy. His main anti-Catholic action was the dissolution of the monasteries. Over nine thousand monks and nuns were turned out and vast land holdings and wealth exchanged hands. With the destruction of the Catholic monasteries the way was open for a gradual but strong Protestant influence to take hold in England.

With Henry's death, the boy-king Edward VI (1547-1553) assumed the throne. Thomas Cranmer, a Calvinist at heart, gained much influence in England. His *Book of Common Prayer* (1549), a liturgical masterpiece, followed the basic outlines of the Catholic Mass but also included some key Reformation doctrines. Cranmer also saw that the *Articles of Religion* were passed in the Parliament. About half of these Articles contained Catholic teaching while the rest adopted Lutheran and Calvinist doctrines.

Catholicism made a comeback and Protestants were persecuted during the reign of Mary (1553-1558), Catholic daughter of Henry and Catherine. When her half-sister Elizabeth (1558-1603), daughter of Henry and Anne Boleyn, assumed the throne, a compromise form of Protestantism was established in England. Elizabeth tried to synthesize Catholic, Lutheran and Calvinist (Puritan) elements in the English church. She allowed Episcopalian (another name for Anglican) bishops to take over, and she herself assumed the leadership of the church. Catholics were fined and even put to death for celebrating the Mass and refusing to take the Oath of Supremacy.

In the 17th century the Puritans were persecuted as the kings tried to revive Catholic traditions in the English church. Around 20,000 Puritans left England in the 1630s for the New World hoping to establish holy commonwealths. These Calvinist communities played a key role in shaping the new American nation.

Anabaptists. The most radical form of Protestantism was Anabaptism (literally, "baptism again") which held that the baptism of infants was invalid. To both Protestants and Catholics of their day, the Anabaptists were heretics. They held that only adults freely convinced of the Christian faith make up the true church. For Anabaptists the church was a voluntary community of adults. To the state officials of the day this was considered rebellious and destructive of the customary church-state relationship, and the Anabaptists were severely persecuted. Like the Puritans, many Anabaptists and their spiritual descendents, the Amish and the Mennonites, emigrated to America.

PROTESTANTISM

The word *protest* means: 1) to object to, especially formally, and 2) to promise or affirm. Protestants got their name because they *protested* ("disagreed") with some of the abuses in the Catholic church and because they *protested* ("proclaimed") certain new beliefs. *Protestant* is an all-encompassing term which includes many sects. Here is a bird's-eye view of the three major Protestant streams which arose in the 16th century.

THREE MAJOR PROTESTANT STREAMS

Luther	*Calvin*	*Anglicanism*
key event:	key event:	key event:
95 Theses posted in 1517	*Institutes of the Christian Religion* published in 1536	Henry VIII established Church of England in 1534
1. Humans are depraved. Faith alone justifies.	1. Human nature since Adam's fall is utterly depraved.	1. The pope is not the universal authority over the whole church.
2. The Bible, not the pope, is the center of authority. Individual interpretation of the Bible.	2. Some are predestined for salvation; others for hell; Christ died only for the elect who cannot resist God's grace or backslide once elected.	2. The king (queen) is head of the church in England.
3. Accepts baptism and the Eucharist. Belief in the Real Presence—consubstantiation—bread and wine and the body and blood of Christ coexist in the elements.	3. Accepts only baptism and the Eucharist. Belief that Christ is only spiritually present in the eucharistic elements. Encourages bible reading, sobriety, thrift, capitalism, a strict Sabbath. All believers are priests—emphasis on political and church democracy.	3. Belief in the seven sacraments, including the priesthood. *Book of Common Prayer.*
4. *Rejects*: holy days, fast days, honoring of saints, indulgences, the rosary, monasticism, other five sacraments.	4. *Rejects*: whatever cannot be found in the Bible: vestments, altar, images, paintings, organs, hymns.	4. *Accepts*: most Roman Catholic beliefs and practices.

WORLD RELIGIOUS BELIEF TODAY AND IN 2000

RELIGION	1980 (numbers in millions)	%	2000 (numbers in millions)	%
Christian	1,433	32.8	2,020	32.3
Roman Catholic	809	18.5	1,169	18.7
Protestant	345	7.9	440	7.0
Eastern Orthodox	124	2.8	153	2.4
Other	155	3.6	258	4.1
Non-religious and atheist	911	20.8	1,334	21.3
Muslim	723	16.5	1,201	19.2
Hindu	583	13.3	859	13.7
Buddhist	274	6.3	359	5.7
Chinese Folk Religion	198	4.5	158	2.5
Tribal and Shamanist	103	2.4	110	1.8
"New Religions"	96	2.2	138	2.2
Jewish	17	.4	20	.3
Other	36	.8	61	1.0

Source: *World Christian Encyclopedia*

UNITED STATES CHURCH MEMBERSHIP

Religious Group	Membership
Protestants and others	72,814,971
Roman Catholics	49,812,178
Jews	5,860,900
Old Catholic, Polish National Church, Armenian Churches	936,801
Buddhist Churches of America	60,000
Miscellaneous	163,185
Total	133,469,690

Source: *1981 Yearbook*

Discuss:

1. Do any of these figures surprise you? Why or why not?

2. How do you account for so many non-believers and atheists?

3. Is Roman Catholicism a growing religion?

CATHOLIC REFORMATION

The church was slow in responding to the Protestants. Consequently by the end of the 1530s all of Scandinavia, the British Isles, and most of Germany, Austria and France had split from Roman Catholicism. Why the delay in dealing with the growing dissatisfaction? Most of the reasons were political. As a temporal ruler the pope was caught between the Hapsburgs and the king of France, both of whom coveted the Italian states. Second, the pope greatly feared a council. Conciliarism was still strong and the popes of the day feared that their very office might be abolished. Third, and perhaps most important, the leaders of the church miscalculated the seriousness of the protest movement, and how seriously it challenged traditional Catholic beliefs. At first Luther was seen as a sincere but misguided reformer who was merely quarrelling with some of the worst abuses of the day.

Council of Trent. Although Luther himself called for a council to examine his doctrines, it wasn't until 1545 that Pope Paul III called the 19th General Council at Trent. Only 40 bishops attended, most of them Italians. The first major decision of the council, which had 25 meetings in three separate sessions between 1545 and 1563, was to deal with both doctrine and discipline simultaneously. The teachings of the Council of Trent shaped modern Catholicism more than any other council until the Second Vatican Council which met in the 1960s.

Here is a partial list of matters taken up at Trent:

Doctrinal Issues

1. *Papal supremacy was reaffirmed.* Although the authority of the Bible was upheld, Trent taught that tradition (the teaching of the church handed down from the time of the apostles) is also a guide to Catholic faith. Against those who argued for private interpretation of the Bible, the council held that it is the church's authority that interprets the Bible for us.

2. *The doctrine of original sin and justification was treated at great length.* The council stressed that while salvation comes from

God as a free gift, it depends on human cooperation as well. The good acts we perform have meaning and gain us merit.

3. *The doctrine of transubstantiation was reaffirmed.* Christ is really present, whole and entire, in both the consecrated bread and wine which have been transformed into his body and blood. As opposed to some of the reformers, Trent also taught that the Mass is a true sacrifice, a renewal of Calvary, and one and the same with it, through which Christ is offered in a new manner. Jesus gave the apostles the power to offer him in this new sacrifice and passed it on to priests through the sacrament of holy orders.

4. Trent taught that *confession and absolution are the normal way by which mortal sins, committed after baptism, are forgiven.* Although confession of venial sin is not necessary, it is a good practice through which Christians can grow in virtue. The council also definitively set the number of sacraments at seven, recognizing that the anointing of the sick and the dying (then called extreme unction) and confirmation are truly sacraments. (Most Protestants claimed that only baptism and the Eucharist were true sacraments since Jesus only explicitly mentioned these two in the gospels.)

5. Many Protestants taught that marriages could be dissolved because of unfaithfulness. Trent denied this and further added that a *wedding must be celebrated before a priest and at least two witnesses.* Marriages between Catholics and Protestants were held to be invalid.

6. Again in opposition to the Protestants *the council declared the existence of purgatory* and that the souls in purgatory can be helped by prayer and especially by the Mass. Prayer to saints for help and veneration of their images and relics were permitted as long as the relics and images were not worshipped for their own sake. The council condemned abuses concerning indulgences but reaffirmed the spiritual value of a true indulgence.

Disciplinary Issues

1. *Clerical abuses were attacked.* It was decided that bishops must reside in their dioceses, priests in their parishes, and monks and nuns in their monasteries and convents.

2. Because training of priests had been dreadfully poor, *the council mandated the establishment of seminaries* for the training of future priests. St. Charles Borromeo created a model seminary in his diocese of Milan. Pope Gregory XIII created many colleges for priests; the most famous is the Gregorian University in Rome.

3. *The council created an* Index of Forbidden Books (finally abolished by Pope Paul VI in our own day). The purpose of the *Index* was to keep Catholics from being contaminated by radical and heretical ideas. Unfortunately, the *Index* kept clergy and laity from reading some of the major intellectual works of the modern era.

BOOKS ON THE INDEX

The *Index of Forbidden Books,* created by the Council of Trent to protect Catholics from writings dangerous to faith and morals, ceased publication in 1966. Here is a list of some famous authors and works which appeared by name on the *Index.*

Author	Country	Year Originally Banned	Work
Thomas Hobbes	England	1649	all works
Rene Descartes	France	1663	all works
John Milton	England	1694	*The State Papers*
Jean-Jacques Rousseau	France	1762 1766	*Émile* *The Social Contract*
Edward Gibbon	England	1783	*The Decline and Fall of the Roman Empire*
Immanuel Kant	Germany	1827	*Critique of Pure Reason*
Victor Hugo	France	1834 1864	*Notre Dame de Paris* *Les Miserables*
Alexandre Dumas	France	1863	all novels (including *The Three Musketeers* and *The Count of Monte Cristo)*
Ernest Renan	France	1863	*Life of Jesus*
Gustave Flaubert	France	1864	*Madame Bovary*
Émile Zola	France	1898	all works
Jean-Paul Sartre	France	1948	all works

St. Ignatius Loyola

Reform Into Action. It was one thing for the Council of Trent to issue decrees of reform; it was quite another to put those decrees into action. Luckily the popes of this age were good men who sincerely wished to reform the church. The first and greatest of the reform popes was Pius V (d. 1572). A highly moral man, he was responsible for publishing a *Catechism* of the council which clearly summarized Catholic beliefs and practices for all to understand. He also reformed the Mass in his *Revised Roman Missal* which imposed a uniform liturgy on the entire Catholic world. His greatest contribution, though, was reformation of the corrupt curia.

Pius' successor, Pope Gregory XIII (d. 1585), reformed the calendar and worked closely with St. Charles Borromeo to implement the various decrees of the council. Pope Sixtus V (d. 1590) appointed good cardinals and put down banditry in the Papal States. The popes were aided in their efforts by many high-minded bishops who established the reforms of Trent by preaching regularly, visiting their parishes, building seminaries, holding annual synods, ordaining worthy candidates to the priesthood, watching the morals of the religious in their dioceses and giving good example themselves.

The popes and bishops received help from some new religious orders: the Theatines, the Barnabites and the Capuchins (an offshoot of the Franciscans who wanted to restore the spirit of St. Francis to their order). But, without a doubt, the most influential order to come on the scene was the Society of Jesus founded by St. Ignatius Loyola.

St. Ignatius Loyola. One of the greatest of the Catholic saints is Ignatius of Loyola, born in the 1490s in the Basque country near the Pyrenees Mountains. A soldier by profession, his career was abruptly ended by a leg wound. While healing he read the life of Jesus and the lives of saints and dedicated himself to becoming a soldier for Jesus Christ. Ignatius spent a year in prayer and meditation at a monastery. During this time, he drafted one of the world's spiritual classics, the *Spiritual Exercises* (1523).

For the next 10 years Ignatius studied at several universities, eventually making his way to Paris. He gathered around him six remarkable men who took vows of poverty and chastity. At the end of his studies Ignatius resolved to make a pilgrimage to Jerusalem but was foiled in his efforts. He and his companions went to Rome, committed themselves to the cause of the pope and received permission in 1540 to organize their religious order: the Society of Jesus.

Until his death in 1556 Ignatius was general of his order, directing the many worthwhile projects the Society was engaged in. He also refined his *Spiritual Exercises,* a four-week program of meditations and growth in the spiritual life. The aim of the exercises is to achieve in the person taking them a total dedication to the Lord Jesus Christ. They appeal to the human will through understanding, imagination and conscience. These exercises have had a powerful impact on the formation of many Christians up to our own day. Many retreats are based on them and many Christians take their spiritual direction from them.

The Jesuits. The Jesuits, members of the Society of Jesus, did much to foster the ideals of the Catholic Reformation. Ignatius insisted that his men be closely linked with the papacy to engage in whatever work the popes wanted them to do. The men were highly trained and very flexible. They were known for the following activities: preaching, teaching, writing, the founding of schools and colleges, retreat work, confessors and missionary work.

The Jesuits' missionary work was astounding. They won back from the Protestants whole regions in Germany and all of Poland. They traveled to the New World where many were martyred. St. Isaac Jogues (1607-1646) and many others in the group canonized under the title North American Martyrs were Jesuits. In South America Jesuits set up model agricultural communities in Paraguay and Brazil, civilizing the Indians there. Francis Xavier (1506-1552) was the grestest Jesuit missionary, preaching the good news in India, Indonesia and Japan. Matteo Ricci (1552-1610) adapted the gospel to Chinese traditions and thought-forms while Robert De Nobili (1577-1656) did the same kind of work in India.

Jesuits were known for their work in education. By 1749 they had founded 800 schools. These schools were open to all classes of people and rarely charged tuition. During the 17th and 18th centuries many of the educated Catholics in Europe received their educations from Jesuit schools. As a result the Jesuits became extremely influential among the learned and powerful.

The most unfortunate part of the Jesuit story took place when the Bourbon kings of Spain and France forced the pope to suppress the Jesuits in 1773. These kings and their allies feared the power of the Jesuits and disliked many of their liberal teachings. Some Jesuits survived in Prussia and Russia. The order was restored by the pope in 1814. Today the Jesuits are the largest and the most important religious order of men in the Catholic church.

TRENT TO VATICAN II

It has often been said that the Council of Trent was responsible for a fortress mentality in Roman Catholicism, that the church became very defensive and dogmatic in its response to the Protestants. If this is true, it is also quite understandable. Besides attacking sinful abuses the reformers also denied many important beliefs and practices of Roman Catholicism. The bishops at the Council of Trent were forced to state very clearly and carefully exactly what Catholics believe in order to clear up the confusion and give the church a clear sense of identity.

Here are some of the key issues debated during the 16th century. Identify the Catholic view by writing the letter C in the space provided. Then check your understanding of Roman Catholic teaching by referring to the answer key (at the bottom of page 188) which follows the presentation of the issues.

The role of the pope

_____ a. his power comes from the community of believers

_____ b. his authority comes from God

_____ c. he is merely the bishop of Rome

_____ d. he is the proper successor to St. Peter and the head of the church

The Real Presence in the Eucharist

_____ a. the Eucharist is a symbol of love

_____ b. Jesus' body and blood are only spiritually present in the Eucharist

_____ c. the bread and wine are changed into Christ's body and blood (transubstantiation)

_____ d. the bread and wine do not change; they coexist with Christ's body and blood (consubstantiation)

The Bible

_____ a. the Bible is the word of God

_____ b. the only source of authority in the church is the Bible

_____ c. Christians can interpret the Bible any way they want to

_____ d. tradition and the Bible are the two sources of teaching about God's revelation

Believers

_____ a. salvation is meant only for the elect

_____ b. original sin means that we are in need of God's grace

_____ c. God predestines only some for salvation

_____ d. good works gain us merit

_____ e. salvation is a free gift of God

Mary and the saints

_____ a. Mary has a special place in God's kingdom

_____ b. devotion to the saints is worthless—no one should come between Christ and believers

_____ c. saints can intercede for us in heaven

_____ d. honoring relics is a form of superstition

Read carefully the following passages from the documents of Vatican II. Then answer the questions which follow.

Who Is a Catholic?

They are fully incorporated into the society of the Church who, possessing the Spirit of Christ, accept her entire system and all the means of salvation given to her, and through union with her visible structure are joined to Christ, who rules her through the Supreme Pontiff and the bishops. This joining is effected by the bonds of professed faith, of the sacraments, of ecclesiastical government, and of communion. He is not saved, however, who, though he is part of the body of the Church, does not persevere in charity. . . . All the sons of the Church should remember that their exalted status is to be attributed not to their own merits but to the special grace of Christ.

—Constitution on the Church, No. 14

On Catholics and Other Christians

The Church recognizes that in many ways she is linked with those who, being baptized, are honored with the name Christian, though they do not profess the faith in its entirety or do not preserve unity of communion with the successor of Peter. For there are many who honor sacred Scripture, taking it as a norm of belief and of action, and who show a true religious zeal. They lovingly believe in God the Father Almighty and in Christ, Son of God and Savior. They are consecrated by baptism, through which they are united with Christ. They also recognize and receive other sacraments within their own Churches or ecclesial communities. Many of them rejoice in the episcopate, celebrate the Holy Eucharist, and cultivate devotion toward the Virgin Mother of God. They also share with us in prayer and other spiritual benefits.

Likewise, we can say that in some real way they are joined with us in the Holy Spirit, for to them also He gives His gifts and graces, and is thereby operative among them with His sanctifying power. Some indeed He has strengthened to the extent of the shedding of their blood. In all of Christ's disciples the Spirit arouses the desire to be peacefully united, in the manner determined by Christ, as one flock under one shepherd, and He prompts them to pursue this goal. Mother Church never ceases to pray, hope, and work that they may gain this blessing. She exhorts her sons to purify and renew themselves so that the sign of Christ may shine more brightly over the face of the Church.

—Constitution on the Church, No. 15

On Ecumenism

There can be no ecumenism worthy of the name without a change of heart. For it is from newness of attitudes (cf. Eph. 4:23), from self-denial and unstinted love, that yearnings for unity take their rise and grow toward maturity. We should therefore pray to the divine Spirit for the grace to be genuinely self-denying, humble, gentle in the service of others and to have an attitude of brotherly generosity toward them. . . .

Let all Christ's faithful remember that the more purely they strive to live according to the gospel, the more they are fostering and even practicing Christian unity. For they can achieve depth and ease in strengthening mutual brotherhood to the degree they enjoy profound communion with the Father, the Word, and the Spirit.

—Catholic Principles on Ecumenism, No. 7

Questions:

1. Answer in your own words: Who is a Catholic?

_____

_____

_____

2. Name four things we have in common with other Christians:

a._____

b._____

c._____

d._____

3. According to the *Constitution on the Church*, what unites all Christians to Christ?

_____

_____

_____

4. Is the Catholic Church in need of purification and renewal before reunion with other Christians can take place? Explain your answer.

_____

_____

_____

5. What is the key to Christian unity?

_____

_____

_____

Discuss: As a class, list 10 ways you can live the gospel in relation to other Christians and thus promote Christian unity.

Answers to quiz (pages 185-186)

Pope: b, d   Believers: b, d, e
Eucharist: a, c   Saints: a, c
Bible: a, d

SIGNS OF THE PILGRIM CHURCH

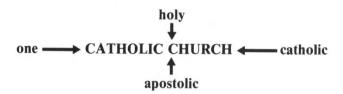

Catholics confirm their belief in the "one, holy, catholic and apostolic" church when they recite the Nicene Creed every Sunday at Mass. These four adjectives are known as the *marks* or *signs* of the church.

All of these signs are linked together in such a way that they manifest the church of Jesus Christ. The church is *one* because of its oneness in the Lord, a oneness which is seen in its belief, its worship and its fidelity to Christ's authority in the church. The church is *holy* because it is united to Jesus Christ, the source of all holiness. As a real presence of the Lord in the world today, the church shares in God's own life. The church is *catholic* (universal) by being for all people in all times in all places. It also is catholic in the sense of fullness. It demonstrates the fullness of what the faith relationship in Jesus Christ calls us to have sacramentally, doctrinally and structurally. Finally, the church is *apostolic* because it professes the same faith as the apostolic church, is essentially the same community founded by Christ, and is ruled by the successors to the apostles.

The signs of the church help strengthen the faith of the believer and can attract the attention of the unbeliever as well. But they also cause questions. The signs of the church are found in a community of people who are on their way, pilgrims who have not yet met their eternal destiny. They exist in a church of very human people, people who sin and sometimes obscure the reality of Jesus they should point to. The church is immersed in and influenced by history. The scandals of the lives of Christians through the ages has, at times, diminished the effectiveness of these authentic signs of Christ's church.

The heart of the church, the presence of the Lord in his Holy

Spirit, has remained the same through the ages, but the members of the Body of Christ in their pilgrimage through time have not always paid attention to the Lord. Think of the scandalous lives of some of the popes during the Age of the Renaissance; they certainly didn't point to the holiness of the Lord Jesus. Or think of the Protestant Reformation. The major split this caused in the church marred the oneness of Christ's body. Despite sin in the church and the paradoxes and tensions of its history, the essence of the church always remains. There were and are today dramatic signs of holiness despite the sinfulness of individual church members. For every corrupt pope, our Lord has raised great saints like Ignatius of Loyola to challenge the church to be true to its real identity.

In this section of the chapter we will define and explain each of these marks or signs of the church. In addition, the tensions and paradoxes in these signs will be illustrated by looking at some of the historical movements of the 17th through 19th centuries.

1. The Church Is One. The church is one because of its oneness with the Lord, a oneness or unity which is seen in its belief, its worship and its fidelity to Christ's authority in the church. When we say the church is one, we mean that members of the church believe the same doctrines (creed), accept the same seven sacraments and worship together at the sacrifice of the Mass (cult) and submit to the same divine authority, Jesus Christ, who rules through the visible head, the pope, and the bishops who are in communion with him (code).

Disputes, the pride and greed of Christians, misunderstandings, weaknesses and abuses have resulted in the tearing of Christ's body. But the Lord's desire remains, as St. John's gospel puts it so well, that all may be one in him.

Through its history the church continuously has to work for unity and against those historical forces which would destroy it. You have read how the teaching of Arius disrupted the unity of the church when he taught that Christ was not divine. You have seen how the Eastern Schism and the Protestant Reformation separated many Christians from unity with the pope. There were also forces at work in the 17th, 18th and 19th centuries which threatened the unity of the church.

Gallicanism. One of these forces, and typical of them, was Gallicanism. Throughout its history the Catholic church has always had to protect its freedom from interference by the state. The danger is always greatest when powerful rulers try to take control of church affairs in their own territories. This same danger threatened the church in France during the last quarter of the 17th century when King Louis XIV, the Sun King, considered himself the very representative of God on earth. He did not want anyone, including the pope, to have influence in France; he wanted the French church to be independent of the Roman pope. This claim to independence is known as Gallicanism (from the Latin name for France).

Louis XIV forced the French clergy to adopt four articles: 1) that the pope and the church have no power over state rulers; 2) that the authority of a general council is greater than that of a pope (conciliarism); 3) that the primacy of the pope must be exercised with due consideration for the customs of the local churches; and 4) that the decrees of the pope on matters of faith are not binding on the faithful until the whole church consents to them. In addition, Louis ordered that these four articles be taught in all French seminaries.

The pope resisted these threats to unity by refusing to appoint bishops. A compromise was reached in 1693 when the pope agreed to appoint bishops if the king agreed to withdraw his order that the four articles be taught in the seminaries. Louis agreed, but the articles were still taught in defiance of the pope. As a result the French clergy were formed with a mistrust of Rome. Similar moves, modeled on Louis' strategy, were made in Austria and in Germany. Rulers throughout Europe wanted the church to be independent of Rome and enacted similar laws to diminish papal authority in their lands. By 1790 there was a real danger that nationalism in Europe would be responsible for destroying the unity of the church.

Revolutions. A number of forces at work in the world at this time gravely upset the unity of the Middle Ages and the medieval church which so marvelously symbolized that unity. These centuries can truly be called the age of revolution.

—*Science*. The Renaissance had prepared the way for some of the startling changes which took place during the Scientific Revolution. The Scientific Revolution stressed independent inquiry and knowledge derived from observable data. This approach was distinct from the medieval and ancient mode of thinking: speculative thought and theoretical conclusions. Using the scientific method thinkers like Copernicus (1473-1543) and Galileo (1564-1642) changed peoples' way of looking at the world. The earth was no longer the center of the universe. The church viewed these new ideas with grave suspicion because they questioned traditional ideas which people had always believed. Galileo's ideas, for example, were condemned by the church at that time.

—*Philosophy*. Simultaneous to the Scientific Revolution was a revolution in ideas known as the Enlightenment. Every country produced "enlightened" thinkers who were characterized by their tremendous confidence in human reason and their optimistic view of the world and human nature. They celebrated human inquiry and criticized institutions they thought diminished human freedom—oppressive governments and the church. These thinkers were hostile toward the supernatural, the concept of divine revelation and every kind of outside authority, especially that of the pope. They ridiculed Catholic beliefs and questioned many church doctrines. They created their own religion—*Deism*—which saw God as a kind of watchmaker who created the world with its own laws and then left it alone.

These new ideas of the world and the role of God in it caused many to relegate religion to a very small part of their lives. Because of the study of comparative religions, some questioned the uniqueness of Christianity. Others adopted an attitude of skepticism and considered religion irrelevant to their practical, everyday lives. More and more people concluded that religion was a private affair with little meaning for the everyday world of politics and culture. This attitude remains with us today.

—*Politics*. Another serious threat to the unity of the church during these centuries was the political revolutions of the day, many of which received their intellectual backing from the Enlightenment. The keynote of the day was freedom.

The French Revolution (begun in 1789) was perhaps the most influential revolution of any era. It began as a serious effort to reform an absolute monarch. It spilled over into many countries and affects the world even to this day. It had serious consequences for the church. During one phase of the revolution the leaders in Paris attempted to destroy the church itself because of its close identification

The people of Paris march on Versailles, October 5, 1789

with the monarchy. They confiscated all church property and destroyed universities, shrines, monasteries and charitable institutions. In their attempt to abolish monarchial absolutism the revolutionaries swept away anything which seemed to them to be associated with it. They even set up their own state church, substituting pagan idols and practices for Catholic devotions.

With Napoleon and the governments which came after him the excesses of the Revolution abated to some degree. But the strongest supporter of the papacy outside of Italy had been destroyed, and the direct papal influence in French government had ended forever. By the mid-19th century French-style revolutions had hit many countries. By 1870 Italy itself was united into a single state, thus signaling the end of the Papal States. No longer would the pope be a secular ruler, heavily involved in controlling territories as an equal to other temporal rulers.

Aftermath. What did these massive historical movements mean? For one thing, they meant that the religious life of Europe was affected. Because the church is a pilgrim in history, many members were attracted to the changes which resulted from the scientific, political and social revolutions; they were lost to the church. For another, the visible unity of the church which had been identified with a united Europe and a common medieval outlook were destroyed. The world had changed and moved into modern times. The church was no longer a political power which could control kings and force them to do its will. Instead the church has had to rely more and more on what is really important: the force of its spiritual message. In a sense the church had made a pilgrimage from being a temporal power to being what it is today—a spiritual power which tries to influence people's lives in light of the gospel. The principle of Catholic unity is a living Lord and the good news he brings.

Throughout this turbulent period and the massive changes which it brought about, the Lord remained with the church. His message was preached. Catholics still worshipped and celebrated the sacraments. They proclaimed a common faith. And they looked to the pope as a symbol of unity who continued to teach as Christ's representative on earth.

EXERCISES

A. *Report*: Make a short report on one of these topics.

1. The causes and results of the French Revolution. Mention at least three results for the Catholic church.

2. The beliefs of the Enlightenment thinkers as shown by one of the following:

    a. René Descartes (1596-1650)
    b. Blaise Pascal (1623-1662)
    c. John Locke (1632-1704)
    d. Jean-Jacques Rousseau (1712-1778)
    e. Francois-Marie Arouet (Voltaire) (1694-1778)

3. Investigate the Galileo Galilei case.

B. *Unity*. Every Catholic has the responsibility to contribute to the unity of the church, Christ's body. Here are some factors which can promote unity. Evaluate your contribution according to the following scale.

5—a very strong point with me   2—I need work on this
4—a good description of me   1—I've got a long way to go
3—this is me some of the time

____ 1. I use some of my money to help others.

____ 2. I take care of my health so that I can use it for others.

____ 3. I value my education, knowing that someday I'll be able to use it to contribute to the well-being of others.

____ 4. I am concerned about the value of human life, even to speaking out for the cause of the helpless.

____ 5. I fully participate in the Mass, showing other believers that my presence is important.

____ 6. I accept the teachings of the Roman Catholic Church.

____ 7. I am a peacemaker when arguments arise.

____ 8. I search out the opinions of others when I am trying to do the right thing.

____ 9. I refrain from cheating because I know that it destroys trust, a key ingredient of unity.

____ 10. I respect others' opinions even if they differ from mine.

____ 11. I appreciate that I have been given gifts to share with others.

____ 12. I respect the teachings of the pope, the bishops and other religious guides.

____ 13. I am willing to say I'm sorry when I've hurt others.

Discuss: What is your greatest contribution to unity at school? at home? as a Catholic young person?

2. The Church Is Holy. The church in its essence is holy because its head is Christ and its soul is the Holy Spirit. As the Council of Trent's catechism puts it:

> The Church is called holy, because she is consecrated and dedicated to God. . . . The Church is holy because she is the Body of Christ, by whom she is sanctified, and in whose blood she is washed.

As the Lord's presence in the world today the church continues his work of sanctifying its members and the world. The church continues this work of the Lord through its teachings, through the seven sacraments, the sacrifice of the Mass and the sacramentals, through various devotions like the rosary, through church law which reminds us of our duty to perform acts of worship, penance and mortification, through various apostolic movements and the religious orders, and through the lives of the saints who hold out to us a model of holiness.

What is holiness? Above all else it is a share in God's own life. One scholar claims that holiness is wholeness, a full and true humanity which is marked by continuous conversion, a turning away from sin and the evils which accompany it. Holiness results from living the virtue of faith—thinking with Christ. Holiness results from living the virtue of hope—a spirit of vital youthfulness which allows God's kingdom to touch our lives and control them. Holiness results from living the virtue of charity—a participation in the divine love which looks out for the welfare of others. Holiness, in short, is a striving to live a fully human life by imitating our Lord and Savior Jesus Christ. It is the result of allowing the Lord to live in us. It manifests itself in the fruits of the Holy Spirit; for example, mercy, kindness, humility, meekness, patience.

Paradox of Holiness. Holiness in the church is a paradox. The church is holy because of the Lord's presence in it; the church is also sinful. As the bride of Christ the church is in constant need of purification (see Ephesians 5). The divine dimension in the church makes it holy; the human dimension has often manifested sinfulness. There have been corrupt popes who lived immoral lives. There have been countless laity whose level of Christianity has bordered on superstition. Christians have organized Inquisitions, cooperated with corrupt governments, tolerated slavery and done countless other sinful actions which have clouded Jesus Christ and his message.

Regardless of these faults, though, in every age the church of Jesus Christ has manifested the holiness of the Lord. The gospel has always been preached. People have always celebrated the sacraments. The presence of the church has from the beginning transformed the world. It has nurtured a profound respect for the value of celibacy and the sacramental nature of marriage. Its message and devotion has brought mercy and compassion for the poor, the sick and the aged. The church today stands as a symbol of peace. It preaches respect for life and continues to share Jesus' love for every creature, no matter how weak and defenseless.

Jansenism and Quietism. In every age, though, it seems that the church needs to keep itself from a false sense of holiness. You might recall that in the ancient church there were those who claimed that one could be holy only if everything connected with the material world was shunned and avoided. Certain gnostic sects certainly taught this.

The 17th century also produced a movement which preached a false spirituality—*Jansenism*—named after Cornelius Jansen (d. 1638), a bishop of Ypres in France. He gathered around him a well-organized and significant number of priests, nuns and laity.

The Council of Trent wisely taught that Catholics should be urged to participate more frequently in the sacraments of reconciliation (penance) and the Holy Eucharist. Both of these had been neglected and were now seen as important ways to achieve holiness. The Jesuits, among others, greatly promoted these two obvious ways to holiness.

The Jansenists, however, taught a doctrine that was very near to Calvinism. In their view original sin radically corrupted human nature so that everything natural is totally evil. They taught that grace is given only to a few, a form of predestination. The Jansenist view maintained that confession of sin was useless unless a person had *perfect* sorrow. They discouraged reception of communion because they felt that communion was only for the very holy people. Their distorted view held that a person showed greater virtue by staying away from communion than by receiving it. They had a superior attitude to other Catholics and considered themselves better than popes and bishops.

The pope condemned Jansenism for teaching strict rigorism in the spiritual life, distrust of the material world, especially human sexuality, and for the attitude of superiority to others. Its influence, however, has remained strong even to this century. Many Catholics have thought that holy communion was a rare privilege for which they had to prepare themselves with the greatest care. In 1904 Pope St. Pius X decreed that all Catholics, including children who have reached the age of reason, should be encouraged to receive the Eucharist as often as possible, not as a prize for holiness we have earned, but as a major means to attain holiness.

Another false heresy of this century—*Quietism*—was condemned by Pope Innocent XI in 1687. It taught that human nature was so powerless that we can do absolutely nothing to grow in the spiritual life. Its founder, a Spanish priest by the name of Molinos, taught that Catholics should not be concerned with the pursuit of virtues or questions like heaven and hell. Temptations should be ignored and not even resisted. For him, temptations were God's will and nothing should be said or done about them, not even in confession.

Both Jansenism and Quietism distorted what it means to pursue holiness.

Saints. There have always been remarkable men and women whose lives have provided an example of true holiness. These men and women we call saints.

In the 16th century, besides the great St. Ignatius Loyola, there were men of the caliber of *St. Philip Neri* (1515-1595) who labored in Rome to renew the quality of priests' lives. He did much through his organization called the Oratory to reform the corrupt curia.

The 16th century also produced some amazing women, most

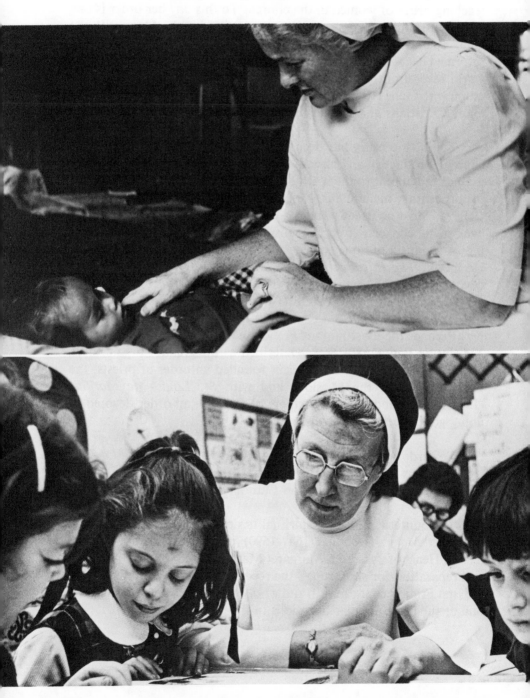

notably *St. Angela Merici* (1470-1540) and *St. Teresa of Avila* (1515-1582). St. Angela, after many years of charitable work caring for young women and the sick, founded the Ursulines, the first teaching order of women in the church. To this day her order is one of the outstanding orders of educators in the church. Along with the great Spanish mystic, St. John of the Cross (1542-91), St. Teresa reformed her religious order, the Carmelites in Spain. She gave to the world several outstanding books on the mystical life of prayer and union with God. Her works have remained a source of inspiration for many Christians and are very popular today.

The 17th century has been called the century of the saints. The church produced an abundance of holy people whose lives dramatically point to the work of God in the world. The great saints of this century include *St. Francis de Sales* (1567-1622), a bishop of Geneva. Most courteous and a shining example of charity, he won back many converts from Calvinism. He is also the source of a saying: A spoonful of honey catches more flies than a barrel of vinegar. His book, *The Introduction to the Devout Life*, is still a popular devotional work. Along with his friend *St. Jane Frances de Chantal* (1572-1641) he founded the Order of Visitation.

Perhaps the most famous French saint of the 17th century is *St. Vincent de Paul* (1580-1660). Described as the greatest organizer of charity who ever lived, St. Vincent founded an order of priests, the Congregation of the Mission, and with *St. Louise de Marillac* (1591-1660) founded the Daughters of Charity, an order devoted to doing good works among the poor.

Toward the end of the 17th century *St. John Baptist de La Salle* (1651-1719) established the Brothers of Christian Schools. This order has had a tremendous impact on Catholic education.

To counteract the false spiritualities of Jansen and Molinos, *St. Margaret Mary Alacoque* (1647-1690) promoted devotion to the Sacred Heart of Jesus. St. Margaret Mary fostered a worship of love and reparation for sin through the reception of holy communion on the first Fridays of the month and a holy hour of prayer. This became one of the most popular devotions in the church.

A WORD ABOUT SAINTS

A saint is someone we believe is in heaven and whom we honor and imitate as having lived a full life in the Lord. The *Constitution on the Church* puts it this way:

> In the lives of those who shared in our humanity and were transformed into especially successful images of Christ (cf. 2 Cor. 3:18), God vividly manifests to men His presence and His face. He speaks to us in them, and gives us a sign of His kingdom, to which we are powerfully drawn, surrounded as we are by so many witnesses (cf. Heb. 12:1), and having such an argument for the truth of the gospel (No. 50).

Saints are offered to us as examples of holiness, as models to imitate. The church is saying if we do as they did, according to our ability, what they have achieved we can achieve also.

Everyone who dies in the friendship of God is with him in heaven. But not everyone who dies in the Lord's friendship is canonized. *Canonization* is a process in the church whereby certain individuals are declared to be in heaven. The process of canonization is quite detailed in today's church. It involves an examination into the holiness of a person's life and his or her teachings and beliefs. A brief is collected in the local diocese and again at Rome. The testimony of witnesses (if possible) is obtained. A historical study of the person's life is constructed. There is a serious investigation to see if miracles were performed through the person's intercession. The cause of the holy person can proceed to *beatification*, that is, the person can be called "Blessed" and a limited cult is permitted, which means he or she can be venerated in a particular town, diocese or religious society. After further miracles are validated the cause of the holy person can proceed to canonization. Today it is the pope who declares both the beatification and canonization of the saint.

A. *Lives of the Saints.* Research and report on the life of one of the Christian heroes mentioned in this chapter. As an alternative, report on the life of the founder of a particular religious order, perhaps an order which teaches at your school.

B. *Life of a Hero.* Write a short biography of a person whom you know and consider to be specially close to the Lord. You may need to interview the person or some people who know him or her well. Report on the following questions:

1. How does this person grow in holiness?

2. What role do prayer, the sacraments, the Mass and other devotions play in this person's life?

3. Has the person done anything extraordinary? Explain.

4. Does the person do anything ordinary in an extraordinary way? Explain.

5. How does he or she demonstrate Christian charity?

6. Would you like to be like this person? Explain.

C. *Holiness and You.* All Christians are called to be holy, to manifest in their lives the life of Jesus Christ. Here is a list of commonly accepted marks of holiness. As a class, discuss what each of these virtues means. Then check two which you yourself exhibit to a fairly good degree. Explain to a friend or classmate how you try to live or manifest these virtues.

A holy person is

___ a loving person; one who looks out for others

___ patient

___ one who heralds the gospel

___ kind

___ prayerful

___ a pilgrim who asks for forgiveness when he or she sins

___ one who makes use of the sacraments

___ humble

___ a community-builder

___ pure

___ gentle

___ merciful, forgiving

___ a person of faith

___ a person of genuine hope

___ long-suffering

___ meek

___ obedient

For further growth:

Mark off one virtue you'd like to improve on in the following month or so. Make a list of three or four concrete ways you can improve.

---

3. The Church Is Catholic. The word *catholic* literally means "general" or "universal." The title was first used by St. Ignatius of Antioch in A.D. 107 in his letter to the Smyrneans, "Where Jesus Christ is, there is the Catholic Church." By the end of the second century it acquired the two meanings now associated with it: "universal" in the sense of spread throughout the world, and "orthodox" or true to all of the Lord's teachings.

The church is catholic first of all because it is made up of many peoples—it is for all people, in all places, in all times. Second, it exhibits the fullness (universality) of faith in the Lord and demonstrates in its sacraments, doctrines and organizational structure the catholicity intended by Jesus Christ. For example, the church continues to teach the good news that Jesus taught, carries out his command to baptize all people in his name, and administers the sacraments as signs of his grace.

A Missionary Church. As a pilgrim, the church has moved out to the rest of the world on its journey to the Father. The Catholic church is a missionary church which has a message to spread. The 16th and 17th centuries gave rise to a missionary movement unparalleled in Christianity except for the very early centuries of its history. The impulse to proclaim the gospel in these two centuries followed the incredible discoveries and explorations that began in the 15th century. North and South America, the East and the Far East and Africa (from 1622) were virgin territory for the missionaries.

Activity in the West. In North and South America, the missionaries converted the native Americans as part of the colonizing effort of the Portuguese and Spanish governments. The story of this cooperation between church and state was not a totally happy one. The conquerers destroyed the native civilizations and imposed on the New World inhabitants a Spanish or Portuguese culture. There was a crusading spirit to the missionary efforts. Forced conversions, extermination of some natives and exploitation of others resulted from this wedding of church missionary efforts to state colonizing activity.

Many good missionaries fought these abuses. Heroic men like Bartolomé de Las Casas, the first priest ordained in the New World (1519), spent their lives trying to get legal rights for the Indians. St. Peter Claver (1580-1654) worked among the slaves in Colombia. Other Jesuits set up model communities in Paraguay and Brazil. Known as the Paraguay Reductions, these communities attempted to preserve native culture while providing education and the benefits of civilization.

Activity in the East. Eastern missionary efforts were quite different from those in the West. Generally the missionaries, exemplified by the astronomer Matteo Ricci in China and Robert de Nobili in India, tried to *adapt* Christianity to certain of the cultural and intellectual features of these Eastern civilizations. The Jesuits maintained that Christianity would only take root in these civilizations if methods of accommodation were used. Unfortunately Rome did not appreciate their methods.

When Dutch and Spanish ships came to Japan, the Japanese thought that the Europeans would try to take control. In 1614 the missionaries were expelled and the fiercest persecution known to Christianity took place. In a 20-year period over 40,000 Christians were martyred. By 1697 only a few of the 300,000 Christians in Japan survived. Much of the work of men like St. Francis Xavier was undone.

St. Francis Xavier, Manapad, India, 1544

With the suppression of the Jesuits and the ferment caused by the Enlightenment and the French Revolution, missionary activity declined in the 18th century and did not pick up again until the 19th century when Pope Pius VII lifted the ban on the Jesuits (1814). Vibrant missionary orders were also founded in the 19th century: the Oblates of Mary Immaculate (1816), the Marists (1817), the Salesians (1859) and the White Fathers (1868).

Tensions of Catholicity. It is true that the church preached the gospel to the world in these centuries, opening the good news to millions of people who had never heard it. But this attempt to preach to all brought some problems with it: 1) With a few exceptions Rome held that native talent and genius should be replaced by European models. In the quest for *one* church, some healthy diversity was eliminated. For example, a liturgy in the native tongue with some recognition of local customs was banned; 2) The missionaries tended to treat the natives as children and by and large failed to develop a native clergy. The natives saw Catholic leadership in terms of white European men; 3) The religious orders carried on intense rivalries in their approach to missionary work, often working at cross purposes; 4) The missionary effort was too closely identified with colonialism, imperialism and exploitation.

4. The Church Is Apostolic. The mark of apostolicity stresses the continuing role of the Holy Spirit in the church. He evokes in the church, a pilgrim traveling through space and time, the same faith held in the church of the apostles. Thus the church is apostolic in three ways: 1) It is the same community as the church of the apostolic age, the same Body of Christ, the same real presence of the Lord; 2) Jesus founded the church on the apostles and it continues to be governed by their successors, the bishops, with the pope as their head; 3) The teaching of Jesus, first preached by the apostles to the world, continues to be taught by the Catholic church.

Liberalism in the 19th Century. The story of the First Vatican Council (1870) must be told against the backdrop of the controversies surrounding the liberals and conservatives in the 19th century. In the aftermath of the French Revolution, there were those who wished to implement many of the ideas of the Enlightenment both in governmental affairs and in the church. Their agenda for change was called liberalism, an outlook which favored the maximum amount of freedom in the social, economic and religious spheres.

In general the 19th-century liberals favored the following: constitutional government, a broadening of the right to vote, complete religious liberty, equality of all citizens, the abolition of established churches and clerical privileges, the separation of church and state and the assumption by the state of functions formerly handled by the church. The liberals wanted the state to control marriage, public charity and education. They tended to view the church as subservient to the state, even in religious affairs.

As a rule the church in the 19th century wanted to *conserve* many of the rights it had gained through the centuries. Thus it challenged many of the liberal movements of the day. Churchmen like the Frenchman Lammenais tried to strike a compromise by looking to Rome for guidance and asking the pope to back liberal ideas, even in the church. But Pope Gregory XVI, who abhorred the excesses of the French Revolution and other liberal revolutions in the 19th century, condemned democratic ideals in the church.

In the light of social reformers like Karl Marx, who wrote that religion is the opiate of the people, the popes of the 19th century were very wary of any tyranny that might emerge in the name of political, economic or social revolution. The church was also wary of liberal thinkers within its own ranks who advocated that it face a changing world rather than taking a defensive posture against it.

Liberal thinkers within the church were particularly active in Germany where the schools of theology were attached to secular universities. The result was that the theologians were more in touch with social and scientific developments and more aware of the need for the church to deal with them rather than condemn them.

Pope Pius IX, fearing the spread of liberal and modern ideas, issued his famous *Syllabus of Errors* in 1864, a list of 80 modern errors including separation of church and state and socialism. A tremendous controversy surrounded the syllabus and its condemnation of strong trends like church accommodation to a changing society or of established rights in some countries like freedom of religion.

A further complication was that the 80 errors were compiled from earlier documents of Pius IX's and were listed without the benefit of the development and explanation contained in those documents. The result was that many of the errors listed were subject to misinterpretation or presentation out of context.

In addition, many of the errors were listed in the context of the immediate problem the papacy was facing in Italy where political figures like Cavour, Mazzini and Garibaldi were advocating violence against the Papal States as they sought to establish the modern Italian nation.

The conservative movement in the church, which wanted to hold on to so many good values of the Middle Ages, attempted to check the absolute belief in human progress and the common assumption that secular life was perfect and didn't need God or religion. Conservative churchmen, the Ultramontines, looked to Rome for guidance in the running of the national churches. They sought a strong unity with Rome and very often got into heated debates with liberal churchmen who wanted more local autonomy in the church and who wanted the church to compromise somewhat with the new ideas of liberalism.

Vatican I. It is against this backdrop of controversy and rapid change that Pius IX called the First Vatican Council to address the issue of papal authority and clarify some traditional Catholic beliefs attacked by Enlightenment thinkers. Seven hundred forty-four bishops attended the council, and thanks to improved means of travel, 46 came from the United States. One of the earliest items discussed was papal infallibility. This was a key issue for the pope, not only to counteract the claims of the liberals that the pope had no ultimate authority in the church, but also to help establish his spiritual authority at a time when his temporal authority was threatened by the loss of the Papal States.

Some of the more liberal bishops did not want the doctrine

defined because they did not think the time was ripe. One of the greatest thinkers of the 19th century, Cardinal Newman, wrote from England that any definition at this time was both premature and unnecessary. At any rate, the doctrine *was* defined even though 60 bishops left the council rather than embarrass the pope by voting against it. Only two of the remaining bishops, one of them Bishop Fitzgerald of Little Rock, Arkansas, voted against it. The doctrine reads:

> The Roman pontiff when he speaks *ex cathedra*, that is, when exercising the office of pastor and teacher of all Christians, he defines with his supreme apostolic authority a doctrine concerning faith or morals to be held by the universal Church, through the divine assistance promised to him in St. Peter, is possessed of that infallibility with which the divine Redeemer willed his Church to be endowed in defining doctrine concerning faith and morals: and therefore such definitions of the Roman Pontiff are irreformable of themselves and not from the consent of the Church.

Aftermath. The doctrine of papal infallibility confirmed what Catholics had always believed. Unfortunately the council was aborted before the issue of the bishops' authority could be addressed. France had to withdraw its troops from Rome leaving the way open for Italian revolutionary troops to occupy the city. Having completely lost the Papal States, the pope became a voluntary prisoner in Vatican City. The lopsided emphasis on the role of the pope was not balanced until Vatican II took up the topic of the bishops and the theme of religious liberty.

The conservatives won the day at the council. Their influence remained dominant during the rest of the 19th century and into the 20th. As a result the church only slowly began to accept new theological ideas and accommodate itself to the world which by and large had adopted many of the liberal notions.

On the positive side, though, the clear sense of identity and church authority which emerged at Vatican I and the desire of the church to preserve a strong international flavor enabled the pilgrim church to emerge from the great upheavals of the 20th century. These upheavals, symbolized in leaders like Hitler, attempted to subordinate the church to the new concept of the state. The church today, a post-Vatican II church, still very much a pilgrim church, shows many signs of new vitality and life.

MORE ON INFALLIBILITY

The doctrine of infallibility causes confusion to both Catholics and non-Catholics. It is important for you to understand it so that you can help clear up difficulties others may have.

In the *Constitution on the Church* Vatican II teaches that infallibility—*preservation from error*—is present in three senses in the church:

1. When the bishops, *in union with the pope*, teach authoritatively on a matter of faith and morals and agree that a particular teaching is to be held definitively and absolutely. This is done most clearly in an ecumenical council. (See No. 25.)

2. The whole body of believers, anointed by Christ, cannot err in matters of belief. "Thanks to a supernatural sense of the faith which characterizes the People as a whole, it manifests this unerring quality when 'from the bishops down to the last member of the laity,' it shows universal agreement in matters of faith and morals" (No. 12).

3. When the pope teaches *ex cathedra*, from the chair of Peter, in a solemn declaration for the whole church on a matter of faith or morals. (See No. 25.)

Papal infallibility is:

- a preservation from error when teaching on matters of faith and morals given to the pope by Christ when he said: "And know that I am with you always; yes, to the end of time"(Mt 28:20)

- concerned with the teachings of the gospels (necessary for salvation)

- addressed to the *whole* church by the pope after consulting the traditional faith of the church

- an explicit statement by the pope that what he is teaching is binding, to be believed by all

- an *ex cathedra* teaching, that is, the pope in his role as the official teacher of the whole church

Papal infallibility **is not**:

- absolute power given to the pope as a person; it belongs to his office
- dependent on numerical acceptance (truth rules, not the majority)
- a guarantee that the pope cannot err in his personal life
- a guarantee that the pope cannot make a mistake in his ordinary judgments.

Exercise:

Given these conditions of papal infallibility, check off any of these which would *not* qualify for a divine protection from error.

_____ 1. The pope solemnly declares that Mary was assumed into heaven.

_____ 2. The pope predicts that the Yankees will win the World Series.

_____ 3. The pope solemnly declares that Jesus was married.

_____ 4. The pope tells Americans not to build any more nuclear power plants.

_____ 5. The pope, *ex cathedra,* proclaims the doctrine of the Immaculate Conception of Mary.

_____ 6. The pope teaches that the Mass must be said in Greek.

Check your answers on page 213.

THE PILGRIM CHURCH TODAY

As a traveler in time and space the *pilgrim* church of the 16th through 19th centuries faced monumental challenges: revolutions in thought which took countless believers away from traditional Catholic belief, incredible changes in the political, social, cultural and economic fields, and many other serious obstacles. Through it all the church survived, even though many predicted its end. And through it all the various other models of the church were reflected in its story.

The Council of Trent reminded God's people that the abuses which caused the Reformation were often the result of sinful Christians. Trent introduced reforms to help make the church a better *sacrament*, a better sign of Christ's presence in the world. Along with Trent, the First Vatican Council clearly taught the primacy of the pope, thus delineating for all Catholics an essential feature of the *institutional* church. Farsighted saints like Ignatius of Loyola established religious orders during this period which exemplified the meaning of Christian *community*. Courageous saints like Francis Xavier *heralded* the gospel in an unprecedented way, even to the ends of the earth. Remarkable men like Vincent de Paul and women like Louise de Marillac witnessed in their lives what church as *servant* means.

The story of the church in these four centuries provides an important lesson for the church today. To be a pilgrim means to weather rough storms. To be a pilgrim means to have the necessities for the long haul and to rid oneself of the excess baggage which gets in the way of a successful journey.

As a member of the pilgrim church, you might ask yourself whether you carry the proper luggage for a successful trip. For example, do you have the virtue of faith—the fundamental belief that our Lord will remain with you through good times and bad? Do you have hope—trust that in your life and in the life of your Christian community good will ultimately conquer evil? Most important of all, do you have Christian charity—love of God and love of neighbor and a healthy love for yourself? As St. Paul says, if we have everything else, but no love, then we are nothing at all. The pilgrim church has often hit rough waters because of a lack of love in either its leaders or its members.

In chapter 13 of First Corinthians St. Paul gives the agenda of love for Christians. Love means patience and kindness. Love is without jealousy and is never boastful or conceited. Love is never rude or selfish. Love does not take offense and is not resentful. Love

delights in the truth and does not take pleasure in others' sins. It is ready to excuse, trust, hope and endure.

Imagine the impact of a pilgrim church which lived these virtues of love! Had they been exhibited to a greater degree in the 14th and 15th centuries the Protestant Reform of the 16th century need never have taken place. Vatican II reminds us that Catholics work best for reunion and demonstrate to the world their faith when they love. This was the challenge for the church in the past; it is our challenge today.

BEING A PILGRIM

If you could choose four of the following for your journey through life, what four would they be? Give reasons for your choices to your classmates.

_____ a thorough knowledge of the Bible

_____ a Ph.D. in physics

_____ a good spouse and three healthy children

_____ an ability to speak five languages

_____ an ability to explain almost anything to almost anyone

_____ a reputation as a generous person

_____ a $75,000 annual income

_____ a skill at fixing almost anything

_____ a knowledge of how to pray

Answers to Infallibility Quiz, page 210

1. Pope Pius XII declared this statement in 1950. It is an infallible statement and reflects the traditional belief in the church about Mary.

2. This is not an infallible statement. It is a private judgment.

3. This is not an infallible statement because it is not supported by the gospel and goes against the traditional belief about Jesus.

4. This would not be infallible because it is not directed to the whole church. It is questionable whether it qualifies as a moral issue necessary for salvation.

5. This is an infallible teaching. It was declared by Pope Pius IX in 1854 and reflects the traditional faith in the church about Mary.

6. This would not be infallible. It is not central to our faith and would not be taught *ex cathedra*.

SUMMARY

1. The pilgrim church exists in space and time. As a community on its way it keeps its eyes turned to its final destiny: perfect salvation and redemption in the Lord Jesus Christ.

2. The following are considered the main causes of the Protestant Reformation: the Renaissance, the debasement of Catholic piety and an anti-intellectual Catholic theology, the Western Schism, the rise of nationalism, the church's identification with Western civilization and the influence of some key personalities.

3. The four acknowledged leaders of the Protestant Reformation were Martin Luther, Ulrich Zwingli, John Calvin and King Henry VIII. Luther believed in justification by faith alone and attacked Catholic belief about good works and practices like indulgences. Zwingli fostered a democratic kind of church rule. Calvin taught the absolute depravity of people due to original sin and believed in the doctrine of predestination. Henry VIII had few doctrinal problems with the church. Rather, because of a moral issue concerning divorce, he declared himself the head of the church in England. Protestantism in England took the form of Anglicanism and was fashioned by Thomas Cranmer and Queen Elizabeth I.

4. The Anabaptists believed that baptism of infants was invalid.

5. The Council of Trent heralded the Catholic Reformation. It reaffirmed papal supremacy and the doctrine of transubstantiation. It taught that good works gain merit and that confession of sin is necessary for mortal sin. It reaffirmed the existence of purgatory and the value of indulgences. Trent also listed the seven sacraments, attacked clerical abuses in the church, and established seminaries for the training of priests.

6. The Catholic Reformation was greatly aided by the Society of Jesus, founded by St. Ignatius Loyola. The Jesuits were known for their work as missionaries, educators, preachers, writers, confessors and defenders of the pope.

7. The church of Christ is marked by four signs: one, holy, catholic and apostolic.

8. The church is one in that members believe the same doctrines, accept the same sacraments and the sacrifice of the Mass and submit to the same authority. A threat to unity during the 17th through 19th centuries was Gallicanism which tried to diminish the pope's authority in France. Other threats to unity included the Scientific Revolution, the Enlightenment and various political revolutions, especially the French Revolution.

9. The church is holy because it is the presence of Jesus and as such is consecrated and dedicated to God. The church is the Body of Christ and through its head Jesus continues to sanctify the world today. False ideas of holiness, like Jansenism, threaten the church. The saints show God's pilgrim people the true meaning of holiness. The 17th century produced some outstanding saints: St. Francis de Sales, St. Vincent de Paul, St. John Baptist de La Salle, St. Jane Frances de Chantal, St. Margaret Mary Alacoque.

10. The church is catholic—universal—in that it is for all people in all places in all times. It is catholic in that it continues to teach all that Jesus taught while he was on earth. The church's missionary efforts in the 16th and 17th centuries extended Christ's message to the West and the East. Unfortunately, missionaries were too identified with colonial efforts and Rome failed to permit a healthy diversity in some of the religious practices in mission lands.

11. The church is apostolic because it lives the faith of the apostles. It is the same faith community founded by the apostles; it is still governed by the successors of the apostles; and it continues to preach what the apostles preached. In the 19th century the doctrine of papal infallibility was defined at the First Vatican Council against the backdrop of the liberal thinking of the day. This doctrine holds that the Lord preserves the pope from error when he is teaching solemnly to the whole church on a matter of faith and morals.

EVALUATION

Essays:

1. Could the Protestant Reformation have been avoided? Explain your answer.

2. List and explain in your own words three teachings of the Council of Trent.

3. In your own words, what is the doctrine of papal infallibility?

Matching:

Here are some important writings of the era just studied. Match the author with the work.

_____ 4. Pope Pius V

_____ 5. John Calvin

_____ 6. St. Ignatius Loyola

_____ 7. Thomas Cranmer

_____ 8. Martin Luther

_____ 9. Philip Melanchthon

_____ 10. Pius IX

_____ 11. St. Francis de Sales

a. *Spiritual Exercises*

b. *95 Theses*

c. *Augsburg Confession*

d. *Syllabus of Errors*

e. *Introduction to the Devout Life*

f. *Book of Common Prayer*

g. *Institutes of the Christian Religion*

h. *Catechism of the Council of Trent*

Who Am I?: Identify the following important persons.

_____ 12. I taught the doctrine of predestination.

_____ 13. I defined the doctrine of papal infallibility.

_____ 14. I established Presbyterianism in Scotland.

_____ 15. I promoted devotion to the Sacred Heart of Jesus.

_____ 16. I was beheaded for not taking my former friend's Oath of Supremacy.

_____ 17. I, the Sun King, attempted to make the church subservient to myself.

_____ 18. I founded the Brothers of the Christian
Schools.

True or False:

____ 19. The doctrine of transubstantiation maintains that the bread
and wine at the sacrifice of the Mass are changed into the
body and blood of Jesus Christ.

____ 20. Luther wanted to break from the church.

____ 21. Nominalism taught that the sacraments are barriers between God and his people.

____ 22. For the church to be one it must be totally uniform, that is,
absolutely the same in all regards.

Define:

23. canonization: _____

_____

_____

24. ex cathedra:_____

_____

_____

25. indulgence: _____

_____

_____

PRAYER REFLECTION

Recite together St. Ignatius Loyola's famous prayer. Then write your
own prayer based on the themes in this prayer.

> Take, Lord, and receive
>   all my liberty, my memory,
>   my understanding, and my entire will,
>   all that I have and possess.
>
> You have given all to me.
>
> To you, Lord, I return it.
> All is yours.
>   Dispose of it wholly according to your will.
>
> Give me your love and your grace,
>   for this is enough for me.

6

The Church as Sacrament: A Sign to the 20th Century

As the Council teaches, "by his Incarnation, he, the Son of God, in a certain way united *himself with each man." The Church therefore sees its fundamental task in enabling that union to be brought about and renewed continually. The Church wishes to serve this single end: that each person may be able to find Christ, in order that Christ may walk with each person the path of life, with the power of the truth about man and the world that is contained in the mystery of the Incarnation and the Redemption and with the power of the love that is radiated by that truth.*

—Pope John Paul II
Redemptor Hominis (No. 13)

In his compelling novel, *The Clowns of God*, author Morris West tells a powerful story of a fictional pope of the future—Gregory XVII—who is granted a vision of the end of the world. Gregory insists that he must tell the world to get ready for the Lord's Second Coming. But his cardinals feel that he is a madman and convince him to resign his office. Gregory's problem in the rest of the book is an age-old one: How can he convey his message to a world that does not want to hear?

Morris West's hero finds a way to get his message out. He does it by being true to his vision and being the same kind of loving, generous and faithful person he has always been. And, believe it or not, some people listen to him.

The church finds itself in a situation similar to Gregory's. As the Body of Christ it has been entrusted with an important message: the good news of Jesus. But it exists in a world that has a hard time seeing Jesus' good news in action and oftentimes doesn't want to believe it even when it does see it.

The *Constitution on the Church* reminds Catholics of an important truth: The church is a sacrament or sign of intimate union with

221

God and with all of humanity because of its relationship to Jesus. This imposes a tremendous responsibility on the church—it must be a sign people can recognize.

In *The Church in the Modern World* the Vatican II fathers stated:

> Although by the power of the Holy Spirit the Church has remained the faithful spouse of her Lord and has never ceased to be the sign of salvation on earth, still she is very well aware that among her members, both clerical and lay, some have been unfaithful to the spirit of God during the course of many centuries. In the present age, too, it does not escape the Church how great a distance lies between the message she offers and the human failings of those to whom the gospel is entrusted (No. 43).

This paragraph suggests that the church has not always been the most effective sign of God's grace in the world. Later the document reminds the church that it must learn from its past mistakes and draw from its rich history to help make God's message come alive for today.

In effect, the story of the church in the 20th century can be told as the story of how the church has come to grips with the modern world. At times during this century the church has shed brilliant light on God's plan for his people; at other times it has taken more halting, groping and unsure steps in its attempt to be a clear sign. With the advent of the Second Vatican Council though, we can confidently say that the Roman Catholic Church has made positive efforts to speak the gospel to the people of the modern world. The church today is very aware of the struggle it is engaged in to be the sacrament/sign of God's presence in the world.

We will look at this period of church history by discussing briefly the following topics:

- the church's prophetic efforts to deal with the new social conditions

- the church's continuous struggle to incorporate new ideas
- the church story through the eyes of 20th-century popes
- Vatican II

BEING A SACRAMENT/SIGN

Not only the church but each individual Christian has the responsibility to be an authentic sign or sacrament of the good news. You let the light of Christ shine through you to others when:

- You are a *prophet*—
  when you proclaim the good news in word or deed (for example, when you study or learn, read the bible, speak the truth, stand up for the defenseless, take a stand on controversial issues, etc.)

- You are a *priest*—
  when you mediate between God and others (for example, when you pray, explain your faith, worship, keep peace, forgive, etc.)

- You are a *king*—
  when you serve as Jesus served; a Christian concept of kingship is one of leadership through service (for example, when you help out at home, spend time with a friend, help someone at school, give money to the poor, join others in a common task, take leadership in righting social injustice, etc.)

Do these two things:

1. As a class, list other activities which you can and do engage in which are truly prophetic, priestly or kingly.

2. Using the grid below, review how you spent your last two days. List significant activities. Then check any of the activities that could be classified as prophetic, priestly or kingly.

ACTIVITY	Time Spent	Prophet	Priest	King

Personal Profile:

In reviewing two days of my life I see that I:

_____ usually let the light of Christ shine through me

_____ sometimes let Christ be seen by others

_____ need to work to become a better sacrament/sign of the Lord

---

NEW SOCIAL CONDITIONS

The church of Pope Pius IX (1846-1878) has been pictured as a fortress which resisted the new ideas and revolutions of the 19th century. After Pius' death the church began to break out of that mold by grappling with the social problems caused by a dramatically changing world.

Industrialization. One of the important phenomena of the 19th century was *industrialization*, that is, the progressive reliance on machines and the concentration of the methods of producing goods in the hands of a few. Industrialization transformed the lives of many people. Railroads, for example, speeded up travel; the telegraph aided communication. Many other inventions literally changed the lives of the average citizens.

The move to factories brought countless numbers off the rural lands and herded them into congested and dingy neighborhoods near smoky, dangerous factories. Workers were subject to abominable conditions. Men, women and children worked up to 15 hours a day for wages that could hardly support a small family. There were no social benefits; if a worker was sick or the victim of an accident—too bad! That person would probably starve to death.

These conditions resulted from an unbridled form of liberal economic ideas known as laissez faire capitalism. The liberal theory rested on the belief that the state should not interfere with the laws of the marketplace, and that private initiative and individual effort should be allowed to generate money without any outside restraint.

Reaction. The laws of the marketplace, of laissez faire capitalism, tended to chew up workers and isolate them from the very work process. Socialism, and especially communism as expounded by Karl Marx in his *Communist Manifesto* (1848) and *Das Kapital* (1867), attracted many workers as a solution to the social abuses of unbridled capitalism. Marx taught that class struggle and warfare in the capitalist states such as England and Germany would lead to revolutions. After the revolutions the proletariat (workers) would rule a society in which everything would be held in common. Marx denied spiritual values and promoted atheism, criticizing religion as "the opiate of the people," too closely associated with the exploiters of the working class.

Because it was generally slow adapting to the many changes of the day, at first the church did not quite know how to respond to the new economic situation. For example, historians acknowledge that French workers were lost to the church by 1880. The reasons seem to stem from the very conservative church leadership in France, the reluctance of Catholics to adopt new democratic procedures and their refusal to accept some of the good ideas of socialism.

Catholic Response. Some Catholic leaders, most notably Bishop William Ketteler of Germany, intervened on behalf of the workers as early as 1848. Bishop Ketteler steered a middle course between socialism and unbridled capitalism. He insisted that workers could form their own associations and called for many reforms including reasonable working hours, rest days, profit sharing, factory inspection and regulation of child labor.

Similar efforts were undertaken elsewhere in both Europe and America. Two pioneers were Cardinal Manning in England who fought for workers' rights and Cardinal Gibbons of Baltimore who backed the Knights of Labor, the most important labor union in America at the time. Some conservative American and Canadian bishops wanted the Knights banned, but Cardinal Gibbons convinced Rome that such a move would be disastrous and might permanently lead to the loss of the workers to the church.

Catholic Social Teaching. In 1891 Pope Leo XIII, the successor of Pius IX, issued one of the most influential encyclicals of modern times. Its title was *Rerum Novarum (On the Condition of Workers)*. *Rerum Novarum* is considered the constitution of Catholic social justice. It summarized the current thought on social problems and clarified the main issues at stake. Most important, *Rerum Novarum* provided the basic framework for Catholic social teaching.

Rerum Novarum steered a middle course between socialism and liberal capitalism. Its main teachings underscored the dignity of the human person. Here are some of its main teachings:

Against socialism	*Against liberal capitalism*
• Private property is a natural right	• Some state intervention is necessary to uphold the spiritual and material interests of the worker
• The family is the primary social unit	• Workers have a right to a living wage
• Class warfare is not inevitable	• Workers have the right to unionize

- Religion has an important role to help build relations of charity and justice among people

Rerum Novarum did not entirely stem the attraction of the workers to Marxist ideals, but it did have considerable impact, especially on the developing Christian trade unions and Christian democratic parties. The Young Christian Workers, an outstanding example of a Christian trade union, was founded by Father Joseph Cardijn (1882-1967). This union was typical of Christian trade unions in that it worked against the socialist doctrine of government ownership of all business and production. Furthermore Christian unions stressed that workers should fight for their rights in a spirit of collaboration. Finally, Christian unions insisted that individuals are tremendously important and should not be subordinated to the state as Karl Marx held.

Father Cardijn's role in church history of this century is most important. In fact, some believe that he was the most influential social thinker in the church in the 20th century. He founded the Young Christian Workers, an organization which grew to number millions in 60 countries within 50 years. He advocated basic worker rights out of a burning desire to correct the abuses he had witnessed firsthand growing up and again when he was assigned to a workers' parish in Brussels a few years after his ordination.

His famous quote, "Observe, act, judge," became the basis for a variety of Catholic action groups and their approach to social issues. His ideas were the basis for the famous social encyclical by Pope John XXIII, *Mater et Magistra* (1961). He also played a major role in the formulation of two very important documents to emerge from Vatican II: the *Constitution on the Laity* and *The Church in the Modern World*. As a result of his work the church became a sign of the meaning of the good news in contemporary society. Cardijn was himself a symbol of that teaching.

With people like Cardijn and some remarkable papal teaching, the church in the 20th century has developed a systematic set of teachings on social justice, that aspect of church teaching and Christian life which tries to apply Jesus' command to love to the structures, systems and institutions of the society in which we live. This teaching has offered to Catholics and to the world a clear alternative to communism and uncontrolled capitalism. It has shown the world how to be a sign, a sacrament of the good news of Jesus.

An Overview. In the following section you will find listed the most important documents which present Catholic social teaching. A short summary of each follows along with a sample passage which touches on an important point of Catholic teaching.

1. *Quadragesimo Anno* (1931) was issued by Pope Pius XI during the height of the Great Depression. It marked the 40th anniversary of *Rerum Novarum*. This encyclical reaffirmed the right to private property but condemned its arbitrary use and its selfish accumulation. Pius XI also endorsed the principle of subsidiarity and taught that justice and charity should dominate the social order.

The Principle of Subsidiarity

Just as it is wrong to withdraw from the individual and commit to the community at large what private initiative and endeavor can accomplish, so it is likewise an injustice, a serious harm, and a disturbance of proper order to turn over to a greater society, of higher rank, functions and services which can be performed by smaller communities on a lower plane (paragraph 79).

2. *Mater et Magistra* (1961) was written by Pope John XXIII on the 70th anniversary of Leo XIII's historic letter, *Rerum Novarum*. Pope John's letter notes development in Catholic teaching over the past century and also calls attention to some important modern developments: 1) the impact of the technological revolution; 2) the rise of the welfare state; and 3) people's growing desire to participate in the political process. Because of these three phenomena Pope John introduced the notion of *socialization* which is both the result and cause of more state intervention in the social and economic order.

While endorsing the principle of subsidiarity, Pope John saw the need for the state to intervene in matters of health care, education and housing.

Definition of the Process of Socialization

. . . the growing interdependence of citizens in a society giving rise to various patterns of group life and activity and in many instances to social institutions established on a juridical basis (paragraph 59).

3. *Pacem in Terris, Peace on Earth* (1963) was also written by Pope John XXIII. This encyclical deals with rights and duties and the necessary conditions for peace in the world.

Rights Listed in Pacem in Terris

. . . the right to life, to bodily integrity, and to the means which are necessary and suitable for proper development of life; these are primarily food, clothing, shelter, rest, medical care, and finally the necessary social services. Therefore a human being also has the right to security in case of sickness, inability to work, widowhood, old age, unemployment or in any case in which he is deprived of the means of subsistence through no fault of his own (paragraph 11).

4. *Gaudium et Spes, The Church in the Modern World* (1965), is an extremely important achievement of Vatican II. This pastoral constitution describes the modern world scene and how the church should interact with it. After discussing human dignity, solidarity and activity, the document shows how the church is vitally interested in the good of people by discussing some principles in regard to marriage, culture, socioeconomic life, politics and world peace.

On Discrimination

With respect to the fundamental rights of the person, every type of discrimination, whether social or cultural, whether based on sex, race, color, social condition, language, or religion, is to be overcome and eradicated as contrary to God's intent (paragraph 29).

On the Arms Race

Therefore, it must be said again: the arms race is an utterly treacherous trap for humanity, and one which injures the poor to an intolerable degree (paragraph 81).

5. *Populorum Progressio, On the Development of Peoples* (1967), was composed by Pope Paul VI and outlines the problems of the underdeveloped countries and pointedly reminds wealthy countries of their obligations to alleviate poverty and to aid the developing nations.

Universal Brotherhood

This duty is the concern especially of more privileged nations. Their obligations stem from a brotherhood that is at once human and supernatural, and take on a threefold aspect: first, the duty of human solidarity—the aid that the rich nations must give to developing countries; next, the duty of social justice—the rectification of inequitable trade relations between the powerful nations and weak nations; finally, the duty of universal charity—the effort to bring about a world that is more human toward all men, where all will be able to give and receive, without one group making progress at the expense of the other. The question is urgent, for on it depends the future of the civilization of the world (paragraph 44).

6. *Octagesima Adveniens* (1971) was also written by Pope Paul VI, this time on the occasion of the 80th anniversary of *Rerum Novarum*. In it Pope Paul insists that sometimes the political sector must get involved to insure basic economic rights for people.

The Christian Meaning of Political Power

Political power, which is the natural and necessary link for ensuring the cohesion of the social body, must have as its aim the development of the common good. While respecting the legitimate liberties of individuals, families and subsidiary groups, it acts in such a way as to create, effectively and for the well-being of all, the conditions required for attaining man's true and complete good, including his spiritual end (paragraph 46).

7. *Justice in the World* (1971) is an important pastoral statement drawn up by the Second Synod of Bishops. This forceful document emphasizes the church as sacrament by stating that justice is an essential ingredient of the church's mission and that the church itself must *be* just in order to be *seen* as a teacher of justice. In other words, the church should practice what it preaches.

The Essential Role of Justice

Action on behalf of justice and participation in the transformation of the world fully appear to us as a constitutive dimension of the preaching of the Gospel, or, in other words, of the Church's mission for the redemption of the human race and its liberation from every oppressive situation (from the Introduction).

8. *Laborem Exercens, On Human Work* (1981) was written by Pope John Paul II on the 90th anniversary of *Rerum Novarum*. After treating the dignity of the human person as worker against rigid capitalism and Marxism, both of which make the person subordinate to labor, Pope John Paul II takes up the rights of workers and develops a spirituality of work.

Family Rights

Experience confirms that there must be a social reevaluation of the mother's role, of the toil connected with it and of the need that children have for care, love and affection in order that they may develop into responsible, morally and religiously mature and psychologically stable persons. It will redound to the credit of society to make it possible for a mother—without inhibiting her freedom, without psychological or practical discrimination, and without penalizing her as compared to other women—to devote herself to taking care of her children and educating them in accordance with their needs, which vary with age. Having to abandon these tasks in order to take up paid work outside the home is wrong from the point of view of the good of society and of the family when it contradicts or hinders these primary goals of the mission of a mother (paragraph 19).

EXERCISES

A. *Discussion:*

1. Over the years the popes and other Catholic leaders have argued that workers have the right to organize into unions for mutual aid, benefit and protection. Catholics in this country have been strong supporters of unions. What do you say to the charge being made today that unions are too strong, that they demand too much and that they share a major blame for today's poor economic situation?

   Optional: Some students may wish to find articles supporting unions in America; others may wish to find articles which attack them. Report on your reading to the rest of the class.

2. Can you think of some ways in which the arms race hurts the poor?

3. Do you want a life in politics? Why or why not? How can a good politician contribute to a just world? (See the quote from *Octagesima Adveniens* on page 230.)

4. What does your class think about Pope John Paul II's quote about employed mothers (page 231)? Does the pope have a good idea? Read this quote to your own mother and ask her opinion. Also interview three mothers who work outside the home to see what they think. Finally, interview some classmates whose mothers work to see what they think and feel about this situation.

B. *Looking at the Documents*: As a class, obtain copies of each of the nine documents discussed in the previous section of this chapter. Assign several people to a document according to length. Divide up the reading. Each person should make a list of five major points. Each small group should share information and then prepare a final report to the rest of the class.

C. *Mini-social justice inventory*

   Some Definitions:

   justice—the virtue which renders to each his or her own

   individual justice—regulates relationships between individuals

   social justice—individuals pay their debts to the common good

   distributive justice—distribution of goods by representatives of the common good

   common good—protection of the rights and the performance of the duties of the human person

Step 1:

Rank the following items 1-2-3.

1. What is the most serious justice problem today?
   ____ the failure to protect unborn life
   ____ the arms race
   ____ roughly two people per minute every day starving to death

2. Which group is most discriminated against in American today?
   ____ women   ____ the handicapped
   ____ blacks   ____ retarded people
   ____ gays   ____ the aged

3. What should our country do to help the underdeveloped nations?
   ____ make fairer trade treaties with them
   ____ give 10% of our military budget for them to use for their development
   ____ give them more food and medical assistance

4. Which right is of most value to you?
   ____ right to a job
   ____ right to medical care
   ____ right to worship as you see fit

5. What should our leaders make the priority in our country today?
   ____ more jobs
   ____ cutting runaway inflation
   ____ the defense program

6. If cutbacks are to be made in our budget, which should go first?
   ____ aid to higher education
   ____ programs for unwed mothers
   ____ benefits for veterans

7. What is in the greatest need of reform in our country?
   ____ prison system
   ____ system of taxation
   ____ welfare system

8. What issue must the church speak out most forcefully about today?
   ____ human rights in totalitarian countries
   ____ world peace
   ____ poverty

Step 2:

Form into small groups of three or so. Rank these again, reaching consensus.

Step 3:

Share your group's rankings with the rest of the class. This time defend your choices in light of the principles of Catholic social justice. Add some research to back up your opinions.

GRAPPLING WITH NEW IDEAS
—TOWARD VATICAN II

Modernism. The church has the task of presenting Jesus' message so that people of every age can understand it. At the same time the church must always present the entire message of Jesus without watering it down. The church must be a sign that people can understand and recognize; simultaneously, the church must authentically and truly reflect Jesus.

In presenting the message of Jesus the church has been generally slow to use new thought forms. This was especially true after the Council of Trent. The wish of the church leaders was to preserve Catholic believers from ideas that might threaten their faith. You read, for example, how Pope Pius IX used extreme caution when dealing with the liberal ideas of his day, many of which attacked outright Catholic religious belief and practice.

In the early part of the 20th century the church also moved cautiously in regard to thinkers who wished to adapt the gospel to new thought forms. Pope St. Pius X (d. 1914) silenced Catholic thinkers who did not take a conservative stance on every issue dealing with church doctrine. He termed the progressive thinkers of his day *Modernists.*

Some of the Modernists were clearly heretical in their views. Alfred Loisy, the French Bible expert, even denied the divinity of Christ. His position had to be condemned; in fact, the pope did so in both a decree and an encyclical. Unfortunately Pius X's condemnation of new Modernist teachings left many scholars with the idea that the new *methods* of learning were also forbidden; for example, studying the Bible in its original languages, using the historical method in getting to the sense of the scriptural text and the studying of Hebrew literature.

The pope required priests to take an anti-Modernist oath. A secret watchdog committee was also formed to advise the pope on seminary professors who gave even the slightest hint that they might be teaching any novel ideas. Sometimes false accusations were made and some scholars lost their reputations. As a result of these moves church historians believe that Catholic theology and scripture scholarship was slow getting under way in this century.

Some Winds of Change. The hindsight of history helps us understand why the pope feared the Modernists. It is true that some traditional doctrines were being seriously questioned and challenged.

But Catholic thought was not sleeping during the 20th century. There were many signs of vitality—a vitality which led up to the calling of the Second Vatican Council. Here is a short list of the kinds of intellectual activity which took place during the 20th century, intellectual activity which prepared the way for the renewal in church life which came with Vatican II.

1. Some scholars devoted themselves to renewing the liturgy. The *liturgical movement* which they inspired emphasized that liturgy was meant for communal worship of God. They stressed that a good sacrament is a sign and good signs are something that people should be able to understand. Their efforts helped prepare the way for the use of vernacular language in the liturgy. Thanks to their preparatory work we celebrate the Mass and the other sacraments in English today.

2. Spurred on by Pope Pius XII's encyclical *Divino Afflante Spiritu* (1943) which encouraged Catholic scholars to use modern methods of scripture research, the *biblical movement* helped lead Catholics back to a love of the scriptures. Bible study is on the upswing today in almost every Catholic community. Bible scholarship has enriched every aspect of church life.

3. The years before the council were noted for *Catholic Action.* Catholic Action stressed the important role the laity has in bringing Catholic values into the secular world. It stressed the need for the laity to witness to the meaning of the gospel in the world and to apply gospel values in the marketplace. It was, in one form or another, the application of Cardinal Cardijn's, "Observe, judge, act." Though after Vatican II Catholic Action seemed to wane a bit, today Pope John Paul II seems to be emphasizing again the key role of the laity

in bringing Christian values to the political, economic and social structures of society.

4. Before the council some Catholics started to get involved in the *ecumenical movement*. Although viewed with some suspicion by the popes because it started as a Protestant movement, some Catholic scholars did push ahead in this area. Their work and the Vatican II document on ecumenism have stimulated the Catholic community to get involved in efforts towards Christian unity. Pope John XXIII, Pope Paul VI and Pope John Paul II have provided strong leadership in this important area as well.

5. The *missionary efforts* in the 20th century became less and less related to colonialism. Popes increasingly supported a native clergy and appointed native bishops to serve in the various mission lands.

6. We have already discussed at some length workers like Cardijn and the profound papal teaching in the area of *social justice*. In many cases Catholic thought in this area was way ahead of its time.

7. All of these various movements and efforts helped to bring about a Catholic *renewal in theology*. This renewal gave to the church outstanding scholars who served as experts at the Second Vatican Council and who often helped write the important documents which emerged from the council. Three notable examples are Karl Rahner, S.J., Henri de Lubac, S.J., and Yves Congar, O.P. Rahner is considered the most influential theologian in all of Catholicism in the 20th century.

CHANGING THE CHANGELESS

The problem every scholar encounters when he or she wishes to try to improve traditional Catholic teaching or practice can be stated this way: When is it harmful to tamper with the essentials? Here is a list of possible changes in Catholic teaching or practice. Check (✔) those which you think are changeable. Then, as a class, discuss why some are unchangeable.

_____ 1. teach that the three members of the Trinity are not distinct persons

____ 2. change the words of consecration at Mass

____ 3. make a law saying that Catholics must perform a certain penance every day during the Advent season

____ 4. permit premarital sexual intercourse

____ 5. find a new way to elect the pope

____ 6. permit Catholics to divorce and remarry

____ 7. teach that Jesus did not believe he was God

____ 8. allow women to be ordained priests

____ 9. teach that Mass attendance for Catholics is optional

____ 10. deny that Mary was a virgin

____ 11. formulate a teaching on how to deal with extraterrestrial life.

THROUGH THE EYES OF THE POPES

In a recent book Francis X. Murphy studies the history of 20th-century Catholicism from the perspective of the papacy. This focus highlights the tremendous effect the popes have had on the church story in this century. Following Father Murphy's lead, here is a list of the popes and their major accomplishments. The list ends with Pope John XXIII who convened the Second Vatican Council, a turning point in church history.

Pius X (1903-1914). We have already referred to Pope Pius X as the pope who condemned Modernism. This condemnation gave a hint of Pius X's interests. Unlike his predecessor, Leo XIII, he made little effort to reconcile the church with the modern world. He was much more dedicated to the tasks of a simple parish priest. His intention was to restore "all things in Christ." He reformed liturgical music, restoring Gregorian chant to the Mass. He instituted the practice of frequent reception of the Eucharist for adults and first communion at age seven for children. He was responsible for a reform in Canon Law, a work not completed and published until after his death. Pope Pius X's personal holiness, simplicity and warmth gained him canonization in 1954.

Benedict XV (1914-1922). A frail, physically unattractive man from a noble family, Pope Benedict XV devoted his papacy to the cause of peace both in the church and in the world. He worked toward peace in the church by calling off the suspicions against the Modernists. He devoted all of his energy to working for world peace during World War I, though his efforts were often misunderstood. Benedict deplored the war, condemning it as unjust and refusing to take sides. This brought him severe criticism from warring parties. He published his peace proposals, many of which seem to have been incorporated into President Woodrow Wilson's *14 Points.*

Benedict helped the church confront the problem of the proper role of Catholics in Italian politics. There had been an uneasy coexistence between church and state in Italy after the Papal States were taken from the church in 1870. Benedict now allowed dependable Catholic politicians to serve in the Italian government. This prepared the way for a more permanent solution under the next pope.

Benedict was known for his incredible charity in organizing relief for the starving and homeless after the war and for his own personal generosity to all who asked him for help of any kind. Today historians view his papacy with much favor.

Pius XI (1922-1939). Pius XI spent most of his priestly life as a librarian. His hobby was mountain climbing, a hobby which characterized his own stoic and stern personality. The first objective of his reign was to reconcile the Vatican to Italy. By giving support to Benito Mussolini's fascist party against the Catholic Popular Party, Pius XI paved the way for the Lateran Concordat and Treaty of 1929. Mussolini gave the pope the equivalent of $70,000,000, recognized Vatican City as a sovereign state and gave the Catholic church special privileges in Italy in return for the church's surrender of papal claims to Italian territory. The Roman Question was solved.

Pius ruled the church during the time when several dictators came to power. His policy was to make *concordats* with them, that is, formal agreements which would respect certain church rights such as the pope's right to appoint bishops, and freedom for the Catholic Action movement. Unfortunately the church has often been wrong in thinking that dictators will keep their promises. When Hitler began to attack the German church, Pius XI wrote an encyclical which was smuggled into Germany by the future American Cardinal Spellman. The encyclical, *Mit brennender Sorge, With Burning Concern*, 1937, confronted and criticized Nazism for its various crimes. It even called Hitler a "mad prophet." Hitler, in return, denounced the encyclical, closed down Catholic publishers, arrested monks and harassed priests by conducting false immorality trials against them.

During his reign Pope Pius also severely condemned atheistic communism, fearing it even more than fascism. He died while preparing two major speeches, rumored to be about his desire to break with the fascist state and a condemnation of its leaders.

Pius XII (1939-1958). Cardinal Eugenio Pacelli served as secretary of state under Pope Pius XI, emerging as the late pope's own candidate to succeed him. He was known as a master diplomat, both intelligent and holy. His election was most predictable. He took the name of Pius XII.

Soon after his election World War II and its terrible furies were unleashed. With Catholics fighting on both sides Pius XII tried to remain impartial. He hated communism and Nazism, though he had a special love for the German people which grew out of his years as a diplomat stationed in Germany. Pius has been accused of not speaking out strongly enough against the crimes committed by Hitler. His reasons were many: the fear that if he spoke out, Hitler would be even more cruel; his belief that he could do more for the victims, especially Jews, behind the Nazis' backs as long as their ire was not aroused; the belief that a major condemnation would do no good; a fear that Hitler would take terrible reprisals on the church. In private, though, Pope Pius did much to help the Jews escape, giving them shelter and finding them homes.

Pius coordinated relief efforts during the war and worked hard to save Rome from destruction.

After the war the papacy was looked on as a symbol of peace. The pope tried to mobilize world opinion against communism, allying the church more and more with Western democracies. In 1949 he decreed that any Catholic who belonged to the Communist party would be excommunicated.

A generally conservative pope who exalted the idea of a monarchial papacy, Pope Pius XII moved the church slowly into the modern world. He gave support to the biblical and liturgical movements. He wrote many important speeches which dealt with important topics like medical ethics. He delivered many significant addresses on peace, especially in his quotable Christmas addresses.

Pope Pius XII is remembered for his own piety and his strong devotion to the Blessed Mother. He declared 1950 a holy year and defined the doctrine of the Assumption of Mary into heaven, the second infallible Marian doctrine in a century. (The first was defined by Pope Pius IX in 1854—the Immaculate Conception.) Millions made a pilgrimage to Rome to celebrate the occasion.

Pius XII died in 1958. After a three-day conclave the cardinals elected an aging compromise pope, the patriarch of Venice, Cardinal Angelo Roncalli. With the election of this man, who would become one of the most beloved men of the 20th century, an exciting new chapter in church history was about to be written.

John XXIII (1958-1963). Pope John XXIII was a remarkable Christian, joyously in love with life and other people. He broke Pius XII's tradition of eating alone by inviting friends to dine with him. He would sneak out of the Vatican to visit people in the streets, hospitals and prisons of Rome. He would tell jokes and poke fun at himself. In a very short time Pope John endeared himself to the world.

There was little in his background to hint that he would call an ecumenical council of the church. He did so, he said, under inspiration of the Holy Spirit. He wanted to bring the church up-to-date, to engage it in *dialogue* with the world.

Unlike most other church councils, Vatican II was not called as a response to heresy. Rather, John XXIII called it specifically to renew

Pope John XXIII

the church and help the church speak better to people in the modern world. Many in the curia, fearful that the council might bring too much change, tried to discourage Pope John from calling it. Failing that, they tried to control the council. As events turned out, their efforts did not succeed. The Spirit was very much alive in the church and helped the 2,600 bishops, the largest assembly of bishops in any church council, to produce some amazing documents which brought the church into the modern world.

Pope John XXIII in his opening address to the bishops set the tone for the whole council. He asked the bishops to be hopeful and expectant, not gloomy and looking for the worst in the modern world. He said that the task of the council was not to suppress heresy, but to find a good way to present the deposit of faith to people today. Mercy rather than severity is the method to be used; the church should "show herself to be the loving mother of all, benign, patient, full of mercy and goodness."

MARY: THE MOTHER OF THE CHURCH

1950 marked a key year in Marian devotion. Thus before looking at the achievements of Vatican II, let us turn to a brief discussion of Mary, the mother of Jesus and the mother of the church. Mary has always held a special and unique place in the history of Catholicism. From the very beginning Christians revered her. Through the course of centuries her influence can be seen in Christian art, music, literature and especially devotions. In the late Middle Ages and again in the past couple of centuries a number of popular devotions sprang up around her.

In an earlier exercise you read that Pope Pius IX defined as a matter of faith the traditional teaching that Mary was conceived without original sin. This doctrine of the *Immaculate Conception* holds that Mary was conceived in God's friendship, a friendship she never lost. You read in this chapter that Pope Pius XII defined the doctrine of the *Assumption of Mary,* the teaching that Mary was assumed body and soul into heaven.

Vatican II eloquently showed how Mary fits into the church. She is, in fact, the model of the church. She is the best Christian example of faith, hope and love. When Mary said yes to the Father's invitation to be mother of his son, she prefigured the yes we say when we accept the Lord into our lives. Her "let it be done" is the supreme act of faith, of surrendering herself to the will of the Father. This is the model for all Christian faith. Mary is, in fact, a symbol of the church as sacrament.

Because Mary is the mother of Christ, Pope Paul VI proclaimed that she is also mother of the church. Pope John Paul II in his first encyclical, *Redeemer of Man,* elaborates on this truth. Mary gave human life to Jesus and remained faithful to him throughout her life. While hanging on the cross Jesus gave his mother to John, the beloved apostle. Christians, in imitation of John, have taken Mary as their mother ever since and have looked to her as an example of what the Christian life is all about.

The *Constitution on the Church* reminds us that the church has used various titles in referring to Mary. The document wisely warns, though:

> These, however, are to be so understood that they neither take away from nor add anything to the dignity and efficacy of Christ the one Mediator (paragraph 62).

The council was aware that some Catholics almost substituted Mary for Christ. But today some Catholics ignore any devotion to Mary.

It is true that Jesus is our unique redeemer, but his mother plays an important role as the greatest Christian saint. She points us to her son. She guides us. She gives an example of what it means to be a totally committed Christian. True devotion to her as our mother leads us to recognize more intensely that Jesus her son is our brother and redeemer.

EXERCISES

A. *Some Reflection and Discussion Questions:*

1. *List* five important virtues of motherhood (for example, caring).

   a. _____

   b. _____

   c. _____

   d. _____

   e. _____

2. What is your own mother's strongest virtue?

   _____

3. *Discuss:*

   More and more women today don't want to be mothers.
   Is this statement true? Is that good or bad?

4. *Discuss:*

   What does it mean to call the church a mother?

B. *Some Research Possibilities:*

1. *Apparitions of Mary.* The church has sometimes sanctioned devotion to Mary as the result of her appearances to certain Christians. Here are three important Marian apparitions. Read about one and report on the devotion which grew out of the apparition.

Our Lady of Guadalupe (1531)

Our Lady of Lourdes (1858)

Our Lady of Fatima (1917)

2. *Portrait of Mary.* Read the following scripture passages and construct a report entitled: Mary in the New Testament.

Lk 1:26-56;2:1-19,41-52

Jn 2:1-12;19:25-27

Mt 1:18-25

Acts 1:14

3. *Research and report* on the life of a great Christian woman. You may choose one of the following or choose another:

Dorothy Day

St. Elizabeth Ann Seton

Catherine de Hueck Doherty

Mother Teresa of Calcutta

C. *Survey on Mary:* Agree (✔) Disagree (X) Don't know (?)

_____ I look to Mary as my mother.

_____ I turn to Mary to ask for help.

_____ I know how to recite the rosary.

_____ Mary is the mother of the church.

_____ Devotion to Mary is an important part of being a *Catholic.*

_____ Devotion to Mary is an important part of being a *Christian.*

_____ Mary was a liberated woman.

_____ Mary is an important Christian symbol.

Share and discuss your choices.

THE SECOND VATICAN COUNCIL

Vatican II is unique among church councils. As you read earlier in the chapter it was called not to stamp out heresy but to help the church enter the modern world. It was the largest council in history and the most representative in terms of cultures and nations. Both non-Catholic and lay observers were invited. It received tremendous press coverage. It was truly an *ecumenical* or worldwide council.

The first session of the council began October 11, 1962; the fourth and final session closed on December 8, 1965, the Feast of the Immaculate Conception.

In all, the council was responsible for 16 documents, seven of which have emerged as the most important. In one way or another all the documents deal either with the inner nature of the church and its workings or with the church in its relationship to the world.

The aftermath of the council has been the introduction of new ways of thinking and doing things in the church. Some Catholics have embraced these new ways with great enthusiasm; others have resisted and feared change.

Following is a list of the seven most important documents of Vatican II with a short synopsis of each. Next you will find a chart on some of the important changes in thought and practice brought on by the council.

SEVEN KEY DOCUMENTS

Title	Some Key Insights
Lumen gentium (Constitution on the Church)	• the church is a mystery, a sacrament, a pilgrim people • the church is the whole people of God • collegiality in the church emphasized • all Christians are called to holiness; the laity have a special vocation • Mary is the model of the church
Gaudium et spes (The Church in the Modern World)	• the church must read the signs of the times and interpret them in light of the gospel • the church is the servant of the world • the church must work for God's kingdom • many traditional social teachings of the church reaffirmed and expanded
Decree on Ecumenism	• gives support to the ecumenical movement • talks of *restoring* Christian unity, rather than a *return* of fallen-away Christians to Roman Catholicism • admits both sides to blame at the time of the Reformation • teaches that other Christian communities have many elements which help constitute the church
Constitution on the Sacred Liturgy	• liturgy is the summit toward which the activity of the church is directed • everyone is encouraged to participate fully in the Eucharist and the other sacraments • allows for liturgy in the language of the people and some variations for different groups

Constitution on Divine Revelation	• sacred tradition, sacred scripture and the church's teaching authority are closely linked together; they come under the action of the Holy Spirit and contribute to salvation
	• revelation is primarily God's disclosure of himself; secondarily, of his will and intentions
	• bible reading encouraged—in the context of the Christian tradition and sensitive to tradition
Declaration on Religious Freedom	• in effect, repudiates Pius IX's *Syllabus of Errors*
	• the dignity of the human person and our faith demand that everyone should be free from coercion in matters of religious belief and practice
	• no one can be compelled to be a Christian
Declaration of the Relationship of the Church to Non-Christian Religions	• the church rejects nothing that is good and true in other religious faiths
	• encourages dialogue in the search for spiritual and moral values
	• special respect and understanding should be given to the Jews; they are not to be blamed for the death of Jesus Christ
	• all kinds of persecution and discrimination are condemned

SOME CHANGES IN THE CHURCH

Pre-Vatican II	**Post-Vatican II**

Leadership:

1. Church is more an institution, a monarchy with bishops and pastors making decisions. Little room for lay participation.	1. Church as the People of God brings a sense of shared responsibility: parish councils, national advisory boards, priests' senates, etc.
	—common priesthood of all believers now emphasized
	—collegial leadership

Liturgy:

2. Emphasis on sacredness of liturgy as a means of salvation. Care in keeping liturgy uniform. Latin used throughout the world. Priests perform, laity observe.

2. Many liturgical changes:

—liturgy as celebration

—vernacular languages

—all participate, allowing for diverse ministries: lay lectors, ministers of the Eucharist, etc.

Ecumenism:

3. Church is the true church of Jesus—no toleration of error. Catholics can't read works of Protestant Reformers.

3. *Ecumenical spirit* encouraged: freedom of inquiry, joint study groups, joint prayer services, common edition of the Bible, respect for dignity of others, intercommunion sometimes permitted with bishop's permission.

Modern World:

4. Only scholasticism allowed. New learning looked on with suspicion.

Catholic participation in politics distrusted in some places.

Traditional forms of spirituality encouraged (rosary, devotion to the Sacred Heart, novenas, benedictions, etc.)

4. *More tolerance:*

—for different kinds of learning: advances in biblical studies; more regard for historical studies

—for dialogue with the modern world

—for new forms of spirituality: all are called to holiness (Catholic Charismatic movement, directed retreats, Marriage Encounter, cursillo)

ACTIVITIES

A. *Mini-Research Topic:*

1. Find an article on the church and its relationship to the modern world. Look at the religion section of *Time* or *Newsweek* or find a relevant article from a recent issue of *St. Anthony Messenger, U.S. Catholic, New Catholic World, Our Sunday Visitor* or *National Catholic Reporter.*

2. Read the article and make a report of it to the class. Then, as a class, compile a list of topics with which today's church seems to be dealing.

B. *The Church as Sacrament/Sign of God's Union With Us in Christ.*

1. For you, what one person today best symbolizes what it means to be a Christian?_____
   Discuss your reasons for choosing this person.

2. If you had to describe the activity of the church today using just one *verb*, what would it be?_____
   Share.

3. What do you think non-Catholics notice most about the Catholic church? In other words, what external activity or image of the church comes to mind when they think *Catholic* church?

   _____

   Would you say this image is positive or negative? Why or why not?

C. *Interview* your parents, your grandparents (or someone of their generation), and a parish priest (or someone who knows the church well). Obtain answers to these questions:

   1. What do you think has been the biggest change in the church since the days of the Second Vatican Council?
   2. Do you consider this change good or bad? Explain.
   3. Is the church better off today than it was when you were my age? Why or why not?
   4. Do you think the laity has a larger role to play in today's church? Could you explain your answer?
   5. Do you have any comments on church leadership today?

   Discuss the interviews:

   1. Share responses.
   2. Did the responses generally support the list of changes on the chart on pages 248-250?
   3. Were you surprised by any of the responses you received? Explain.

BEING A SACRAMENT

The history of the Roman Catholic Church in the 20th century is very much the story of how the church came to grips with its identity as Christ's sacrament. A sacrament is an external sign which points to an invisible grace and helps that grace come about. The external element draws the people to embrace the spiritual reality behind it. Thanks to Vatican II, the church today is grappling with how it can be a good sign for modern people, many of whom have great difficulty seeing Jesus Christ in today's world.

The church needs to be the kind of herald which speaks in a language and with thought patterns people can understand. It wants to be the kind of *institution* that rules as a *servant*. This means, as Vatican II pointed out, that the church is not just buildings or priests or laws. Rather, the church is the *whole* People of God, a *community* where shared responsibility and full participation of all are possible. Finally, Vatican II reminded Catholics that the church is a *pilgrim* which can learn much from good people of other faiths in attempting to spread God's kingdom: the work of reconciliation, peacemaking, healing, justice and the like.

To say the church is a sacrament is to say that it presents externally to the world the Jesus who is the head of the church, the love of God who is active in the world. As a member of the church, you are also a sacrament of the Lord. He is present in the world through you. You are his light which shines on others. You are the salt which gives flavor to the world. You are his hands that do good deeds, his eyes that forgive, his comforting words. He is present in the world through an external sign—you, his disciple.

Your task, and the task of the church, is to be a sign that people understand and recognize. Through your deeds people will know you. Through your deeds people will recognize the Spirit who is in you. Through you Jesus reveals himself to the world. Your challenge: Be a sacrament of Jesus Christ. Be a good sign.

EXAMINATION OF CONSCIENCE

Suppose that you really want to be an active and good member of the Lord's body, his church. What if you had to apply for membership to this community? How would you measure up? Here is an "application blank" for membership in the church. Complete these questions.

Your name:_____

Date of birth:_____

1. Why do you want to belong to the Roman Catholic Church? List three reasons.

   a. _____

   _____

   b. _____

   _____

   c. _____

   _____

2. Name three of your personal strengths which can help the church in its mission to show Jesus Christ to the world.

   a. _____

   _____

   b. _____

   _____

   c. _____

   _____

3. Have you had a significant experience which reveals that you are a person of love? Describe.

   _____

   _____

   _____

   _____

   _____

4. Explain how membership in the Roman Catholic Church can help you personally in your relationship to God and to others.

_____

_____

_____

_____

_____

5. It is quite possible that in the near future Christians in this community will have to suffer for Jesus Christ. Are you prepared to do so? Give some evidence that you are the kind of person who is willing to make sacrifices.

_____

_____

_____

_____

6. What do you believe about:

a. Jesus Christ?_____

_____

_____

b. his church? _____

_____

_____

7. Before admitting you to the church we need two character references. Please list them:

_____

_____

Ask someone who knows you well to write a short note telling us what kind of Catholic you would make. (This person may be a classmate.)

Discussion:

1. Share responses, including your note of recommendation.

2. What did you learn about yourself? about the church?

SUMMARY

1. The church is a sacrament/sign of God's intimate union with all of humanity in Jesus Christ. Its mission is to be an authentic, true sign.

2. Industrialization brought many improvements in the way people lived; unfortunately, it brought with it many social problems, too. Liberal capitalism and communism both attempted to deal with the new conditions.

3. At first, the church as a whole was slow to respond to the changed social order. But by the end of the 19th century the church began to develop a social justice teaching that protected the dignity of all men, women and children. This teaching is presented in some remarkable documents of which the following are the most important: *Rerum Novarum* (1891), *Quadragesimo Anno* (1931), *Mater et Magistra* (1961), *Peace on Earth* (1963), *The Church in the Modern World* (1965), *On the Development of Peoples* (1967), *Octagesima Adveniens* (1971), *Justice in the World* (1971) and *On Human Work* (1981).

4. Social justice applies Jesus' command to love to the structures, systems and institutions of society.

5. The Modernists went overboard in trying to update the church; they were condemned by Pope Pius X. The Modernist controversy slowed Catholic scholarship for a generation.

6. Certain winds of change helped prepare for the Second Vatican Council. Among them were the liturgical, biblical, ecumenical, missionary, Catholic Action and social justice movements and a theological renewal.

7. The 20th century has been blessed with some outstanding popes. Pope John XXIII in particular boldly faced the new era by convening Vatican II.

8. Mary, the mother of God, plays a key role in the church. Honored as the mother of the church, she is *the* model Christian—a symbol of Christian faith, hope and love. True devotion to her leads to a closer relationship to her son Jesus.

9. Vatican II produced 16 documents. Seven of them are considered most influential and reflect the new directions taken in the church.

Constitution on the Church—church as People of God, sacrament, pilgrim

The Church in the Modern World—church as servant to the world

Decree on Ecumenism—a mandate to work for Christian unity

Constitution on the Sacred Liturgy—full participation by all in the vernacular language

Constitution on Revelation—revelation is primarily God's disclosing of himself; Bible study encouraged

Declaration on Religious Freedom—human dignity means that people's freedom to worship is guaranteed

Declaration of the Relationship of the Church to Non-Christian Religions—all forms of religious persecution and discrimination condemned

EVALUATION

_____ 1. Because the church is a sign of Christ, it is without sin. (True or False)

_____ 2. Mothers of small children should not be *forced* to work. (True or False)

3. To fulfill our Christ-given *kingly* mission, we Christians must _____ others.

Matching:

_____ 4. Pope Pius X	a.	fought for peace in the church and the world
_____ 5. Pope Benedict XV		
_____ 6. Pope Pius XI	b.	*Peace on Earth*
_____ 7. Pope Pius XII	c.	defined the doctrine of Mary's Assumption
_____ 8. Pope John XXIII	d.	permitted reception of the Eucharist at age 7
	e.	made a Concordat with Mussolini

Principles:

Check off any of the following statements which are *not* principles of Catholic social justice.

_____ 9. The family is the primary social unit.

_____ 10. Citizens should work against interdependence among nations.

_____ 11. Conflict between workers and employers is inevitable.

_____ 12. Society owes the aged some form of social security.

_____ 13. The state has a right to intervene in economic affairs.

_____ 14. Rich nations must rectify bad trade treaties with poor nations.

_____ 15. Limited nuclear war is permissible.

_____ 16. Working for justice in the social order is an essential part of the gospel.

_____ 17. Workers have the right to collective bargaining.

_____ 18. People have the unlimited right to private property.

Identify:

19. principle of subsidiarity:_____

20. Joseph Cardijn: _____

_____

_____

21. Modernists: _____

_____

_____

22. Immaculate Conception:_____

_____

_____

Essay:

How is the church of today different from the pre-Vatican II church? List and discuss at least five examples of change.

PRAYER REFLECTION

Recite as a class the five decades of the Rosary, a traditional prayer which focuses on key events in the lives of Jesus and Mary. These events are called Mysteries because they are signs of God's love for us.

Joyful mysteries

The Annunciation
The Visit of Mary to Elizabeth
The Birth of Jesus
The Presentation of Jesus in the Temple
The Finding of Jesus in the Temple.

Sorrowful mysteries

The Agony of Jesus in the Garden
The Scourging at the Pillar
The Crowning With Thorns
The Carrying of the Cross
The Crucifixion and Death of Jesus

Glorious mysteries

The Resurrection of Jesus
The Ascension of Jesus Into Heaven
The Descent of the Holy Spirit Upon the Apostles
The Assumption of Mary Into Heaven
The Crowning of Mary as the Queen of Heaven

7
The Church as Servant: The Church Today

When he had washed their feet and put on his clothes again he went back to the table. "Do you understand" he said "what I have done to you? You call me Master and Lord, and rightly; so I am. If I, then, the Lord and Master, have washed your feet, you should wash each other's feet. I have given you an example so that you may copy what I have done to you.

"I tell you most solemnly,
no servant is greater than his master,
no messenger is greater than the man who sent him."
—John 13:12-16

Modern society more or less dictates to us who our heroes should be. Without a doubt the media make stars and superstars out of those in the entertainment industries. Who are these superstar-heroes paraded before us today? Examine the media and discover the kinds of people who are held up for your admiration. Aren't you supposed to admire the burly professional football player or the baseball all-star who can command millions of dollars a year? Aren't you supposed to care about the lifestyles of TV and movie stars, and even buy the products they claim to use in the ads to which they lend their names? Aren't you supposed to hang on every word of the latest rock star?

The media seem to value how much money we make, how physically attractive we are, how much power we have over people. We are given the distinct idea that if we are not rich, beautiful or powerful we are not worth too much.

Our Christian community has a different set of values; ideally we should admire those who serve as Jesus served. Our heroes are the mothers and fathers who not only want to have children but patiently, day in, day out, take care of them. Our superstars are women like

261

Mother Teresa who ministers to the homeless in the wretched streets of Calcutta or men like Jean Vanier of Canada who cares for helpless and handicapped people.

These people and countless others like them are really foot-washers, people who are serving others in imitation of the Lord Jesus. Today the church is very conscious of its role as *servant* of God's kingdom. In many ways, the servant image clarifies the other images we have been studying in this book. If the church is to be a believable *sacrament/sign* of God's kingdom, it must serve. An extremely important way of *heralding* the gospel is through service of others. The church discovers the true meaning of *pilgrim, community* and *institution* when it thinks of itself as a *serving* pilgrim, a *serving* community and a *serving* institution.

In looking at today's church through the image of servant we will examine the following topics:

- The post-Vatican II church
- Some contemporary issues
- Parish and ministry
- Who is a Catholic?

EXERCISE

Heroes: Answer these questions and share your responses and reasons.

1. Whom do you admire?

2. Who inspires you?

3. On whom would you like to model your life?

Discuss: Do the people you named show the values promoted by the media, or do they exemplify Christian values? Explain.

POST-VATICAN II CHURCH

The post-Vatican II Catholic church has undergone a troublesome time in its struggles to come to grips with the contemporary world. A revolution has taken place in some areas of church life; but the revolution has caused its share of grief.

Perhaps the most significant change at Vatican II was in the way church officials understood themselves. Prior to Vatican II many church leaders saw the church in terms of a monarchial church and tended to emphasize the institutional model. Vatican II, on the other hand, stressed the community model of the church, emphasizing the fact that the church is the whole People of God.

Results of a Changed Understanding. Stressing the church as the *whole* People of God brought, among others, these changes in the post-Vatican II church:

1. In the area of *spirituality* it became clear that lay people, not just nuns and priests and brothers, were called to holiness and active spiritual lives.

One important outgrowth of this new emphasis on an active lay spirituality was the phenomenon of the Catholic Charismatic Movement. Catholic charismatics emphasize the power of the Holy Spirit. They pray together, receiving what they call the "baptism of the Holy Spirit," an adult acceptance of their faith and new commitment to it. Sometimes they receive gifts (charisms) which are meant to build up the community in the service of others. The greatest of these gifts, as St. Paul taught, is love. Other gifts include speaking in tongues, prophecy and healing.

Since the council many lay people have been involved in various other forms of spirituality as well. Bible study groups, Marriage Encounters, cursillos, parish renewals, retreats and classes on meditation are some of the more popular means used by today's lay people in their pursuit of holiness.

2. Many changes were made in the *liturgy and in our understanding of the sacraments*. At Mass the celebrant faces the people and is closer to them. People participate more actively now; for example, they hear and speak their own language, sing, present readings, distribute communion. Communion may be received in the hand and consecrated wine is sometimes offered as well. The sacrament of reconciliation allows the option of face-to-face confession to emphasize the personal nature of the forgiveness our Lord offers. The sacrament of the sick emphasizes physical as well as spiritual healing. A revised rite of Christian initiation of adults underscores the serious adult commitment demanded by Catholicism. In many places the age of confirmation is later and coincides more closely with the psychological readiness of the young people who receive it. The sacrament of marriage demands more serious premarital preparation and allows for more involvement of the bride and the groom in the ceremony.

3. In the area of *ecumenism* dialogue has opened up with the Orthodox and some Protestant groups, most notably the Anglicans and the Lutherans. Significant progress has been made toward a common understanding of the real presence of Jesus in the Eucharist and on the issue of the Mass as a sacrifice. Better understandings are being forged on the role of the pope. However, much work still needs to be done on the role of Mary in the history of salvation.

4. Vatican II probably introduced some of the most controversial expectations in the area of *church authority*. In general Vatican II supported the principle of subsidiarity, the principle which holds that affairs should, if at all possible, be handled on the local level. In addition the council supported the principle of collegiality, that is, consultation and mutual decision-making between the bishops and the pope. At the same time Vatican II reasserted the doctrines of papal primacy and papal infallibility which had been defined at the First Vatican Council.

For many Catholics a serious shock wave hit the church when Pope Paul VI issued his encyclical *On Human Life* (*Humanae Vitae*) in 1968. Pope Paul VI assumed the throne of St. Peter when Pope John XXIII died in 1963, before the second session of the council opened. He continued Pope John's spirit of renewal and saw the council to its completion.

But Pope Paul had the difficult task of implementing the changes of Vatican II. Extreme conservatives complained that the pope was moving too fast and destroying the church which they had always known. Extreme liberals accused the pope of being too indecisive and not moving fast enough to bring the church into the modern world.

On Human Life, the so-called birth-control encyclical, was an explosive document mainly for two reasons: 1) Many Catholics thought the pope would allow some change in the traditional church teaching about birth control. They were greatly disappointed when he reaffirmed the church's ban on artificial means of contraception. The pope taught that *every* act of sexual intercourse in a marriage must be open to both life and love. To exclude one or the other was to exclude an essential aspect of the meaning of lovemaking. To frustrate one or the other of these purposes—to use an artificial means of birth control, for example—is, therefore, gravely wrong. 2) Some theologians and bishops were upset because the pope went against the majority of the advisers he had assembled to study the issue and make recommendations. The majority on the pope's commission recommended some limited change in the church's traditional teaching. Because the pope did not follow the advice of his commission, some people interpreted this as a violation of the principle of collegiality.

Humanae Vitae and its aftermath presented a modern-day crisis of papal authority. Some theologians rebelled. Some national conferences of bishops published pastoral letters which upheld the teaching of the encyclical on the one hand, but on the other restated the church's teaching on the role of a Christian's conscience in personal decision-making. More and more Catholics realized that they had to assume personal responsibility in deciding the issue through a more responsible formation of conscience. Papal teaching was no longer accepted in a vacuum separated from all other sources of learning.

Pope Paul VI

5. *Other phenomena.* For good or ill, the following have occurred in the post-Vatican II church:

1) There has been greater involvement of Catholic people in their church. An example, very popular in Latin America, is a phenomenon known as "base communities." These communities are an attempt to organize Christians into a vital church. They are small groups and are typically made up of Catholics from similar backgrounds. Most of the communities arise among the poor. Lay involvement is strong. Members usually meet in a member's home for bible reading, the sharing of the sacraments, ecumenical discussions and projects to promote sharing the gospel with others. Some are very active in making their members aware of the rich social justice message of Catholicism.

2) Although many lay Catholics are more involved in the church today, many others have stopped going to Mass. For some, disillusionment set in because the changes were too slow in coming; for others, bitterness took over because they thought the changes which did come destroyed their church. In addition, a great number of Catholics have ceased the practice of *frequent* confession.

3) Vocations have declined dramatically and there has also been a substantial exodus of priests, nuns and brothers from their ministries. It has been estimated that approximately 8,000 priests left their ministry between 1966 and 1972. That is 30 times the rate in any comparable period before the council. Some scholars attribute this to an identity crisis in the priesthood (With more lay participation, what is so special about the priest?) and controversy over the celibacy issue. We might add, though, that today vocations seem to be on the upswing.

4) Although the Catholic school system is quite healthy in the United States today, many parochial schools closed in the late 1960s and the 1970s as the numbers of religious declined and the schools became more expensive to operate.

IN GREATER DEPTH

A. *Lay Spirituality.* Read an article or interview someone connected with one of the following: Catholic Charismatic Movement, cursillo, Marriage Encounter or parish renewal. Report to the class. You may wish to invite a representative from one of these groups to come to class and report on the benefit of the movement for lay spiritual growth.

B. *Prayer and You.* Prayer is the basis for spiritual life. Reflect on the current status of your own prayer life. Mark according to this scale:

> U—usually
> S—sometimes
> R—rarely

_____ When I pray I sense the presence of God.

_____ When I pray I put myself into God's presence.

_____ When I think about it I realize that God speaks to me through other people and events in my ordinary life.

_____ When I read scripture I try to listen to what the Lord is saying to me.

_____ My prayer involves asking for things.

_____ My prayer involves asking for God's forgiveness.

_____ My prayer involves thanking God for what he has given me.

_____ My prayer involves praising God.

_____ My prayers are informal.

Explain why prayer is easy or difficult for you:

_____

_____

_____

Give an example of a time prayer helped you:

_____

_____

Optional: Share your responses with a friend.

C. *Different Views*: One of the most serious problems in the post-Vatican II church, especially during the late 1960s and most of the 1970s, was polarization in the church. *Polarization* refers to the camps which formed and argued over how much and how fast change should take place in the church.

In a community as broad as Roman Catholicism it is not surprising to find Catholics holding any of the following four views (greatly simplified here):

radical (**RA**)	—advocates fast change; wants some things destroyed; questions almost everything and advocates change for the sake of change
liberal (**L**)	—wants change in the spirit of Vatican II in order to move into the modern world; does not desire the destruction of the good things from the past, but does want steady progress
conservative (**C**)	—desires extreme caution and does not want change for the sake of change; wants to preserve the best from the past; questions the need for change
reactionary (**RE**)	—desires things the way they were after the Council of Trent; thinks that Vatican II was not needed; wants to reverse many of the concessions made in the church to accommodate itself to modern developments

Here are some statements which one might hear in the post-Vatican II church. Some of these positions cause bitter arguments among the various groups in the church. See if you can identify which group (**RA, L, C** or **RE**) would most likely support a given statement.

_____ 1. Let's hire a lay budget director for the parish.

_____ 2. Students should be taught religion from a catechism, preferably the Baltimore Catechism.

_____ 3. English in the Mass is fine, but let's allow those who want to go to a Latin Mass the opportunity to do so.

_____ 4. Teachers of religion don't need texts. Texts limit the freedom teachers need to teach properly.

_____ 5. We had better ordain women—and fast.

_____ 6. We should think twice about abolishing the Catholic schools; they are a chief means of passing on Catholic identity.

_____ 7. Let's organize a Bible study group to meet in our homes.

_____ 8. Let's follow the lead of our bishops and support the lettuce boycott.

_____ 9. A priest who leaves the active ministry (except for health reasons) should be excommunicated.

_____ 10. While it is praiseworthy that the focus of spirituality today is on Jesus, especially in the Mass, it is still a shame that so many people have given up saying the rosary.

Share your responses and the reasons for them. Which of these might you yourself say? Why?

SOME CONTEMPORARY ISSUES

Shortly before his death the popular American preacher, Archbishop Fulton J. Sheen, wrote that he belonged to the Catholic church because the church loves and serves three things: life, truth and love. His portrayal of the church is quite accurate. Despite the sins and failings of Catholics throughout the course of history, the People of God has still been concerned about life, truth and love. This is also true today.

The Church Serves Life. In the past few years, the Catholic church has taken a forceful stance on many life issues. Here are two which are perhaps the two most important moral issues of our day.

Nuclear Weapons. An increasing number of Catholic moralists have stated that the nuclear arms race dwarfs all other moral and human issues because of its present and future consequences. Consider these facts:

1. America now has a nuclear stockpile which can destroy every major Soviet city 40 times over; the Soviet Union has a stockpile which can destroy every major American city 17 times over.

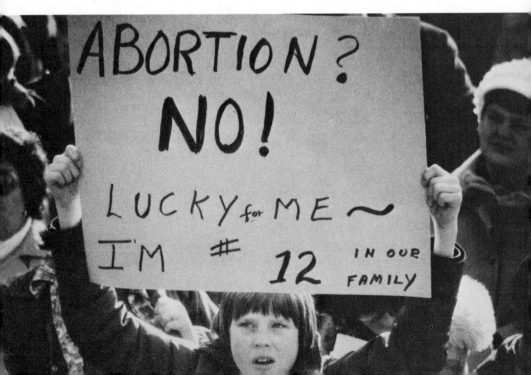

2. It is estimated that by 1986 the United States will spend just under $1 billion dollars per day on the military.

3. If a 10-megaton bomb exploded where you are now, it is likely that everyone in a three-mile radius would die and everything would be leveled. In the next six-mile ring, one out of two persons would die and nine out of ten would be severely burned by radiation.

The popes from Pius XII to John Paul II have condemned nuclear weapons. World peace has been the theme of many of Pope John Paul II's speeches. When he visited Hiroshima, he had this to say:

> To remember Hiroshima is to abhor nuclear war. To remember Hiroshima is to commit oneself to peace. . . . Let us promise our fellow human beings that we will work untiringly for disarmament and the banishing of all nuclear weapons; let us replace violence and hate with confidence and caring.

The church is striving to remind the world of the Lord's, "Blessed are the peacemakers."

Abortion. John Powell, S.J., an outstanding Catholic writer and teacher, has written a book entitled *Abortion: The Silent Holocaust.* His thesis is that what is taking place in America since the 1973 Supreme Court decision allowing abortion on demand is similar to what Hitler did when he tried to exterminate the Jews. The difference this time is that the 1,500,000 unborn babies who are killed annually cannot speak for themselves.

Time and again the church has spoken strongly and repeatedly on the gross immorality of abortion. It is a strong advocate of the human life amendment to the United States Constitution and offers support to organizations like Birthright, a group which gives emotional and physical aid to expectant mothers, whether married or not.

The church has struggled in recent years to reach a pro-life position which is consistent. This means that the church has begun to rethink its stance on capital punishment and the morality of war itself. Furthermore, the church has increasingly spoken out for human rights in totalitarian countries. Recall, also, the church's stand on social justice issues as discussed in the last chapter.

The Church Serves Truth. The church has the continual task of being faithful to Jesus who said, "I am the Truth" (Jn 14:6). Service of the truth implies that the church must safeguard the basic truths of the faith. The teaching authority of the church—the bishops in union with the pope—has as one of its primary functions this very task.

One of the values of having a hierarchical church is that there are official teachers who ensure that the truth of the gospel message is taught in an age which does not always want to hear the truth. For example, the church's teaching about the need to love our enemies, the need to share our goods with the less fortunate, the need for us to respect our bodies by refraining from drugs for the sake of recreation, and the need to respect the sexuality of ourselves and others are not popular messages today. Nonetheless the church must still teach these messages.

Evangelization. A common theme of the church in recent years is *evangelization*, the process of preaching the good news of God's love for us. Its purpose is to arouse the beginnings of faith. Its aim is conversion to the gospel of Jesus. Evangelization takes place most obviously in mission lands where people have never heard the name of Jesus. Evangelization must also take place in Christian and Catholic lands. Because of the distractions of our contemporary world—appeals to pleasure, power and money—many Christians and Catholics have never really *heard* the good news of the Lord. An ongoing task of the church is to preach the word of God so that people can truly hear it.

Catechesis. The church today is also very much concerned with *catechesis*, that process of instruction which helps a person's faith become alive, active and conscious. The church's parochial school system, religious education classes, youth programs, sacramental preparation programs, adult education classes, radio and television programs, newspapers, magazines and books all represent a tremendous investment of time, energy, personnel and money to further the good news about God's kingdom.

Evangelization and catechesis are both ministries of teaching. The ministry of teaching is one of the church's chief forms of service to our Lord's unchanging good news.

The Church Serves Love. *Love* is a slippery word in English. For one person it means friendship; for another, sex. Some mean *like* while others have in mind the teaching of Jesus about turning the other cheek.

Families. The church has the Christ-given mandate to spread the message of love both in word and deed. Without a doubt it must remind people today that love is seen in a special way in the family. The family is the basic unit of society and the basic unit of the church.

All that threatens family life is of deep concern to the church. Thus the church teaches Jesus' message that sexual love is a special sharing in God's own creative activity. It demands the fidelity and commitment of marriage. The church must also teach that true love is forever. It is not a passing fancy but demands sacrifice and commitment—in sickness, in health, in riches, in poverty, until death. Parents must hear the message that they are worthwhile and communicate love to their children by respecting, caring for, listening to and guiding them. Children must hear the message that they are God's own images, of tremendous worth, and gifts to their parents. Love within the family is the most basic ingredient for true Christian community on a larger scale.

Laity. Love is more than words. St. John writes:

> My children,
> our love is not to be just words or mere talk,
> but something real and active;
> only by this can we be certain
> that we are children of the truth (1 Jn 3:18-19).

Today, perhaps more than ever in its long history, the church is reminding the laity that it is the church—"The people are the church'' as a popular book once put it—and must bring God's love into the marketplace.

Until modern times various historical factors made the laity second-class citizens in the church. Among these factors were the development of monasticism which tended to emphasize religious life as "superior" to the lay state; the fact that kings patronized mostly clerics, thus giving them a privileged status in society; and the reality that, until recent centuries, only the clergy were educated.

During this century, however, the laity has come into its own. As both the *Constitution on the Church* (Chapter 4) and the *Decree on the Apostolate of the Laity* make quite clear, the lay person can and does participate in the apostolate of the church's saving mission.

> The laity are called in a special way to make the Church present and operative in those places and circumstances where only through them can she become the salt of the earth (*Constitution on the Church*, No. 33).

What Vatican II taught is that lay people are the church-in-the-world. Lay people today must realize that they have a unique vocation of serving and building God's kingdom in the world: through business, the trades, commerce, the arts, politics and the various professions. They must increase their awareness that they serve God's cause by bringing God's love to the world. Leadership, for example, is a tremendous way to serve the good news. Lay people, in fact, serve the cause of love in their work as housewives, bricklayers, political and social leaders, white-collar workers, nurses, lawyers, accountants and so on.

The service of love demands that God's people witness to the values of the gospel on the job. It means that they energetically support social service and the works of mercy: feeding the hungry, educating the ignorant, comforting the elderly, healing the sick, reforming the prisons, caring for the orphans, finding jobs for the unemployed. At the same time, it means a commitment to social action, to social justice, to changing unjust practices and policies of institutions; for example, policies which keep certain racial groups from getting equal rights and opportunities.

One can safely predict that the church of our day—clergy and laity—will strive more and more to understand the tremendous role we all have in the service of life, truth and love.

EXERCISES

A. *What Can You Do About Abortions*? Here is a checklist of things *you* can do to promote the pro-life movement. Resolve to get involved by doing at least one of the following:

- Prepare a lecture on the sacredness of human life.
- Read a book on a pro-life topic so that you know something about the issues involved.
- Join a pro-life group.
- Write pro-life letters to government representatives, newspapers, television stations, magazines.
- March at a pro-life rally or attend a pro-life convention in your area.
- Raise money (car wash, bake sale, youth dance, walkathon, etc.) to support a local pro-life group.
- Ask your parish priest to preach on this topic.
- Ask your teachers to sponsor a pro-life unit in one of your classes.
- Advertise the pro-life movement by wearing a pro-life bracelet or rose applique, use bumper stickers, etc.
- Pray, pray, pray . . . for pregnant women, for people who support abortion, for pro-lifers that they continue their battle for life, for divine forgiveness for the taking of innocent lives.

B. *Action Research*

1. Interview a Catholic adult who is in a career or profession you might like to pursue someday.
2. Discover how that person brings gospel values to his or her work. If possible spend a day with the person at his or her place of work.
3. Report on your findings to the class.

C. *Reading*

1. Read Chapter 4 of the *Constitution on the Church*.
2. Find a definition of the term *laity* (see paragraph 31) and then list three or four significant things the council teaches about the laity.

D. *Some Other Issues:*

Research and debate one of these three topics.

1. *Clerical Celibacy*

   a. What is clerical celibacy?

   b. When and why did the Roman Catholic Church develop the discipline of clerical celibacy?

   c. Should priests be allowed to marry?

   d. What is the pope's stand on this issue?

   e. Interview at least two priests to get their opinions on this topic.

2. *Ordination of Women.* The role of women in today's church is a burning issue. Women's rights movements in the larger society have also made an impact on the church. Many historical factors, which we don't have the space to study here, have been responsible for making our church male and clerically dominated. Today, though, many Catholics are trying to figure out the proper role of women in the church. The issues involved have often focused on the topic of ordination of women to the priesthood. Do some research on this lively topic.

   a. What are the arguments for and against the ordination of women?

   b. What position has the official teaching authority taken on this issue?

   c. What do you think?

   d. Interview your mother, father, a nun and a priest to get their opinions on this topic. Report their views.

3. *Catholic Schools.* Some people think it is wrong for the church to spend millions of dollars to support the massive parochial school system. They argue that the money could be spent to develop excellent parish school of religion programs with countless dollars left over for social service and social action projects. What do you think?

   Discuss:

   Is there a need for the church to support special schools; for example, schools in urban areas among the underprivileged?

   Debate:

   Should the church continue to support the parochial school system?

PARISH AND MINISTRY

For most of us the church means our parish. Parish is the church-in-miniature. The parish is a community of Christians whose daily struggles make the church come alive in the here and now. The parish, usually organized according to territory, is made up of families and individuals who come to worship the Lord and to carry on his mission. In an organizational flow chart, parishes make up a diocese; and dioceses are like spokes in a wheel that make up the worldwide church.

Ministries in the Parish. A modern, post-Vatican II concept in today's church is the idea of ministry. Parishes could not exist without ministers.

Ministry fits into the servant model of church simply because ministry means service. Ministers are those who serve. Ministry is an act of service which the church designates as necessary for the fulfillment of its mission. Among these works are preaching, teaching, almsgiving, leading in worship, the works of mercy and the like. Ministry, in fact, applies to any act of Christian service. It means making the Lord present to the world, especially to those in need.

Parish Ministers. Some people are formally appointed in each parish to engage in ministry and work to build up the Body of Christ on the local level. Some of the following are ministers one can typically find in parishes today:

- *Pastor*—the spiritual leader and focus of unity in the parish.

- *Associate or Assistant Pastor*—a priest who shares in the spiritual leadership role with the pastor.

- *Deacon*—a man called to serve the community by proclaiming God's word, by assisting at worship and through works of charity.

- *Director of Religious Education* (*DRE*)—a trained catechist who coordinates all parish catechetical activities.

- *Sisters*—women who live in religious community. Sisters have various ministries: education, social, hospital and parish work.

- *Music Minister*—leads the worshipping community in music and singing.

- *School Principal*—provides educational leadership in either the parish elementary or high school.

- *Parish Council Members*—either elected or appointed members of an advisory board who help the ministerial team and pastor make decisions.

- *Pastoral Ministers*—some of these can be found in many parishes today: youth ministers, eucharistic ministers, ministers to the elderly, ministers to the sick.

In the post-Vatican II church more parishes seem to be adopting the concept of *team ministry*. Various parish ministers and other representatives, led by the pastor, make joint decisions, usually by consensus.

Not everyone has an official ministry in a parish but everyone is

called to minister. By living the Christian life and witnessing to it, you are engaged in ministerial work. Perhaps you have gone on a youth retreat or renewal and have subsequently helped give another one. If so you were involved in *peer ministry*. Peer ministry is becoming more popular in the church, especially among young people. Peer ministers support, help, encourage, challenge, listen and witness to each other. Your involvement in parish youth groups and parish projects of one kind or another is an example of ministry in the broader sense. Your living the gospel in front of your classmates, friends and everyone you meet is serving to spread the Lord's message. It is the work of ministry.

ACTIVITIES

A. *Parish History*. A small group of students may wish to research and write the history of their parish. Some possible research questions:

1. Who founded the parish? When?
2. What was the ethnic makeup of the parish when it was founded? How has this changed?
3. Discover five significant people who were parishioners and contributed to parish or civic life.
4. Report on five significant events in the life of the parish.
5. What is the current population of the parish?

B. *Parish Ministry*. Ministry often takes the form of committees and organizations of people who see that certain things get done. Look into your own parish organizations. List the groups or organizations in your parish which are involved in the following:

Religious Education

Worship and Prayer

Social Justice and Social Action

Interfaith Affairs

Parish Finances, Buildings and Grounds

Which organizations are open to young people?

C. *Task Force*. Divide into groups of five or six. Imagine that your parish council has appointed your group to come up with some ideas for a possible youth group.

1. What are the five greatest needs of the young people in your parish? Rank them in order.

2. What can adults do to get the young people more involved in parish life?

3. Should the parish begin a youth group? If so, should the emphasis be on 1) social activities; 2) education; 3) prayer; 4) athletics; or 5) community service? Explain your choice.

4. If you decide to form a youth group, construct a budget for it. How much money should the group be given or allowed to raise and for what purposes?

The small groups should report their discussions to the class as a whole.

D. *Making a Judgment*. Now that you have studied all six models of the church, evaluate them here. In a few short words, describe what each means to you. Then rank them in order of importance to you.

MODEL	DESCRIPTION	RANKING
Community		
Herald		
Institution		
Pilgrim		
Sacrament		
Servant		

Write a brief statement on how your parish could improve if it operated more under the influence of the model you chose as most important. Share your statement with your classmates.

_____

_____

_____

_____

_____

_____

WHO IS A CATHOLIC?

Let's pause here and reflect on the precise identity of a Catholic Christian. Who is a Catholic?

Vatican II taught that a Catholic:

1. has faith in Jesus as Lord and Savior by reason of the gift of the Holy Spirit;

2. is joined to the community of faith in Jesus and accepts the entire system of the Catholic church and the means of salvation given to the church;

3. is joined to the Body of Christ and the Lord himself through union with the church's visible structure;

4. professes a common faith, the seven sacraments, a community in which the Lord lives and a church government through which Christ rules in the pope and the bishops.

(See the *Constitution on the Church*, No. 14.)

Why Be a Catholic? This is a more difficult question to answer. Different Catholics will answer this question in different ways. It is a question that every thinking Catholic must reflect on sometime along the way.

Here is one approach to the question:

I am Catholic because *I have been chosen*. Like most Catholics, I was born into a faith community which believes that Jesus is the Lord and Savior of all people. My parents, close friends and relatives believe this. I also believe it and realize that I need a faith community to help me in my journey to the Father.

But this is not enough. I am Catholic because I believe that *Jesus Christ is the center of human history*. I believe he is the center of my life. I believe his good news that God is incredible love. I believe the good news that I am worth something, that I am worth God's Son offering his life for my salvation. I believe that life will conquer death. I believe that struggling to live a good life is the way to find true happiness. I believe that good will triumph over evil, and that if I'm sorry, my own sins will be forgiven by my loving Father.

But this is still not enough, because all Christians believe this, too. I am Catholic because I firmly believe that *the fullness of what the Lord intended his church to be can be found in the Catholic community.* I find that I need other people on my journey to the Father. The Catholic church is a people church, open to all kinds of sinners, even people like me. The Catholic church has struggled through its long history—a history that can be traced to the Lord himself—to try to be faithful to all that Jesus taught. True, there are some things in the church's story which turn me off, some times when people simply failed to be what the Lord called them to be. At the same time, though, I admire so much about this pilgrim people. Somehow the church has always kept alive some very important realities:

- The church has always taught that the material world is good and that God can be found in it. I'm proud of the church's efforts to support art, music, architecture, literature and the like.

- The church has emphasized that in the sacraments God mysteriously connects with my deepest concerns. For example, in the sacrament of reconciliation, he's there to forgive my sins. He's ready to give me strength when I'm sick or dying. He's there—body and blood—in the Eucharist to give me his very self so that I can be Jesus for others.

- The church has produced some remarkable men and women: great minds like Thomas Aquinas, missionaries like Francis Xavier, martyrs like Margaret Clitherow, peacemakers like Francis of Assisi, and countless other saints, all of whom are related to me and concerned with my welfare. The church has also produced witnesses to the kingdom in our own times: martyrs like Maximilian Kolbe, canonized in 1982, and the women missionaries martyred in El Salvador; social justice workers like Dorothy Day; workers among the poor and dying like Mother Teresa.

- The church has kept alive a devotion to Mary, the mother of the Lord and my mother.

- The church has always been *catholic*: open to ideas that help to get the Lord's message across; never excluding the good news from anyone.

Furthermore, I am Catholic because I believe that our Lord wanted to guide his church through St. Peter and the apostles and their successors: the popes and the bishops. I appreciate the value of a strong leadership, but a leadership that encourages people to handle their own affairs if possible. I appreciate a church which speaks out on moral issues—even if in doing so it is not popular. I am glad to be part of a community of people who set a high ideal for me but at the same time is willing to forgive me if I fall short of the ideal. I am proud to be a member of a community which sees service as vitally important, a community which is willing to take a stand for the poor, for the sick, for the aged, for the dispossessed, for the underdog, for those whom nobody else wants.

To be a Catholic means to be for all of the above. To be a Catholic means to be part of something larger than oneself: the Body of the Lord. It means recognizing that we are all brothers and sisters and should care for each other. It means that we have some great news—God loves us and has an incredible future in store for us. Finally, to be a Catholic means to *do* something: to love as Jesus loved; to herald his gospel; to wash feet; to be light and salt; to support each other on our journey through life; to praise and thank God for all he has done for us in his Son Jesus Christ.

BEING CATHOLIC

A. Make a statement on what it means to be a Catholic for you. Possible approaches:
   1. Make a collage
   2. Make a slide show with music
   3. Write a prayer/poem; illustrate with pictures
   4. Write an essay: Why *I* Am a Catholic
   5. Write a creed, a statement of your beliefs

B. Interview at least one person whom you greatly admire. Ask, "What does it mean for you to be a Catholic?" Share with your classmates.

SUMMARY

1. The Second Vatican Council was revolutionary in some ways. For example, the laity is called to a more mature spirituality than usual in recent history. The Charismatic Movement is one form of spirituality which has attracted many Catholics in the post-Vatican II church.

2. Vatican II brought with it the renewal of the Mass and the seven sacraments, advances in the area of ecumenism, and more emphasis on shared responsibility.

3. Pope Paul VI's encyclical *Humanae Vitae* restated and reaffirmed the traditional Catholic teaching on birth control. Its publication, however, touched off a crisis in papal authority.

4. While many lay people seem more involved in today's church, others have stopped going to Mass. In recent years vocations to the religious life have also declined. The post-Vatican II church has at times been polarized between those who think change has taken place too fast and those who think change has not been rapid enough.

5. The church as servant seeks to serve life, truth and love. For example, the church serves life by speaking out on the nuclear arms and abortion issues; it serves truth by a deep commitment to evangelization and catechetical efforts; it serves love by reaffirming the values of good family life and by stressing the absolutely crucial role the laity have in spreading Christ's good news.

6. The parish is the church-in-miniature. There are many ministries in the parish. Some of these are officially recognized by the church as necessary for the fulfillment of its mission: the pastor, associate pastor, deacon, director of religious education, teaching sister, minister of music, parish council member, and so on. Other ministries are performed by any Catholic who serves others.

7. To be a Catholic means to affirm the good news of Jesus, the rich history of the church, the value of the seven sacraments, fellow believers, all creation, hierarchical leadership and the responsibility to be heralds, servants and living signs of God's kingdom.

EVALUATION

Essays:

1. Write a 300-word essay responding to this question: What is the Roman Catholic Church?

2. Write a 200-word essay responding to this question: Who is a Catholic today?

PRAYER REFLECTION

The church is always in need of our prayers because by praying for the church we are praying for ourselves. Here is a time-honored prayer by William Laud (d. 1645) for the church. Recite it with faith that our Father will shower his blessings on his Son's church.

> Gracious Father,
> we pray to you for your holy Catholic church.
> Fill it with your truth.
> Keep it in your peace.
> Where it is corrupt, reform it.
> Where it is in error, correct it.
> Where it is right, defend it.
> Where it is in want, provide for it.
> Where it is divided, reunite it;
> for the sake of your Son, our Savior Jesus Christ.